# MUSICIANS OF TO-DAY

# MUSICIANS OF TO-DAY

BY

ROMAIN ROLLAND

TRANSLATED BY

MARY BLAIKLOCK

WITH AN INTRODUCTION BY

CLAUDE LANDI

*Essay Index Reprint Series*

 BOOKS FOR LIBRARIES PRESS

FREEPORT, NEW YORK

First Published 1915
Reprinted 1969

STANDARD BOOK NUMBER:
8369-1188-1


LIBRARY OF CONGRESS CATALOG CARD NUMBER:
72-86777


PRINTED IN THE UNITED STATES OF AMERICA

# CONTENTS

# INTRODUCTION

It is perhaps fitting that the series of volumes comprising *The Musician's Bookshelf* should be inaugurated by the present collection of essays. To the majority of English readers the name of that strange and forceful personality, Romain Rolland, is known only through his magnificent, intimate record of an artist's life and aspirations, embracing ten volumes, *Jean-Christophe*. This is not the place in which to discuss that masterpiece. A few biographical facts concerning the author may not, however, be out of place here.

Romain Rolland is forty-eight years old. He was born on January 29, 1866, at Clamecy (Nièvre), France. He came very early under the influence of Tolstoy and Wagner and displayed a remarkable critical faculty. In 1895 (at the age of twenty-nine) we find him awarded the coveted Grand Prix of the Académie Française for his work *Histoire de l'Opéra en Europe avant Lulli et Scarlatti*, and in the same year he sustained, before the faculty of the Sorbonne —where he now occupies the chair of musical criticism—a remarkable dissertation on *The Origin of the Modern Lyrical Drama*—his thesis for the Doctorate. This, in reality, is a vehement protest against the indifference for the Art of Music which, up to that time, had always been displayed by the University. In 1903 he published a remarkable *Life of Beethoven*, followed by a *Life of Hugo Wolf* in 1905. The present volume, together with its companion, *Musiciens d'Autrefois*, appeared in 1908. Both form remarkable essays and reveal a consummate and most intimate knowledge of the life and works of our great contemporaries. A just estimate of a composer's work is not to be arrived at without a study of his works and of the conditions under which these were produced. To take, for instance, the case of but one of the composers treated in this volume, Hector Berlioz. No composer has been so misunderstood, so vilified as he, simply because those who have written about him, either wilfully or through ignorance, have grossly misrepresented him.

The essay on Berlioz, in the present volume, reveals a true insight into the personality of this unfortunate and great artist, and removes any false misconceptions which unsympathetic and superficial handling may have engendered. Indeed, the same introspective faculty is displayed in all the other essays which form this volume, which, it is believed, will prove of the greatest value not only to

the professional student, but also to the *intelligent
listener*, for whom the present series of volumes has
been primarily planned. We hear much, nowadays,
of the value of "Musical Appreciation." It is high
time that something was done to educate our
audiences and to dispel the hitherto prevalent
fallacy that Music need not be regarded seriously.
We do not want more creative artists, more executants ; the world is full of them—good, bad and
indifferent—but we *do* want more *intelligent listeners*.

I do not think it is an exaggeration to assert that
the majority of listeners at a high-class concert or
recital are absolutely bored. How can it be otherwise, when the composers represented are mere names
to them ? Why should the general public appreciate a Bach fugue, an intricate symphony or a
piece of chamber-music ? Do we professional
musicians appreciate the technique of a wonderful
piece of sculpture, of an equally wonderful feat of
engineering or even of a miraculous surgical opera-
tion ? It may be argued that an analogy between
sculpture, engineering, surgery and music is absurd,
because the three former do not appeal to the masses
in the same manner as music does. Precisely : it
is because of this universal appeal on the part of
music that the public should be educated to *listen*
to *good* music ; that they should be given, in a
general way, a chance to acquaint themselves with

the laws underlying the " Beautiful in Music " and should be shown the demands which a right appreciation of the Art makes upon the Intellect and the Emotions.

And, surely, such a " desideratum " may best be effected by a careful perusal of the manuals to be included in the present series. It is incontestable that the reader of the following pages—apart from a knowledge of the various musical forms, of orchestration, etc.—all of which will be duly treated in successive volumes—will be in a better position to appreciate the works of the several composers to which he may be privileged to listen. The last essay, especially, will be read with interest to-day, when we may hope to look forward to a cessation of race-hatred and distrust, and to what a writer in the *Musical Times* (September, 1914) has called, "a new sense of the emotional solidarity of mankind. From that sense alone," he adds, " can the real music of the future be born."

CLAUDE LANDI.

# MUSICIANS OF TO-DAY

## BERLIOZ

### I

IT may seem a paradox to say that no musician is
so little known as Berlioz. The world thinks it
knows him. A noisy fame surrounds his person
and his work. Musical Europe has celebrated his
centenary. Germany disputes with France the
glory of having nurtured and shaped his genius.
Russia, whose triumphal reception consoled him
for the indifference and enmity of Paris,[1] has said,
through the voice of Balakirew, that he was " the
only musician France possessed." His chief compositions are often played at concerts ; and some
of them have the rare quality of appealing both to
the cultured and the crowd ; a few have even reached
great popularity. Works have been dedicated to
him, and he himself has been described and criticised by many writers. He is popular even to his
face ; for his face, like his music, was so striking
and singular that it seemed to show you his character
at a glance. No clouds hide his mind and its
creations, which, unlike Wagner's, need no initia-

[1] " And you, Russia, who have saved me. . . ." (Berlioz,
*Mémoires*, II, 353, Calmann-Lévy's edition, 1897).

B

tion to be understood; they seem to have no
hidden meaning, no subtle mystery; one is instantly their friend or their enemy, for the first
impression is a lasting one.

That is the worst of it; people imagine that they
understand Berlioz with so very little trouble.
Obscurity of meaning may harm an artist less than
a seeming transparency; to be shrouded in mist
may mean remaining long misunderstood, but those
who wish to understand will at least be thorough
in their search for the truth. It is not always
realised how depth and complexity may exist in a
work of clear design and strong contrasts—in the
obvious genius of some great Italian of the Renaissance as much as in the troubled heart of a Rem-
brandt and the twilight of the North.

That is the first pitfall; but there are many more
that will beset us in the attempt to understand
Berlioz. To get at the man himself one must break
down a wall of prejudice and pedantry, of convention and intellectual snobbery. In short, one
must shake off nearly all current ideas about his
work if one wishes to extricate it from the dust that
has drifted about it for half a century.

Above all, one must not make the mistake of
contrasting Berlioz with Wagner, either by sacri-
ficing Berlioz to that Germanic Odin, or by forcibly
trying to reconcile one to the other. For there are
some who condemn Berlioz in the name of Wagner's
theories; and others who, not liking the sacrifice,
seek to make him a forerunner of Wagner, or kind of
elder brother, whose mission was to clear a way and

prepare a road for a genius greater than his own. Nothing is falser. To understand Berlioz one must shake off the hypnotic influence of Bayreuth. Though Wagner may have learnt something from Berlioz, the two composers have nothing in common ; their genius and their art are absolutely opposed ; each one has ploughed his furrow in a different field.

The Classical misunderstanding is quite as dangerous. By that I mean the clinging to super-stitions of the past, and the pedantic desire to enclose art within narrow limits, which still flourish among critics. Who has not met these censors of music ? They will tell you with solid complacence how far music may go, and where it must stop, and what it may express and what it must not. They are not always musicians themselves. But what of that ? Do they not lean on the example of the past ? The past ! a handful of works that they themselves hardly understand. Meanwhile, music, by its unceasing growth, gives the lie to their theories, and breaks down these weak barriers. But they do not see it, do not wish to see it ; since they cannot advance themselves, they deny pro-gress. Critics of this kind do not think favourably of Berlioz's dramatic and descriptive symphonies. How should they appreciate the boldest musical achievement of the nineteenth century ? These dreadful pedants and zealous defenders of an art that they only understand after it has ceased to live are the worst enemies of unfettered genius, and may do more harm than a whole army of ignorant people. For in a country like ours, where musical education is poor, timidity is great in the presence of a strong, but only half-understood, tradition ; and anyone who has the boldness to break away from it is condemned without judgment. I doubt if Berlioz would have obtained any consideration at all from lovers of classical music in France if he had not found allies in that country of classical music, Germany—"the oracle of Delphi," "Germania alma parens,"[1] as he called her. Some of the young German school found inspiration in Berlioz. The dramatic symphony that he created flourished in its German form under Liszt ; the most eminent German composer of to-day, Richard Strauss, came under his influence ; and Felix Weingartner, who with Charles Malherbe edited Berlioz's complete works, was bold enough to write, "In spite of Wagner and Liszt, we should not be where we are if Berlioz had not lived." This unexpected support, coming from a country of traditions, has thrown the partisans of Classic tradition into confusion, and rallied Berlioz's friends.

But here is a new danger. Though it is natural that Germany, more musical than France, should recognise the grandeur and originality of Berlioz's music before France, it is doubtful whether the German nature could ever fully understand a soul so French in its essence. It is, perhaps, what is exterior in Berlioz, his positive originality, that the Germans appreciate. They prefer the *Requiem* to *Roméo*. A Richard Strauss would be attracted by an almost insignificant work like the *Ouverture du*

[1] *Mémoires*, II, 149.

*roi Lear ;* a Weingartner would single out for notice works like the *Symphonie fantastique* and *Harold*, and exaggerate their importance. But they do not feel what is intimate in him. Wagner said over the tomb of Weber, "England does you justice, France admires you, but only Germany loves you ; you are of her own being, a glorious day of her life, a warm drop of her blood, a part of her heart. . . ." One might adapt his words to Berlioz ; it is as difficult for a German really to love Berlioz as it is for a Frenchman to love Wagner or Weber. One must, therefore, be careful about accepting unreservedly the judgment of Germany on Berlioz ; for in that would lie the danger of a new misunderstanding. You see how both the followers and opponents of Berlioz hinder us from getting at the truth. Let us dismiss them.

Have we now come to the end of our difficulties ? Not yet ; for Berlioz is the most illusive of men, and no one has helped more than he to mislead people in their estimate of him. We know how much he has written about music and about his own life, and what wit and understanding he shows in his shrewd criticisms and charming *Mémoires.*[1]

[1] The literary work of Berlioz is rather uneven. Beside passages of exquisite beauty we find others that are ridiculous in their exaggerated sentiment, and there are some that even lack good taste. But he had a natural gift of style, and his writing is vigorous, and full of feeling, especially towards the latter half of his life. The *Procession des Rogations* is often quoted from the *Mémoires ;* and some of his poetical text, particularly that in *L'Enfance du Christ* and in *Les Troyens,* is written in beautiful language and with a fine sense of rhythm. His *Mémoires* as a whole is one of the most delightful books ever written by an artist. Wagner was a greater poet, but as a

One would think that such an imaginative and skilful writer, accustomed in his profession of critic to express every shade of feeling, would be able to tell us more exactly his ideas of art than a Beethoven or a Mozart. But it is not so. As too much light may blind the vision, so too much intellect may hinder the understanding. Berlioz's mind spent itself in details ; it reflected light from too many facets, and did not focus itself in one strong beam which would have made known his power. He did not know how to dominate either his life or his work; he did not even try to dominate them. He was the incarnation of romantic genius, an unrestrained force, unconscious of the road he trod. I would not go so far as to say that he did not understand himself, but there are certainly times when he is past understanding himself. He allows himself to drift where chance will take him,[1] like an old Scandinavian pirate laid at the bottom of his boat, staring up at the sky ; and he dreams and groans and laughs and gives himself up to his feverish delusions. He lived with his emotions as uncertainly as he lived with his art. In his music, as in his criticisms of music, he often contradicts himself, hesitates, and turns back ; he is not sure either of his feelings or his thoughts. He has poetry in his soul, and strives to write operas ; but his admiration wavers between Gluck and Meyerbeer. He has a popular genius, but despises the people. He is a daring musical revolutionary,

prose writer Berlioz is infinitely superior. See Paul Morillot's essay on *Berlioz écrivain*, 1903, Grenoble.

[1] " Chance, that unknown god, who plays such a great part in my life " (*Mémoires*, II, 161).

but he allows the control of this musical movement to be taken from him by anyone who wishes to have it. Worse than that : he disowns the movement, turns his back upon the future, and throws himself again into the past. For what reason ? Very often he does not know. Passion, bitterness, caprice, wounded pride—these have more influence with him than the serious things of life. He is a man at war with himself.

Then contrast Berlioz with Wagner. Wagner, too, was stirred by violent passions, but he was always master of himself, and his reason remained unshaken by the storms of his heart or those of the world, by the torments of love or the strife of political revolutions. He made his experiences and even his errors serve his art ; he wrote about his theories before he put them into practice ; and he only launched out when he was sure of himself, and when the way lay clear before him. And think how much Wagner owes to this written expression of his aims and the magnetic attraction of his arguments. It was his prose works that fascinated the King of Bavaria before he had heard his music ; and for many others also they have been the key to that music. I remember being impressed by Wagner's ideas when I only half understood his art ; and when one of his compositions puzzled me, my confidence was not shaken, for I was sure that the genius who was so convincing in his reasoning would not blunder ; and that if his music baffled me, it was I who was at fault. Wagner was really his own best friend, his own most trusty champion ; and his was the

guiding hand that led one through the thick forest
and over the rugged crags of his work.

Not only do you get no help from Berlioz in this
way, but he is the first to lead you astray and
wander with you in the paths of error. To understand his genius you must seize hold of it unaided.
His genius was really great, but, as I shall try to
show you, it lay at the mercy of a weak character.

.     .     .     .     .     .

Everything about Berlioz was misleading, even
his appearance. In legendary portraits he appears
as a dark southerner with black hair and sparkling
eyes. But he was really very fair and had blue
eyes,[1] and Joseph d'Ortigue tells us they were
deep-set and piercing, though sometimes clouded
by melancholy or languor.[2] He had a broad forehead furrowed with wrinkles by the time he was
thirty, and a thick mane of hair, or, as E. Legouvé
puts it, " a large umbrella of hair, projecting like a
movable awning over the beak of a bird of prey.[3]
His mouth was well cut, with lips compressed and
puckered at the corners in a severe fold, and his
chin was prominent. He had a deep voice,[4] but his

---

[1] " I was fair," wrote Berlioz to Bülow (unpublished letters,
1858). " A shock of reddish hair," he wrote in his *Mémoires*,
I, 165. " Sandy-coloured hair," said Reyer. For the colour
of Berlioz's hair I rely upon the evidence of Mme. Chapot,
his niece.

[2] Joseph d'Ortigue, *Le Balcon de l'Opéra*, 1833.

[3] E. Legouvé, *Soixante ans de souvenirs*. Legouvé describes
Berlioz here as he saw him for the first time.

[4] " A passable baritone," says Berlioz (*Mémoires*, I, 58). In
1830, in the streets of Paris, he sang " a bass part " (*Mémoires*,
I, 156). During his first visit to Germany the Prince of
Hechingen made him sing " the part of the violoncello " in one
of his compositions (*Mémoires*, II, 32).

speech was halting and often tremulous with emotion ; he would speak passionately of what interested him, and at times be effusive in manner, but more often he was ungracious and reserved. He was of medium height, rather thin and angular in figure, and when seated he seemed much taller than he really was.[1] He was very restless, and inherited from his native land, Dauphiné, the mountaineer's passion for walking and climbing, and the love of a vagabond life, which remained with him nearly to his death.[2] He had an iron constitution, but he wrecked it by privation and excess, by his walks in the rain, and by sleeping out-of-doors in all weathers, even when there was snow on the ground.[3]

But in this strong and athletic frame lived a feverish and sickly soul that was dominated and tormented by a morbid craving for love and sympathy: " that imperative need of love which is killing me. . . ."[4] To love, to be loved—he would give up all for that. But his love was that of a youth who lives in dreams ; it was never the strong, clear-eyed passion of a man

[1] There are two good portraits of Berlioz. One is a photograph by Pierre Petit, taken in 1863, which he sent to Mme. Estelle Fornier. It shows him leaning on his elbow, with his head bent, and his eyes fixed on the ground as if he were tired. The other is the photograph which he had reproduced in the first edition of his *Mémoires*, and which shows him leaning back, his hands in his pockets, his head upright, with an expression of energy in his face, and a fixed and stern look in his eyes.

[2] He would go on foot from Naples to Rome in a straight line over the mountains, and would walk at one stretch from Subiaco to Tivoli.

[3] This brought on several attacks of bronchitis and frequent sore throats, as well as the internal affection from which he died.

[4] " Music and love are the two wings of the soul," he wrote in his *Mémoires*.

who has faced the realities of life, and who sees the
defects as well as the charms of the woman he
loves. Berlioz was in love with love, and lost
himself among visions and sentimental shadows.
To the end of his life he remained " a poor little
child worn out by a love that was beyond him."[1]
But this man who lived so wild and adventurous a
life expressed his passions with delicacy ; and one
finds an almost girlish purity in the immortal
love passages of *Les Troyens* or the *"nuit sereine"*
of *Roméo et Juliette*. And compare this Virgilian
affection with Wagner's sensual raptures. Does it
mean that Berlioz could not love as well as Wagner ?
We only know that Berlioz's life was made up of
love and its torments. The theme of a touching
passage in the Introduction of the *Symphonie
fantastique* has been recently identified by M.
Julien Tiersot, in his interesting book,[2] with a
romance composed by Berlioz at the age of twelve,
when he loved a girl of eighteen " with large eyes
and pink shoes "—Estelle, *Stella montis, Stella
matutina*. These words—perhaps the saddest he
ever wrote—might serve as an emblem of his life,
a life that was a prey to love and melancholy,
doomed to wringing of the heart and awful loneliness;
a life lived in a hollow world, among worries that
chilled the blood ; a life that was distasteful and
had no solace to offer him in its end.[3] He has
himself described this terrible *" mal de l'isolement,"*

[1] *Mémoires*, I, 11.
[2] Julien Tiersot, *Hector Berlioz et la société de son temps*,
1903, Hachette.
[3] See the *Mémoires*, I, 139.

which pursued him all his life, vividly and minutely.[1]
He was doomed to suffering, or, what was worse, to
make others suffer.

Who does not know his passion for Henrietta
Smithson ? It was a sad story. He fell in love with
an English actress who played Juliet (Was it she or
Juliet whom he loved ?). He caught but a glance of
her, and it was all over with him. He cried out,
" Ah, I am lost ! " He desired her ; she repulsed
him. He lived in a delirium of suffering and passion ;
he wandered about for days and nights like a
madman, up and down Paris and its neighbourhood,

[1] " I do not know how to describe this terrible sickness. . . .
My throbbing breast seems to be sinking into space ; and my
heart, drawing in some irresistible force, feels as though it would
expand until it evaporated and dissolved away. My skin
becomes hot and tender, and flushes from head to foot. I want
to cry out to my friends (even those I do not care for) to help
and comfort me, to save me from destruction, and keep in the
life that is ebbing from me. I have no sensation of impending
death in these attacks, and suicide seems impossible ; I do not
want to die—far from it, I want very much to live, to intensify
life a thousandfold. It is an excessive appetite for happiness,
which becomes unbearable when it lacks food ; and it is only
satisfied by intense delights, which give this great overflow of
feeling an outlet. It is not a state of spleen, though that may
follow later . . . spleen is rather the congealing of all these
emotions—the block of ice. Even when I am calm I feel a
little of this ' isolement ' on Sundays in summer, when our
towns are lifeless, and everyone is in the country ; for I know
that people are enjoying themselves away from me, and I feel
their absence. The *adagio* of Beethoven's symphonies, certain
scenes from Gluck's *Alceste* and *Armide*, an air from his Italian
opera *Telemacco*, the Elysian fields of his *Orfeo*, will bring on
rather bad attacks of this suffering ; but these masterpieces
bring with them also an antidote—they make one's tears flow,
and then the pain is eased. On the other hand, the *adagio* of
some of Beethoven's sonatas and Gluck's *Iphigénie en Tauride*
are full of melancholy, and therefore provoke spleen . . . it is
then cold within, the sky is grey and overcast with clouds, the
north wind moans dully. . . ." (*Mémoires*, I, 246).

without purpose or rest or relief, until sleep overcame him wherever it found him—among the
sheaves in a field near Villejuif, in a meadow near
Sceaux, on the bank of the frozen Seine near
Neuilly, in the snow, and once on a table in the
Café Cardinal, where he slept for five hours, to the
great alarm of the waiters, who thought he was
dead.[1]  Meanwhile, he was told slanderous gossip
about Henrietta, which he readily believed.  Then
he despised her, and dishonoured her publicly in
his *Symphonie fantastique*, paying homage in his
bitter resentment to Camille Moke, a pianist, to
whom he lost his heart without delay.

After a time Henrietta reappeared.  She had now
lost her youth and her power; her beauty was
waning, and she was in debt.  Berlioz's passion was
at once rekindled.  This time Henrietta accepted
his advances.  He made alterations in his symphony,
and offered it to her in homage of his love.  He won
her, and married her, with fourteen thousand francs
debt.  He had captured his dream—Juliet! Ophelia!
What was she really ?  A charming Englishwoman,
cold, loyal, and sober-minded, who understood
nothing of his passion ; and who, from the time she
became his wife, loved him jealously and sincerely,
and thought to confine him within the narrow world
of domestic life.  But his affections became restive,
and he lost his heart to a Spanish actress (it was
always an actress, a virtuoso, or a part) and left poor
Ophelia, and went off with Marie Recio, the Inès of
*Favorite*, the page of *Comte Ory*—a practical, hard-

[1] *Mémoires*, I, 98.

headed woman, an indifferent singer with a mania for singing. The haughty Berlioz was forced to fawn upon the directors of the theatre in order to get her parts, to write flattering notices in praise of her talents, and even to let her make his own melodies discordant at the concerts he arranged.[1] It would all be dreadfully ridiculous if this weakness of character had not brought tragedy in its train.

So the one he really loved, and who always loved him, remained alone, without friends, in Paris, where she was a stranger. She drooped in silence and pined slowly away, bedridden, paralysed, and unable to speak during eight years of suffering. Berlioz suffered too, for he loved her still and was torn with pity—" pity, the most painful of all emotions."[2]  But of what use was this pity? He left Henrietta to suffer alone and to die just the same. And, what was worse, as we learn from Legouvé, he let his mistress, the odious Recio, make a scene before poor Henrietta.[3]  Recio told him of it and boasted about what she had done. And

[1] " Isn't it really devilish," he said to Legouvé, " tragic and silly at the same time?  I should deserve to go to hell if I wasn't there already."

[2] *Mémoires*, II, 335. See the touching passages he wrote on Henrietta Smithson's death.

[3] " One day, Henrietta, who was living alone at Montmartre, heard someone ring the bell, and went to open the door.

" ' Is Mme. Berlioz at home?'

" ' I am Mme. Berlioz.'

" ' You are mistaken;  I asked for Mme. Berlioz.'

" ' And I tell you, I am Mme. Berlioz.'

" ' No, you are not.  You are speaking of the old Mme. Berlioz, the one who was abandoned;  I am speaking of the young and pretty and loved one.  Well, that is myself!'

" And Recio went out and banged the door after her.

" Legouvé said to Berlioz, ' Who told you this abominable

Berlioz did nothing—" How could I ?   I love her."
One would be hard upon such a man if one was
not disarmed by his own sufferings.  But let us go on.
I should have liked to pass over these traits, but I
have no right to;  I must show you the extraordinary feebleness of the man's character.  " Man's
character," did I say ?   No, it was the character of
a woman without a will, the victim of her nerves.[1]

.     .     .     .     .     .

Such people are destined to unhappiness ;  and if
they make other people suffer, one may be sure that
it is only half of what they suffer themselves.  They
have a peculiar gift for attracting and gathering

thing ?  I suppose she who did it ;  and then she boasted about
it into the bargain.  Why didn't you turn her out of the house ? '
' How could I ? ' said Berlioz in broken tones, ' I love her ' "
(*Soixante ans de souvenirs*).

[1] From this woman's nature came his love of revenge, " a
thing needless, and yet necessary," he said to his friend Hiller,
who, after having made him write the *Symphonie fantastique* to
spite Henrietta Smithson, next made him write the wretched
fantasia *Euphonia* to spite Camille Moke, now Mme. Pleyel.
One would feel obliged to draw more attention to the way he
often adorned or perverted the truth if one did not feel it arose
from his irrepressible and glowing imagination far more than
from any intention to mislead ;  for I believe his real nature to
have been a very straightforward one.  I will quote the story of
his friend Crispino, a young countryman from Tivoli, as a
characteristic example.  Berlioz says in his *Mémoires* (I, 229) :
" One day when Crispino was lacking in respect I made him a
present of two shirts, a pair of trousers, and three good kicks
behind."  In a note he added, " This is a lie, and is the result of
an artist's tendency to aim at effect.  I never kicked Crispino."
But Berlioz took care afterwards to omit this note.  One attaches
as little importance to his other small boasts as to this one.
The errors in the *Mémoires* have been greatly exaggerated ;  and
besides, Berlioz is the first to warn his readers that he only
wrote what pleased him, and in his preface says that he is not
writing his Confessions. Can one blame him for that ?

up trouble ; they savour sorrow like wine, and do not lose a drop of it. Life seemed desirous that Berlioz should be steeped in suffering ; and his misfortunes were so real that it would be unnecessary to add to them any exaggerations that history has handed down to us.

People find fault with Berlioz's continual complaints ; and I, too, find in them a lack of virility and almost a lack of dignity. To all appearances, he had far fewer material reasons for unhappiness than—I won't say Beethoven—Wagner and other great men, past, present, and future. When thirty-five years old he had achieved glory ; and Paganini proclaimed him Beethoven's successor. What more could he want? He was discussed by the public, disparaged by a Scudo and an Adolphus Adam, and the theatre only opened its doors to him with difficulty. It was really splendid !

But a careful examination of facts, such as that made by M. Julien Tiersot, shows the stifling mediocrity and hardship of his life. There were, first of all, his material cares. When thirty-six years old "Beethoven's successor" had a fixed salary of fifteen hundred francs as assistant keeper of the Conservatoire Library, and not quite as much for his contributions to the *Débats*—contributions which exasperated and humiliated him, and were one of the crosses of his life, as they obliged him to speak anything but the truth.[1] That made a total of three thousand francs, hardly gained, on which he

---

[1] *Mémoires*, II, 158. The heartaches expressed in this chapter will be felt by every artist.

had to keep a wife and child—" *même deux*," as
M. Tiersot says. He attempted a festival at the
Opera; the result was three hundred and sixty
francs loss. He organised a festival at the 1844
Exhibition; the receipts were thirty-two thousand
francs, out of which he got eight hundred francs.
He had the *Damnation de Faust* performed; no one
came to it, and he was ruined. Things went better
in Russia; but the manager who brought him to
England became bankrupt. He was haunted by
thoughts of rents and doctors' bills. Towards the
end of his life his financial affairs mended a little,
and a year before his death he uttered these sad
words: " I suffer a great deal, but I do not want
to die now—I have enough to live upon."

One of the most tragic episodes of his life is that of
the symphony which he did not write because of
his poverty. One wonders why the page that
finishes his *Mémoires* is not better known, for it
touches the depths of human suffering.

At the time when his wife's health was causing
him most anxiety, there came to him one night an
inspiration for a symphony. The first part of it—
an allegro in two-four time in A minor—was ringing
in his head. He got up and began to write, and
then he thought :—

" If I begin this bit, I shall have to write the
whole symphony. It will be a big thing, and I
shall have to spend three or four months over it.
That means I shall write no more articles and earn
no money. And when the symphony is finished

I shall not be able to resist the temptation of having it copied (which will mean an expense of a thousand or twelve hundred francs), and then of having it played. I shall give a concert, and the receipts will barely cover half the cost. I shall lose what I have not got ; the poor invalid will lack necessities ; and I shall be able to pay neither my personal expenses nor my son's fees when he goes on board ship. . . . These thoughts made me shudder, and I threw down my pen, saying, ' Bah ! to-morrow I shall have forgotten the symphony.' The next night I heard the allegro clearly, and seemed to see it written down. I was filled with feverish agitation ; I sang the theme ; I was going to get up . . . but the reflections of the day before restrained me ; I steeled myself against the temptation, and clung to the thought of forgetting it. At last I went to sleep ; and the next day, on waking, all remembrance of it had, indeed, gone for ever."[1]

That page makes one shudder. Suicide is less distressing. Neither Beethoven nor Wagner suffered such tortures. What would Wagner have done on a like occasion ? He would have written the symphony without doubt—and he would have been right. But poor Berlioz, who was weak enough to sacrifice his duty to love, was, alas ! also heroic enough to sacrifice his genius to duty.[2]

[1] *Memoires*, II, 319.
[2] Berlioz has already touchingly replied to any reproaches that might be made in the words that follow the story I have quoted. " ' Coward ! ' some young enthusiast will say, ' you

C

And in spite of all this material misery and the sorrow of being misunderstood, people speak of the glory he enjoyed. What did his compeers think of him—at least, those who called themselves such ? He knew that Mendelssohn, whom he loved and esteemed, and who styled himself his " good friend," despised him and did not recognise his genius.[1] The large-hearted Schumann, who was, with the exception of Liszt,[2] the only person who intuitively felt his greatness, admitted that he used sometimes to wonder if he ought to be looked upon as " a genius or a musical adventurer."[3] Wagner, who treated his symphonies with scorn before he had

ought to have written it ; you should have been bold.' Ah, young man, you who call me coward did not have to look upon what I did ; had you done so you, too, would have had no choice. My wife was there, half dead, only able to moan ; she had to have three nurses, and a doctor every day to visit her ; and I was sure of the disastrous result of any musical adventure. No, I was not a coward ; I know I was only human. I like to believe that I honoured art in proving that she had left me enough reason to distinguish between courage and cruelty " (Mémoires, II, 350).

[1] In a note in the Mémoires, Berlioz publishes a letter of Mendelssohn's which protests his " good friendship," and he writes these bitter words : " I have just seen in a volume of Mendelssohn's Letters what his friendship for me consisted of. He says to his mother, in what is plainly a description of myself, '—— is a perfect caricature, without a spark of talent . . . there are times when I should like to swallow him up ' " (Mémoires, II, 48). Berlioz did not add that Mendelssohn also said: " They pretend that Berlioz seeks lofty ideals in art. I don't think so at all. What he wants is to get himself married." The injustice of these insulting words will disgust all those who remember that when Berlioz married Henrietta Smithson she brought as dowry nothing but debts ; and that he had only three hundred francs himself, which a friend had lent him.

[2] Liszt repudiated him later.

[3] Written in an article on the Ouverture de Waverley (Neue Zeitschrift für Müsik),

even read them,[1] who certainly understood his
genius, and who deliberately ignored him, threw
himself into Berlioz's arms when he met him in
London in 1855. " He embraced him with fervour,
and wept ; and hardly had he left him when *The
Musical World* published passages from his book,
*Oper und Drama*, where he pulls Berlioz to pieces
mercilessly." [2]   In France, the young Gounod, *doli
fabricator Epeus*, as Berlioz called him, lavished
flattering words upon him, but spent his time in
finding fault with his compositions,[3] or in trying to
supplant him at the theatre. At the Opera he was
passed over in favour of a Prince Poniatowski.
He presented himself three times at the Academy,
and was beaten the first time by Onslow, the second
time by Clapisson, and the third time he conquered
by a majority of one vote against Panseron, Vogel,
Leborne, and others, including, as always, Gounod.
He died before the *Damnation de Faust* was appreciated in France, although it was the most remarkable musical composition France had produced.
They hissed its performance ?   Not at all ; " they
were merely indifferent "—it is Berlioz who tells us
this.   It passed unnoticed.   He died before he had
seen *Les Troyens* played in its entirety, though it

---

[1] Wagner, who had criticised Berlioz since 1840, and who
published a detailed study of his works in his *Oper und Drama*
in 1851, wrote to Liszt in 1855: " I own that it would interest
me very much to make the acquaintance of Berlioz's symphonies,
and I should like to see the scores.  If you have them, will you
lend them to me ? "
  [2] See Berlioz's letter, cited by J. Tiersot, *Hector Berlioz et
la société de son temps*, p. 275.
  [3] *Roméo, Faust, La Nonne sanglante*.

was one of the noblest works of the French lyric
theatre that had been composed since the death
of Gluck.[1] But there is no need to be astonished.
To hear these works to-day one must go to Germany.
And although the dramatic work of Berlioz has
found its Bayreuth—thanks to Mottl, to Karlsruhe
and Munich—and the marvellous *Benvenuto Cellini*
has been played in twenty German towns,[2] and
regarded as a masterpiece by Weingartner and
Richard Strauss, what manager of a French theatre
would think of producing such works ?

But this is not all. What was the bitterness of
failure compared with the great anguish of death ?
Berlioz saw all those he loved die one after the
other : his father, his mother, Henrietta Smithson,
Marie Recio. Then only his son Louis remained.

[1] I shall content myself here with noting a fact, which I shall
deal with more fully in another essay at the end of this book : it
is the decline of musical taste in France—and, I rather think, in
all Europe—since 1835 or 1840. Berlioz says in his *Mémoires* :
" Since the first performance of *Roméo et Juliette* the indifference of the French public for all that concerns art and literature has grown incredibly " (*Mémoires*, II, 263). Compare the
shouts of excitement and the tears that were drawn from the
dilettanti of 1830 (*Mémoires*, I, 81), at the performances of
Italian operas or Gluck's works, with the coldness of the public
between 1840 and 1870. A mantle of ice covered art then. How
much Berlioz must have suffered. In Germany the great romantic
age was dead. Only Wagner remained to give life to music ;
and he drained all that was left in Europe of love and enthusiasm
for music. Berlioz died truly of asphyxia.

[2] Here is an official list of the towns where *Benvenuto* has
been played since 1879 (I am indebted for this information to
M. Victor Chapot, Berlioz's grandnephew). They are, in alpha-
betical order : Berlin, Bremen, Brunswick, Dresden, Frankfort-
on-Main, Freiburg-im-Breisgau, Hamburg, Hanover, Karlsruhe,
Leipsic, Mannheim, Metz, Munich, Prague, Schwerin, Stettin,
Strasburg, Stuttgart, Vienna, and Weimar.

He was the captain of a merchant vessel; a clever, good-hearted boy, but restless and nervous, irresolute and unhappy, like his father. "He has the misfortune to resemble me in everything," said Berlioz; "and we love each other like a couple of twins."[1] "Ah, my poor Louis," he wrote to him, "what should I do without you?" A few months afterwards he learnt that Louis had died in far-away seas.

He was now alone.[2] There were no more friendly voices; all that he heard was a hideous duet between loneliness and weariness, sung in his ear during the bustle of the day and in the silence of the night.[3] He was wasted with disease. In 1856, at Weimar, following great fatigue, he was seized with an internal malady. It began with great mental distress; he used to sleep in the streets. He suffered constantly; he was like "a tree without leaves, streaming with rain." At the end of 1861, the disease was in an acute stage. He had attacks of pain sometimes lasting thirty hours, during which he would writhe in agony in his bed. "I live in the midst of my physical pain, overwhelmed with weariness. Death is very slow."[4]

Worst of all, in the heart of his misery, there was

[1] *Mémoires*, II, 420.

[2] "I do not know how Berlioz has managed to be cut off like this. He has neither friends nor followers; neither the warm sun of popularity nor the pleasant shade of friendship" (Liszt to the Princess of Wittgenstein, 16 May, 1861).

[3] In a letter to Bennet he says, "I am weary, I am weary. . . ." How often does this piteous cry sound in his letters towards the end of his life. "I feel I am going to die. . . . I am weary unto death" (21 August, 1868—six months before his death).

[4] Letter to Asger Hammerick, 1865.

nothing that comforted him. He believed in
nothing—neither in God nor immortality.

> "I have no faith. . . . I hate all philosophy
> and everything that resembles it, whether religious
> or otherwise. . . . I am as incapable of making a
> medicine of faith as of having faith in medicine."[1]
> "God is stupid and cruel in his complete
> indifference."[2]

He did not believe in beauty or honour, in mankind or himself.

> "Everything passes. Space and time consume
> beauty, youth, love, glory, genius. Human life
> is nothing ; death is no better. Worlds are born
> and die like ourselves. All is nothing. Yes, yes,
> yes ! All is nothing. . . . To love or hate, enjoy
> or suffer, admire or sneer, live or die—what does
> it matter ? There is nothing in greatness or little-
> ness, beauty or ugliness. Eternity is indifferent ;
> indifference is eternal."[3]
> "I am weary of life ; and I am forced to see
> that belief in absurdities is necessary to human
> minds, and that it is born in them as insects are
> born in swamps."[4]

[1] Letters to the Princess of Wittgenstein, 22 July, 21 September, 1862 ; and August, 1864.
[2] *Mémoires*, II, 335. He shocked Mendelssohn, and even
Wagner, by his irreligion. (See Berlioz's letter to Wagner,
10 September, 1855.)
[3] *Les Grotesques de la Musique*, pp. 295–6.
[4] Letter to the Abbé Girod. See Hippeau, *Berlioz intime*,
p. 434.

" You make me laugh with your old words about a mission to fulfil. What a missionary! But there is in me an inexplicable mechanism which works in spite of all arguments; and I let it work because I cannot stop it. What disgusts me most is the certainty that beauty does not exist for the majority of these human monkeys." [1]

" The unsolvable enigma of the world, the existence of evil and pain, the fierce madness of mankind, and the stupid cruelty that it inflicts hourly and everywhere on the most inoffensive beings and on itself—all this has reduced me to the state of unhappy and forlorn resignation of a scorpion surrounded by live coals. The most I can do is not to wound myself with my own dart." [2]

" I am in my sixty-first year; and I have no more hopes or illusions or aspirations. I am alone; and my contempt for the stupidity and dishonesty of men, and my hatred for their wicked cruelty, are at their height. Every hour I say to Death, ' When you like! ' What is he waiting for ? " [3]

And yet he fears the death he invites. It is the strongest, the bitterest, the truest feeling he has. No musician since old Roland de Lassus has feared it with that intensity. Do you remember Herod's sleepless nights in *L'Enfance du Christ*, or Faust's soliloquy, or the anguish of Cassandra, or the burial of

---

[1] Letter to Bennet. He did not believe in patriotism. " Patriotism ? Fetichism! Cretinism! " (*Mémoires*, II, 261).
[2] Letter to the Princess of Wittgenstein, 22 July, 1862.
[3] *Mémoires*, II, 391

Juliette ?—through all this you will find the whispered fear of annihilation. The wretched man was haunted by this fear, as a letter published by M. Julien Tiersot shows :—

" My favourite walk, especially when it is raining, really raining in torrents, is the cemetery of Montmartre, which is near my house. I often go there ; there is much that draws me to it. The day before yesterday I passed two hours in the cemetery ; I found a comfortable seat on a costly tomb, and I went to sleep. . . . Paris is to me a cemetery and her pavements are tomb-stones. Everywhere are memories of friends or enemies that are dead. . . . I do nothing but suffer unceasing pain and unspeakable weariness. I wonder night and day if I shall die in great pain or with little of it—I am not foolish enough to hope to die without any pain at all. Why are we not dead ? "[1]

His music is like these mournful words ; it is perhaps even more terrible, more gloomy, for it breathes death.[2] What a contrast : a soul greedy of life and preyed upon by death. It is this that makes his life such an awful tragedy. When Wagner met Berlioz he heaved a sigh of relief—he had at last found a man more unhappy than himself.[3]

[1] Letters to the Princess of Wittgenstein, 22 January, 1859 ; 30 August, 1864 ; 13 July, 1866 ; and to A. Morel, 21 August, 1864.
[2]      " . . . Qui viderit illas
         De lacrymis factas sentiet esse meis,"
wrote Berlioz, as an inscription for his *Tristes* in 1854.
[3] " One instantly recognises a companion in misfortune ; and I found I was a happier man than Berlioz " (Wagner to Liszt, 5 July, 1855).

On the threshold of death he turned in despair to the one ray of light left him—*Stella montis*, the inspiration of his childish love ; Estelle, now old, a grandmother, withered by age and grief. He made a pilgrimage to Meylan, near Grenoble, to see her. He was then sixty-one years old and she was nearly seventy. " The past ! the past ! O Time ! Nevermore ! Nevermore ! "[1]

Nevertheless, he loved her, and loved her desperately. How pathetic it is. One has little inclination to smile when one sees the depths of that desolate heart. Do you think he did not see, as clearly as you or I would see, the wrinkled old face, the indifference of age, the "*triste raison*," in her he idealised ? Remember, he was the most ironical of men. But he did not wish to see these things, he wished to cling to a little love, which would help him to live in the wilderness of life.

> " There is nothing real in this world but that which lives in the heart. . . . My life has been wrapped up in the obscure little village where she lives. . . . Life is only endurable when I tell myself : ' This autumn I shall spend a month beside her.' I should die in this hell of a Paris 'if she did not allow me to write to her, and if from time to time I had not letters from her."

So he spoke to Legouvé ; and he sat down on a stone in a Paris street, and wept. In the meantime, the old lady did not understand this foolishness ; she hardly tolerated it, and sought to undeceive him.

[1] *Mémoires*, II, 396.

" When one's hair is white one must leave dreams—even those of friendship. . . . Of what use is it to form ties which, though they hold to-day, may break to-morrow ? "

What were his dreams ?   To live with her ?   No ; rather to die beside her ; to feel she was by his side when death should come.

" To be at your feet, my head on your knees, your two hands in mine—so to finish."[1]

He was a little child grown old, and felt bewildered and miserable and frightened before the thought of death.

Wagner, at the same age, a victor, worshipped, flattered, and—if we are to believe the Bayreuth legend—crowned with prosperity ; Wagner, sad and suffering, doubting his achievements, feeling the inanity of his bitter fight against the mediocrity of the world, had " fled far from the world "[2] and thrown himself into religion ; and when a friend looked at him in surprise as he was saying grace at table, he answered :   " Yes, I believe in my Saviour."[3]

---

[1] *Mémoires*, II, 415.

[2] " Yes, it is to that escape from the world that *Parsifal* owes its birth and growth.   What man can, during a whole lifetime, gaze into the depths of this world with a calm reason and a cheerful heart ?   When he sees murder and rapine organised and legalised by a system of lies, impostures, and hypocrisy, will he not avert his eyes and shudder with disgust ? " (Wagner, *Representations of the Sacred Drama of Parsifal at Bayreuth, in 1882.*)

[3] The scene was described to me by his friend, Malwida von Meysenbug, the calm and fearless author of *Mémoires d'une Idéaliste.*

Poor beings ! Conquerors of the world, conquered and broken !

But of the two deaths, how much sadder is that of the artist who was without a faith, and who had neither strength nor stoicism enough to be happy without one ; who slowly died in that little room in the rue de Calais amid the distracting noise of an indifferent and even hostile Paris ; [1] who shut himself up in savage silence ; who saw no loved face bending over him in his last moments ; who had not the comfort of belief in his work ; [2] who could not think calmly of what he had done, nor look proudly back over the road he had trodden, nor rest content in the thought of a life well lived ; and who began and closed his *Mémoires* with Shakespeare's gloomy words, and repeated them when dying :—

> " Life's but a walking shadow, a poor player
> That struts and frets his hour upon the stage
> And then is heard no more : it is a tale
> Told by an idiot, full of sound and fury,
> Signifying nothing." [3]

[1] " I have only blank walls before my windows. On the side of the street a pug dog has been barking for an hour, a parrot screaming, and a parroqueet imitating the chirp of sparrows. On the side of the yard the washerwomen are singing, and another parroqueet cries incessantly, ' Shoulder arrms ! ' How long the day is ! "

" The maddening noise of carriages shakes the silence of the night. Paris wet and muddy ! Parisian Paris ! Now everything is quiet . . . she is sleeping the sleep of the unjust " (Written to Ferrand, *Lettres intimes*, pp. 269 and 302).

[2] He used to say that nothing would remain of his work ; that he had deceived himself ; and that he would have liked to burn his scores.

[3] Blaze de Bury met him one autumn evening, on the quay, just before his death, as he was returning from the Institute. " His face was pale, his figure wasted and bent, and his expression dejected and nervous ; one might have taken him for a walking

Such was the unhappy and irresolute heart that
found itself united to one of the most daring geniuses
in the world. It is a striking example of the difference that may exist between genius and greatness
—for the two words are not synonymous. When
one speaks of greatness, one speaks of greatness
of soul, nobility of character, firmness of will,
and, above all, balance of mind. I can understand how people deny the existence of these
qualities in Berlioz; but to deny his musical
genius, or to cavil about his wonderful power—
and that is what they do daily in Paris—is lamentable and ridiculous. Whether he attracts one or
not, a thimbleful of some of his work, a single part
in one of his works, a little bit of the *Fantastique*
or the overture of *Benvenuto*, reveal more genius
—I am not afraid to say it—than all the French
music of his century. I can understand people
arguing about him in a country that produced
Beethoven and Bach; but with us in France, who
can we set up against him? Gluck and César
Franck were much greater men, but they were
never geniuses of his stature. If genius is a
creative force, I cannot find more than four or
five geniuses in the world who rank above him.
When I have named Beethoven, Mozart, Bach,

shadow. Even his eyes, those large round hazel eyes, had ex-
tinguished their fire. For a second he clasped my hand in his
own thin, lifeless one, and repeated, in a voice that was hardly
more than a whisper, Æschylus's words : ' Oh, this life of man !
When he is happy a shadow is enough to disturb him ; and
when he is unhappy his trouble may be wiped away, as with a
wet sponge, and all is forgotten ' " (*Musiciens d'hier et d'aujourd'-
hui*).

Handel; and Wagner, I do not know who else is superior to Berlioz ; I do not even know who is his equal.

He is not only a musician, he is music itself. He does not command his familiar spirit, he is its slave. Those who know his writings know how he was simply possessed and exhausted by his musical emotions. They were really fits of ecstasy or convulsions. At first " there was feverish excitement ; the veins beat violently and tears flowed freely. Then came spasmodic contractions of the muscles, total numbness of the feet and hands, and partial paralysis of the nerves of sight and hearing ; he saw nothing, heard nothing ; he was giddy and half faint." And in the case of music that displeased him, he suffered, on the contrary, from " a painful sense of bodily disquiet and even from nausea."[1]

The possession that music held over his nature shows itself clearly in the sudden outbreak of his genius.[2] His family opposed the idea of his becoming a musician ; and until he was twenty-two or twenty-three years old his weak will sulkily gave way to their wishes. In obedience to his father he began his studies in medicine at Paris. One evening he heard *Les Danaïdes* of Salieri. It came upon him like a thunderclap. He ran to the Conservatoire library and read Gluck's scores. He forgot to eat

---

[1] *A travers chants*, pp. 8–9.

[2] In truth, this genuis was smouldering since his childhood ; it was there from the beginning ; and the proof of it lies in the fact that he used for his *Ouverture des Francs-Juges* and for the *Symphonie fantastique* airs and phrases of quintets which he had written when twelve years old (see *Mémoires*, I, 16–18).

and drink ; he was like a man in a frenzy. A performance of *Iphigénie en Tauride* finished him. He
studied under Lesueur and then at the Conservatoire. The following year, 1827, he composed
*Les Francs-Juges ;* two years afterwards the *Huit
scènes de Faust*, which was the nucleus of the future
*Damnation ;*[1] three years afterwards, the *Symphonie
fantastique* (commenced in 1830).[2] And he had not
yet got the *Prix de Rome !* Add to this that in
1828 he had already ideas for *Roméo et Juliette*,
and that he had written a part of *Lelio* in 1829.
Can one find elsewhere a more dazzling musical
debut ? Compare that of Wagner who, at the same
age, was shyly writing *Les Fées, Défense d'aimer*,
and *Rienzi*. He wrote them at the same age, but
ten years later ; for *Les Fées* appeared in 1833,
when Berlioz had already written the *Fantastique*,
the *Huit scènes de Faust, Lelio*, and *Harold ; Rienzi*
was only played in 1842, after *Benvenuto* (1835),
*Le Requiem* (1837), *Roméo* (1839), *La Symphonie
funèbre et triomphale* (1840)—that is to say, when

----

[1] The *Huit scènes de Faust* are taken from Goethe's tragedy,
translated by *Gérard de Nerval*, and they include : (1) *Chants de
la fête de Pâques ;* (2) *Paysans sous les tilleuls ;* (3) *Concert des
Sylphes ;* (4 and 5) *Taverne d'Auerbach*, with the two songs of
the Rat and the Flea ; (6) *Chanson du roi de Thulé ;* (7) *Romance
de Marguerite*, " D'amour, l'ardente flamme," and *Chœur de
soldats ;* (8) *Sérénade de Méphistophélès*—that is to say, the
most celebrated and characteristic pages of the *Damnation* (see
M. Prudhomme's essays on *Le Cycle de Berlioz*).

[2] One could hardly find a better manifestation of the soul of
a youthful musical genius than that in certain letters written at
this time ; in particular the letter written to Ferrand on 28 June,
1828, with its feverish postscript. What a life of rich and overflowing vigour ! It is a joy to read it ; one drinks at the source
of life itself.

Berlioz had finished all his great works, and after he had achieved his musical revolution. And that revolution was effected alone, without a model, without a guide. What could he have heard beyond the operas of Gluck and Spontini while he was at the Conservatoire ? At the time when he composed the *Ouverture des Francs-Juges* even the name of Weber was unknown to him,[1] and of Beethoven's compositions he had only heard an *andante*.[2]

Truly, he is a miracle and the most startling phenomenon in the history of nineteenth-century music. His audacious power dominates all his age ; and in the face of such a genius, who would not follow Paganini's example, and hail him as Beethoven's only successor ?[3] Who does not see what a poor figure the young Wagner cut at that time, working away in laborious and self-satisfied mediocrity ? But Wagner soon made up for lost ground ; for he knew what he wanted, and he wanted it obstinately.

The zenith of Berlioz's genius was reached, when he was thirty-five years old, with the *Requiem* and *Roméo*. They are his two most important works, and are two works about which one may feel very differently. For my part, I am very fond of the

---

[1] *Mémoires*, I, 70.

[2] *Ibid*. To make amends for this he published, in 1829, a biographical notice of Beethoven, in which his appreciation of him is remarkably in advance of his age. He wrote there : " The *Choral Symphony* is the culminating point of Beethoven's genius," and he speaks of the Fourth Symphony in C sharp minor with great discernment.

[3] Beethoven died in 1827, the year when Berlioz was writing his first important work, the *Ouverture des Francs-Juges*.

one, and I dislike the other ; but both of them
open up two great new roads in art, and both are
placed like two gigantic arches on the triumphal
way of the revolution that Berlioz started. I will
return to the subject of these works later.

But Berlioz was already getting old. His daily
cares and stormy domestic life,[1] his disappointments
and passions, his commonplace and often degrading
work, soon wore him out and, finally, exhausted his
power. " Would you believe it ? " he wrote to his
friend Ferrand, " that which used to stir me to
transports of musical passion now fills me with
indifference, or even disdain. I feel as if I were
descending a mountain at a great rate. Life is so
short ; I notice that thoughts of the end have been
with me for some time past." In 1848, at forty-five
years old, he wrote in his *Mémoires :* " I find myself
so old and tired and lacking inspiration." At forty-
five years old, Wagner had patiently worked out
his theories and was feeling his power ; at forty-
five he was writing *Tristan* and *The Music of the
Future*. Abused by critics, unknown to the public,
" he remained calm, in the belief that he would be
master of the musical world in fifty years' time."[2]

Berlioz was disheartened. Life had conquered
him. It was not that he had lost any of his artistic
mastery ; on the contrary, his compositions became
more and more finished ; and nothing in his earlier
work attained the pure beauty of some of the pages
of *L'Enfance du Christ* (1850-4), or of *Les Troyens*

[1] He left Henrietta Smithson in 1842 ; she died in 1854.
[2] Written by Berlioz himself, in irony, in a letter of 1855.

(1855-63). But he was losing his power; and his intense feeling, his revolutionary ideas, and his inspiration (which in his youth had taken the place of the confidence he lacked) were failing him. He now lived on the past—the *Huit scènes de Faust* (1828) held the germs of *La Damnation de Faust* (1846); since 1833 he had been thinking of *Béatrice et Bénédict* (1862); the ideas in *Les Troyens* were inspired by his childish worship of Virgil, and had been with him all his life. But with what difficulty he now finished his task! He had only taken seven months to write *Roméo*, and " on account of not being able to write the *Requiem* fast enough, he had adopted a kind of musical shorthand ";[1] but he took seven or eight years to write *Les Troyens*, alternating between moods of enthusiasm and disgust, and feeling indifference and doubt about his work. He groped his way hesitatingly and unsteadily; he hardly understood what he was doing. He admired the more mediocre pages of his work : the scene of the Laocoon, the finale of the last act of the *Les Troyens à Troie*, the last scene with Æneas in *Les Troyens à Carthage*.[2] The empty pomposities of Spontini mingle with the loftiest conceptions. One might say that his genius became a stranger to him : it was the mechanical work of

---

[1] *Mémoires*, I, 307.

[2] About this time he wrote to Liszt regarding *L'Enfance du Christ :* " I think I have hit upon something good in Herod's scena and air with the soothsayers ; it is full of character, and will, I hope, please you. There are, perhaps, more graceful and pleasing things, but with the exception of the Bethlehem duet, I do not think they have the same quality of originality " (17 December, 1854).

D

an unconscious force, like " stalactites in a dripping
grotto." He had no impetus. It was only a matter
of time before the roof of the grotto would give way.
One is struck with the mournful despair with which
he works ; it is his last will and testament that he
is making. And when he has finished it, he will
have finished everything. His work is ended ; if
he lived another hundred years he would not have
the heart to add anything more to it. The only
thing that remains—and it is what he is about to
do—is to wrap himself in silence and die.

Oh, mournful destiny ! There are great men
who have outlived their genius ; but with Berlioz
genius outlived desire. His genius was still there ;
one feels it in the sublime pages of the third act
of *Les Troyens à Carthage*. But Berlioz had ceased
to believe in his power ; he had lost faith in everything. His genius was dying for want of nourishment ; it was a flame above an empty tomb. At
the same hour of his old age the soul of Wagner
sustained its glorious flight ; and, having conquered everything, it achieved a supreme victory
in renouncing everything for its faith. And the
divine songs of Parsifal resounded as in a splendid
temple, and replied to the cries of the suffering
Amfortas by the blessed words : " *Selig in Glauben !*
*Selig in Liebe !* "

## II

Berlioz's work did not spread itself evenly over his life ; it was accomplished in a few years. It was not like the course of a great river, as with Wagner and Beethoven ; it was a burst of genius, whose flames lit up the whole sky for a little while, and then died gradually down.[1] Let me try to tell you about this wonderful blaze.

Some of Berlioz's musical qualities are so striking that it is unnecessary to dwell upon them here. His instrumental colouring, so intoxicating and exciting,[2] his extraordinary discoveries concerning timbre, his inventions of new nuances (as in the famous combining of flutes and trombones in the *Hostias et preces* of the *Requiem,* and the curious use of the harmonics of violins and harps), and his huge and nebulous orchestra—all this lends itself to the most subtle expression of thought.[3] Think of the effect that such works must have produced at

[1] In 1830, old Rouget de Lisle called Berlioz, " a volcano in eruption " (*Mémoires,* I, 158).

[2] M. Camille Saint-Saëns wrote in his *Portraits et Souvenirs,* 1900 : " Whoever reads Berlioz's scores before hearing them played can have no real idea of their effect. The instruments appear to be arranged in defiance of all common sense ; and it would seem, to use professional slang, that *cela ne dut pas sonner,* but *cela sonne* wonderfully. If we find here and there obscurities of style, they do not appear in the orchestra ; light streams into it and plays there as in the facets of a diamond."

[3] See the excellent essay of H. Lavoix, in his *Histoire de l'Instrumentation.* It should be noticed that Berlioz's observations in his *Traité d'instrumentation et d'orchestration modernes* (1844) have not been lost upon Richard Strauss, who has just published a German edition of the work, and some of whose most famous orchestral effects are realisations of Berlioz's ideas.

that period.  Berlioz was the first to be astonished
when he heard them for the first time.  At the
*Ouverture des Francs-Juges* he wept and tore his
hair, and fell sobbing on the kettledrums.  At the
performance of his *Tuba mirum*, in Berlin, he nearly
fainted.  The composer who most nearly approached
him was Weber, and, as we have already seen, Berlioz
only knew him late in life.  But how much less rich
and complex is Weber's music, in spite of its nervous
brilliance and dreaming poetry.  Above all, Weber
is much more mundane and more of a classicist ;
he lacks Berlioz's revolutionary passion and
plebeian force ;  he is less expressive and less
grand.

How did Berlioz come to have this genius for
orchestration almost from the very first ?  He himself
says that his two masters at the Conservatoire
taught him nothing in point of instrumentation :—

> "Lesueur had only very limited ideas about
> the art.  Reicha knew the particular resources
> of most of the wind instruments ; but I think
> that he had not very advanced ideas on the subject
> of grouping them."

Berlioz taught himself.  He used to read the
score of an opera while it was being performed.

> "It was thus," he says,[1] "that I began to get

[1] One may judge of this instinct by one fact :  he wrote the
overtures of *Les Francs-Juges* and *Waverley* without really
knowing if it were possible to play them.  "I was so ignorant,'
he says, " of the mechanism of certain instruments, that after
having written the solo in D flat for the trombone in the Intro-

familiar with the use of the orchestra, and to
know its expression and timbre, as well as the
range and mechanism of most of the instruments.
By carefully comparing the effect produced with
the means used to produce it, I learned the
hidden bond which unites musical expression to
the special art of instrumentation; but no one
put me in the way of this. The study of the
methods of the three modern masters, Beethoven,
Weber, and Spontini, the impartial examination
of the traditions of instrumentation and of little-
used forms and combinations, conversations with
virtuosi, and the effects I made them try on their
different instruments, together with a little
instinct, did the rest for me."[1]

That he was an originator in this direction no
one doubts. And no one disputes, as a rule, "his
devilish cleverness," as Wagner scornfully called it,
or remains insensible to his skill and mastery in the
mechanism of expression, and his power over
sonorous matter, which make him, apart from his
creative power, a sort of magician of music, a king
of tone and rhythm. This gift is recognised even
by his enemies—by Wagner, who seeks with some
unfairness to restrict his genius within narrow
limits, and to reduce it to " a structure with wheels

duction of *Les Francs-Juges*, I feared it would be terribly difficult
to play. So I went, very anxious, to one of the trombonists of
the Opera orchestra. He looked at the passage and reassured
me. ' The key of D flat is,' he said, ' one of the pleasantest for
that instrument; and you can count on a splendid effect for
that passage ' " (*Mémoires*, I, 63).

[1] *Mémoires*, I, 64.

of infinite ingenuity and extreme cunning . . . a marvel of mechanism.''[1]

But though there is hardly anyone that Berlioz does not irritate or attract, he always strikes people by his impetuous ardour, his glowing romance, and his seething imagination, all of which makes and will continue to make his work one of the most picturesque mirrors of his age. His frenzied force of ecstasy and despair, his fulness of love and hatred, his perpetual thirst for life, which " in the heart of the deepest sorrow lights the Catherine wheels and crackers of the wildest joy ''[2]—these are the qualities that stir up the crowds in *Benvenuto* and the armies in the *Damnation*, that shake earth, heaven, and hell, and are never quenched, but remain devouring and " passionate even when the subject is far removed from passion, and yet also express sweet and tender sentiments and the deepest calm.''[3]

[1] " Berlioz displayed, in calculating the properties oɪ mechanism, a really astounding scientific knowledge. If the inventors of our modern industrial machinery are to be considered benefactors of humanity to-day, Berlioz deserves to be considered as the true saviour of the musical world ; for, thanks to him, musicians can produce surprising effects in music by the varied use of simple mechanical means. . . . Berlioz lies hopelessly buried beneath the ruins of his own contrivances '' (*Oper und Drama*, 1851).

[2] Letter from Berlioz to Ferrand.

[3] " The chief characteristics of my music are passionate expression, inward warmth, rhythmic in pulses, and unforeseen effects. When I speak of passionate expression, I mean an expression that desperately strives to reproduce the inward feeling of its subject, even when the theme is contrary to passion, and deals with gentle emotions or the deepest calm. It is this kind of expression that may be found in *L'Enfance du Christ,* and, above all, in the scene of *Le Ciel* in the *Damnation de Faust* and in the *Sanctus* of the *Requiem* '' (*Mémoires*, II, 361).

Whatever one may think of this volcanic force, of this torrential stream of youth and passion, it is impossible to deny them ; one might as well deny the sun.

And I shall not dwell on Berlioz's love of Nature, which, as M. Prudhomme shows us, is the soul of a composition like the *Damnation* and, one might say, of all great compositions. No musician, with the exception of Beethoven, has loved Nature so profoundly. Wagner himself did not realise the intensity of emotion which she roused in Berlioz,[1] and how this feeling impregnated the music of the *Damnation*, of *Roméo*, and of *Les Troyens*.

But this genius had other characteristics which are less well known, though they are not less unusual. The first is his sense of pure beauty. Berlioz's exterior romanticism must not make us blind to this. He had a Virgilian soul ; and if his colouring recalls that of Weber, his design has often an Italian suavity. Wagner never had this love of beauty in the Latin sense of the word. Who has understood the Southern nature, beautiful form, and harmonious movement like Berlioz ? Who, since Gluck, has recognised so well the secret of classical beauty ? Since *Orfeo* was composed, no one has carved in music a bas-relief so perfect as

[1] " So you are in the midst of melting glaciers in your *Niebelungen !* To be writing in the presence of Nature herself must be splendid. It is an enjoyment which I am denied. Beautiful landscapes, lofty peaks, or great stretches of sea, absorb me instead of evoking ideas in me. I feel, but I cannot express what I feel. I can only paint the moon when I see its reflection in the bottom of a well " (Berlioz to Wagner, 10 September, 1855).

the entrance of Andromache in the second act of
*Les Troyens à Troie.*  In *Les Troyens à Carthage,*
the fragrance of the Æneid is shed over the night
of love, and we see the luminous sky and hear the
murmur of the sea.  Some of his melodies are like
statues, or the pure lines of Athenian friezes, or the
noble gesture of beautiful Italian girls, or the
undulating profile of the Albanian hills filled with
divine laughter.  He has done more than felt and
translated into music the beauty of the Mediterranean—he has created beings worthy of a Greek
tragedy.  His Cassandre alone would suffice to
rank him among the greatest tragic poets that
music has ever known.  And Cassandre is a worthy
sister of Wagner's Brünnhilde ; but she has the
advantage of coming of a nobler race, and of
having a lofty restraint of spirit and action that
Sophocles himself would have loved.

Not enough attention has been drawn to the
classical nobility from which Berlioz's art so spon-
taneously springs.  It is not fully acknowledged that
he was, of all nineteenth-century musicians, the
one who had in the highest degree the sense of
plastic beauty.  Nor do people always recognise
that he was a writer of sweet and flowing melodies.
Weingartner expressed the surprise he felt when,
imbued with current prejudice against Berlioz's
lack of melodic invention, he opened, by chance,
the score of the overture of *Benvenuto* and found in
that short composition, which barely takes ten
minutes to play, not one or two, but four or five
melodies of admirable richness and originality :—

"I began to laugh, both with pleasure at having discovered such a treasure, and with annoyance at finding how narrow human judgment is. Here I counted five themes, all of them plastic and expressive of personality ; of admirable workmanship, varied in form, working up by degrees to a climax, and then finishing with strong effect. And this from a composer who was said by critics and the public to be devoid of creative power ! From that day on there has been for me another great citizen in the republic of art."[1]

Before this, Berlioz had written in 1864 :—

" It is quite easy for others to convince themselves that, without even limiting me to take a very short melody as the theme of a composition— as the greatest musicians have often done—I have always endeavoured to put a wealth of melody into my compositions. One may, of course, dispute the worth of these melodies, their distinction, originality, or charm—it is not for me to judge them—but to deny their existence is either unfair or foolish. They are often on a large scale ; and an immature or short-sighted musical vision may not clearly distinguish their form ; or, again, they may be accompanied by secondary melodies which, to a limited vision, may veil the form of the principal ones. Or, lastly, shallow musicians may find these melodies so unlike the funny little things that they call

[1] *Musikführer*, 29 November, 1903.

melodies, that they cannot bring themselves to
give the same name to both."[1]

And what a splendid variety there is in these
melodies : there is the song in Gluck's style (Cassandre's airs), the pure German *lied* (Marguerite's
song, " D'amour l'ardente flamme "), the Italian
melody, after Bellini, in its most limpid and happy
form (arietta of Arlequin in *Benvenuto*), the broad
Wagnerian phrase (finale of *Roméo*), the folk-song
(chorus of shepherds in *L'Enfance du Christ*),
and the freest and most modern recitative (the
monologues of Faust), which was Berlioz's own
invention, with its full development, its pliant
outline, and its intricate nuances.[2]

I have said that Berlioz had a matchless gift for
expressing tragic melancholy, weariness of life, and
the pangs of death. In a general way, one may say
that he was a great elegist in music. Ambros, who
was a very discerning and unbiassed critic, said :
" Berlioz feels with inward delight and profound
emotion what no musician, except Beethoven, has
felt before." And Heinrich Heine had a keen
perception of Berlioz's originality when he called
him " a colossal nightingale, a lark the size of an
eagle." The simile is not only picturesque, but of
remarkable aptness. For Berlioz's colossal force
is at the service of a folorn and tender heart ; he
has nothing of the heroism of Beethoven, or Handel,

[1] *Mémoires*, II, 361.
[2] M. Jean Marnold has remarked this genius for monody in
Berlioz in his article on *Hector Berlioz, musicien* (*Mercure de
France*, 15 January, and 1 February, 1905).

or Gluck, or even Schubert. He has all the charm
of an Umbrian painter, as is shown in *L'Enfance du
Christ*, as well as sweetness and inward sadness, the
gift of tears, and an elegiac passion.

.　.　.　.　.　.

Now I come to Berlioz's great originality, an
originality which is rarely spoken of, though it
makes him more than a great musician, more than
the successor of Beethoven, or, as some call him,
the forerunner of Wagner. It is an originality that
entitles him to be known, even more fitly than
Wagner himself, as the creator of " an art of the
future," the apostle of a new music, which even
to-day has hardly made itself felt.

Berlioz is original in a double sense. By the
extraordinary complexity of his genius he touched
the two opposite poles of his art, and showed us
two entirely different aspects of music—that of a
great popular art, and that of music made free.

We are all enslaved by the musical tradition of
the past. For generations we have been so accustomed to carry this yoke that we scarcely notice it.
And in consequence of Germany's monopoly of
music since the end of the eighteenth century,
musical traditions—which had been chiefly Italian
in the two preceding centuries—now became almost
entirely German. We think in German forms : the
plan of phrases, their development, their balance,
and all the rhetoric of music and the grammar of
composition comes to us from foreign thought,
slowly elaborated by German masters. That

domination has never been more complete or more
heavy since Wagner's victory. Then reigned over
the world this great German period—a scaly monster
with a thousand arms, whose grasp was so extensive that it included pages, scenes, acts, and whole
dramas in its embrace. We cannot say that French
writers have ever tried to write in the style of
Goethe or Schiller; but French composers have
tried and are still trying to write music after the
manner of German musicians.

Why be astonished at it? Let us face the
matter plainly. In music we have not, so to speak,
any masters of French style. All our greatest
composers are foreigners. The founder of the first
school of French opera, Lulli, was Florentine; the
founder of the second school, Gluck, was German;
the two founders of the third school were Rossini,
an Italian, and Meyerbeer, a German; the creators
of *opéra-comique* were Duni, an Italian, and Gretry,
a Belgian; Franck, who revolutionised our modern
school of opera, was also Belgian. These men
brought with them a style peculiar to their race;
or else they tried to found, as Gluck did, an " international " style,[1] by which they effaced the more
individual characteristics of the French spirit.
The most French of all these styles is the *opéra-
comique*, the work of two foreigners, but owing
much more to the *opéra-bouffe* than is generally
admitted, and, in any case, representing France very
insufficiently. Some more rational minds have tried

---

[1] Gluck himself said this in a letter to the *Mercure de France*,
February, 1773.

to rid themselves of this Italian and German influence, but have mostly arrived at creating an intermediate Germano-Italian style, of which the operas of Auber and Ambroise Thomas are a type.

Before Berlioz's time there was really only one master of the first rank who made a great effort to liberate French music : it was Rameau ; and, despite his genius, he was conquered by Italian art.[1]

By force of circumstance, therefore, French music found itself moulded in foreign musical forms. And in the same way that Germany in the eighteenth century tried to imitate French architecture and literature, so France in the nineteenth century acquired the habit of speaking German in music. As most men speak more than they think, even thought itself became Germanised ; and it was difficult then to discover, through this traditional insincerity, the true and spontaneous form of French musical thought.

But Berlioz's genius found it by instinct. From the first he strove to free French music from the oppression of the foreign tradition that was suffocating it.[2]

[1] I am not speaking of the Franco-Flemish masters at the end of the sixteenth century : of Jannequin, Costeley, Claude le Jeune, or Mauduit, recently discovered by M. Henry Expert, who are possessed of so original a flavour, and have yet remained almost entirely unknown from their own time to ours. Religious wars bruised France's musical traditions and defiled some of the grandeur of her art.

[2] It is amusing to find Wagner comparing Berlioz with Auber, as the type of a true French musician—Auber and his mixed Italian and German opera. That shows how Wagner, like most Germans, was incapable of grasping the real originality of French music, and how he saw only its externals. The best way to find out the musical characteristics of a nation is to study

He was fitted in every way for the part, even by his deficiencies and his ignorance. His classical education in music was incomplete. M. Saint-Saëns tells us that "the past did not exist for him; he did not understand the old composers, as his knowledge of them was limited to what he had read about them." He did not know Bach. Happy ignorance! He was able to write oratorios like *L'Enfance du Christ* without being worried by memories and traditions of the German masters of oratorio. There are men like Brahms who have been, nearly all their life, but reflections of the past. Berlioz never sought to be anything but himself. It was thus that he created that masterpiece, *La Fuite en Égypte*, which sprang from his keen sympathy with the people.

He had one of the most untrammelled spirits that ever breathed. Liberty was for him a desperate necessity. "Liberty of heart, of mind, of soul—of everything. . . . Real liberty, absolute and immense!"[1] And this passionate love of liberty, which was his misfortune in life, since it deprived him of the comfort of any faith, refused him any refuge for his thoughts, robbed him of peace, and even of the soft pillow of scepticism—this "real liberty" formed the unique originality and grandeur of his musical conceptions.

its folk-songs. If only someone would devote himself to the study of French folk-song (and there is no lack of material), people would realise perhaps how much it differs from German folk-song, and how the temperament of the French race shows itself there as being sweeter and freer, more vigorous and more expressive.

[1] *Mémoires*, I, 221.

" Music," wrote Berlioz to C. Lobe, in 1852,
" is the most poetic, the most powerful, the most
living of all arts. She ought to be the freest, but
she is not yet. . . . Modern music is like the
classic Andromeda, naked and divinely beautiful.
She is chained to a rock on the shores of a vast
sea, and awaits the victorious Perseus who shall
loose her bonds and break in pieces the chimera
called Routine."

The business was to free music from its limited
rhythms and from the traditional forms and rules
that enclosed it ;[1] and, above all, it needed to be
free from the domination of speech, and to be
released from its humiliating bondage to poetry.
Berlioz wrote to the Princess of Wittgenstein, in
1856 :—

" I am for free music. Yes, I want music to
be proudly free, to be victorious, to be supreme. I
want her to take all she can, so that there may
be no more Alps or Pyrenees for her. But she

[1] " Music to-day, in the vigour of her youth, is emancipated
and free and can do what she pleases. Many old rules have no
longer any vogue ; they were made by unreflecting minds, or
by lovers of routine for other lovers of routine. New needs of
the mind, of the heart, and of the sense of hearing, make necessary new endeavours and, in some cases, the breaking of ancient
laws. Many forms have become too hackneyed to be still
adopted. The same thing may be entirely good or entirely bad,
according to the use one makes of it, or the reasons one has for
making use of it. Sound and sonority are secondary to thought,
and thought is secondary to feeling and passion." (These
opinions were given with reference to Wagner's concerts in Paris,
in 1860, and are taken from *A travers chants*, p. 312.)

Compare Beethoven's words : " There is no rule that one may
not break for the advancement of beauty."

must achieve her victories by fighting in person, and not rely upon her lieutenants. I should like her to have, if possible, good verse drawn up in order of battle ; but, like Napoleon, she must face the fire herself, and, like Alexander, march in the front ranks of the phalanx. She is so powerful that in some cases she would conquer unaided ; for she has the right to say with Medea : ' I, myself, am enough.' "

Berlioz protested vigorously against Gluck's impious theory[1] and Wagner's " crime " in making music the slave of speech. Music is the highest poetry and knows no master.[2] It was for Berlioz, therefore, continually to increase the power of expression in pure music. And while Wagner, who was more moderate and a closer follower of tradition, sought to establish a compromise (perhaps an impossible one) between music and speech, and to create the new lyric drama, Berlioz, who was

[1] Is it necessary to recall the *épître dédicatoire* of *Alceste* in 1769, and Gluck's declaration that he " sought to bring music to its true function—that of helping poetry to strengthen the expression of the emotions and the interest of a situation . . . and to make it what fine colouring and the happy arrangement of light and shade are to a skilful drawing " ?

[2] This revolutionary theory was already Mozart's : " Music should reign supreme and make one forget everything else. . . .. In an opera it is absolutely necessary that Poetry should be Music's obedient daughter " (Letter to his father, 13 October, 1781). Despairing probably at being unable to obtain this obedience, Mozart thought seriously of breaking up the form of opera, and of putting in its place, in 1778, a sort of melodrama (of which Rousseau had given an example in 1773), which he called " duodrama," where music and poetry were loosely associated, yet not dependent on each other, but went side by side on two parallel roads (Letter of 12 November, 1778).

more revolutionary, achieved the dramatic symphony, of which the unequalled model to-day is still *Roméo et Juliette*.

The dramatic symphony naturally fell foul of all formal theories. Two arguments were set up against it : one derived from Bayreuth, and by now an act of faith ; the other, current opinion, upheld by the crowd that speaks of music without understanding it.

The first argument, maintained by Wagner, is that music cannot really express action without the help of speech and gesture. It is in the name of this opinion that so many people condemn *a priori* Berlioz's *Roméo*. They think it childish to try and *translate* action into music. I suppose they think it less childish to *illustrate* an action by music. Do they think that gesture associates itself very happily with music ? If only they would try to root up this great fiction, which has bothered us for the last three centuries ; if only they would open their eyes and see—what great men like Rousseau and Tolstoy saw so clearly—the silliness of opera ; if only they would see the anomalies of the Bayreuth show. In the second act of *Tristan* there is a celebrated passage, where Ysolde, burning with desire, is waiting for Tristan ; she sees him come at last, and from afar she waves her scarf to the accompaniment of a phrase repeated several times by the orchestra. I cannot express the effect produced on me by that *imitation* (for it is nothing else) of a series of sounds by a series of gestures ; I can never see it without indignation or without laughing.

E

The curious thing is that when one hears this
passage at a concert, one sees the gesture. At the
theatre either one does not " see " it, or it appears
childish. The natural action becomes stiff when
clad in musical armour, and the absurdity of trying
to make the two agree is forced upon one. In the
music of *Rheingold* one pictures the stature and gait
of the giants, and one sees the lightning gleam and
the rainbow reflected on the clouds. In the theatre
it is like a game of marionettes ; and one feels the
impassable gulf between music and gesture. Music
is a world apart. When music wishes to depict the
drama, it is not real action which is reflected in it,
it is the ideal action transfigured by the spirit, and
perceptible only to the inner vision. The worst
foolishness is to present two visions—one for the
eyes and one for the spirit. Nearly always they kill
each other.

The other argument urged against the symphony
with a programme is the pretended classical argument (it is not really classical at all). " Music,"
they say, " is not meant to express definite subjects ;
it is only fitted for vague ideas. The more indefinite
it is, the greater its power, and the more it suggests."
I ask, What is an indefinite art ? What is a vague
art ? Do not the two words contradict each other ?
Can this strange combination exist at all ? Can an
artist write anything that he does not clearly conceive ? Do people think he composes at random as
his genius whispers to him ? One must at least
say this : A symphony of Beethoven's is a " definite"
work down to its innermost folds ; and Beethoven

had, if not an exact knowledge, at least a clear
intuition of what he was about. His last quartets
are descriptive symphonies of his soul, and very
differently carried out from Berlioz's symphonies.
Wagner was able to analyse one of the former
under the name of " A Day with Beethoven."
Beethoven was always trying to translate into
music the depths of his heart, the subtleties of his
spirit, which are not to be explained clearly by
words, but which are as definite as words—in fact,
more definite ; for a word, being an abstract thing,
sums up many experiences and comprehends many
different meanings. Music is a hundred times more
expressive and exact than speech ; and it is not
only her right to express particular emotions and
subjects, it is her duty. If that duty is not fulfilled,
the result is not music—it is nothing at all.

Berlioz is thus the true inheritor of Beethoven's
thought. The difference between a work like
*Roméo* and one of Beethoven's symphonies is that
the former, it would seem, endeavours to express
objective emotions and subjects in music. I do
not see why music should not follow poetry in
getting away from introspection and trying to
paint the drama of the universe. Shakespeare is as
good as Dante. Besides, one may add, it is always
Berlioz himself that is discovered in his music : it
is his soul starving for love and mocked at by
shadows which is revealed through all the scenes
of *Roméo*.

I will not prolong a discussion where so many
things must be left unsaid. But I would suggest

that, once and for all, we get rid of these absurd
endeavours to fence in art. Do not let us say:
Music can . . . Music cannot express such-and-
such a thing. Let us say rather, If genius pleases,
everything is possible ; and if music so wishes, she
may be painting and poetry to-morrow. Berlioz
has proved it well in his *Roméo*.

This *Roméo* is an extraordinary work : " a
wonderful isle, where a temple of pure art is set up."
For my part, not only do I consider it equal to the
most powerful of Wagner's creations, but I believe
it to be richer in its teaching and in its resources
for art—resources and teaching which contemporary
French art has not yet fully turned to account.
One knows that for several years the young French
school has been making efforts to deliver our music
from German models, to create a language of
recitative that shall belong to France and that the
*leitmotif* will not overwhelm ; a more exact and
less heavy language, which in expressing the freedom
of modern thought will not have to seek the help
of the classical or Wagnerian forms. Not long ago,
the *Schola Cantorum* published a manifesto that
proclaimed " the liberty of musical declamation . . .
free speech in free music . . . the triumph of
natural music with the free movement of speech and
the plastic rhythm of the ancient dance "—thus
declaring war on the metrical art of the last three
centuries.[1]

Well, here is that music ; you will nowhere
find a more perfect model. It is true that many

[1] *Tribune de Saint Gervais*, November, 1903.

who profess the principles of this music repudiate
the model, and do not hide their disdain for Berlioz.
That makes me doubt a little, I admit, the results
of their efforts. If they do not feel the wonderful
freedom of Berlioz's music, and do not see that it was
the delicate veil of a very living spirit, then I think
there will be more of archaism than real life in
their pretensions to " free music." Study, not
only the most celebrated pages of his work, such as
the *Scène d'amour* (the one of all his compositions
that Berlioz himself liked best),[1] *La Tristesse de
Roméo*, or *La Fête des Capulet* (where a spirit like
Wagner's own unlooses and subdues again tempests
of passion and joy), but take less well-known pages,
such as the *Scherzetto chanté de la reine Mab*, or the
*Réveil de Juliette*, and the music describing the
death of the two lovers.[2] In the one what light
grace there is, in the other what vibrating passion,
and in both of them what freedom and apt expression of ideas. The language is magnificent, of
wonderful clearness and simplicity ; not a word too
much, and not a word that does not reveal an
unerring pen. In nearly all the big works of Berlioz
before 1845 (that is up to the *Damnation*) you will
find this nervous precision and sweeping liberty.

Then there is the freedom of his rhythms. Schumann, who was nearest to Berlioz of all musicians

[1] *Mémoires*, II, 365.

[2] " This composition contains a dose of sublimity much too
strong for the ordinary public ; and Berlioz, with the splendid
insolence of genius, advises the conductor, in a note, to turn
the page and pass it over " (Georges de Massougnes, *Berlioz*).
This fine study by Georges de Massougnes appeared in 1870,
and is very much in advance of its time.

of that time, and, therefore, best able to understand
him, had been struck by this since the composition
of the *Symphonie fantastique*.[1]   He wrote :—

   " The present age has certainly not produced a
work in which similar times and rhythms combined
with dissimilar times and rhythms have been
more freely used.   The second part of a phrase
rarely corresponds with the first, the reply to
the question.   This anomaly is characteristic of
Berlioz, and is natural to his southern temperament."

Far from objecting to this, Schumann sees in it
something necessary to musical evolution.

   " Apparently music is showing a tendency to
go back to its beginnings, to the time when the
laws of rhythm did not yet trouble her ; it seems
that she wishes to free herself, to regain an
utterance that is unconstrained, and raise herself to the dignity of a sort of poetic language."

And Schumann quotes these words of Ernest
Wagner :  " He who shakes off the tyranny of time
and delivers us from it will, as far as one can see,
give back freedom to music."[2]

   [1] " Oh, how I love, honour, and reverence Schumann for
having written this article alone " (Hugo Wolf, 1884).
   [2] *Neue Zeitschrift für Musik*.   See *Hector Berlioz und Robert
Schumann*.   Berlioz was constantly fighting for this freedom of
rhythm—for " those harmonies of rhythm," as he said.   He
wished to form a Rhythm class at the Conservatoire (*Mémoires*,
II, 241), but such a thing was not understood in France.
Without being as backward as Italy on this point, France is
still resisting the emancipation of rhythm (*Mémoires*, II, 196).
But during the last ten years great progress in music has been
made in France.

Remark also Berlioz's freedom of melody. His
musical phrases pulse and flow like life itself.
"Some phrases taken separately," says Schumann,
"have such an intensity that they will not bear
harmonising—*as in many ancient folk-songs*—and
often even an accompaniment spoils their fulness."[1]
These melodies so correspond with the emotions,
that they reproduce the least thrills of body and
mind by their vigorous workings-up and delicate
reliefs, by splendid barbarities of modulation and
strong and glowing colour, by gentle gradations
of light and shade or imperceptible ripples of
thought, which flow over the body like a steady tide.
It is an art of peculiar sensitiveness, more delicately
expressive than that of Wagner; not satisfying
itself with the modern tonality, but going back to
old modes—a rebel, as M. Saint-Saëns remarks,
to the polyphony which had governed music since
Bach's day, and which is perhaps, after all, "a
heresy destined to disappear."[2]

How much finer, to my idea, are Berlioz's recitatives, with their long and winding rhythms,[3] than

---

[1] *Ibid.* "A rare peculiarity," adds Schumann, "which
distinguishes nearly all his melodies." Schumann understands
why Berlioz often gives as an accompaniment to his melodies a
simple bass, or chords of the augmented and diminished fifth—
ignoring the intermediate parts.

[2] "What will then remain of actual art? Perhaps Berlioz
will be its sole representative. Not having studied the pianoforte, he had an instinctive aversion to counterpoint. He is in
this respect the opposite of Wagner, who was the embodiment
of counterpoint, and drew the utmost he could from its laws"
(Saint-Saëns).

[3] Jacques Passy notes that with Berlioz the most frequent
phrases consist of twelve, sixteen, eighteen, or twenty bars.
With Wagner, phrases of eight bars are rare, those of four more

Wagner's declamations, which—apart from the climax of a subject, where the air breaks into bold and vigorous phrases, whose influence elsewhere is often weak—limit themselves to the quasi-notation of spoken inflections, and jar noisily against the fine harmonies of the orchestra. Berlioz's orchestration, too, is of a more delicate temper, and has a freer life than Wagner's, flowing in an impetuous stream, and sweeping away everything in its course; it is also less united and solid, but more flexible; its nature is undulating and varied, and the thousand imperceptible impulses of the spirit and of action are reflected there. It is a marvel of spontaneity and caprice.

In spite of appearances, Wagner is a classicist compared with Berlioz; he carried on and perfected the work of the German classicists; he made no innovations; he is the pinnacle and the close of one evolution of art. Berlioz began a new art; and one finds in it all the daring and gracious ardour of youth. The iron laws that bound the art of Wagner are not to be found in Berlioz's early works, which give one the illusion of perfect freedom.[1]

common, those of two still more so, while those of one bar are most frequent of all (*Berlioz et Wagner*, article published in *Le Correspondant*, 10 June, 1888).

[1] One must make mention here of the poorness and awkwardness of Berlioz's harmony—which is incontestable—since some critics and composers have been able to see (Am I saying something ridiculous ?—Wagner would say it for me) nothing but "faults of orthography" in his genius. To these terrible grammarians—who, two hundred years ago, criticised Molière on account of his "jargon"—I shall reply by quoting Schumann.

"Berlioz's harmonies, in spite of the diversity of their effect, obtained from very scanty material, are distinguished

As soon as the profound originality of Berlioz's music has been grasped, one understands why it encountered, and still encounters, so much secret hostility. How many accomplished musicians of distinction and learning, who pay honour to artistic tradition, are incapable of understanding Berlioz because they cannot bear the air of liberty breathed by his music. They are so used to thinking in German, that Berlioz's speech upsets and shocks them. I can well believe it. It is the first time a French musician has dared to think in French ; and that is the reason why I warned you of the danger of accepting too meekly German ideas about Berlioz. Men like Weingartner, Richard Strauss, and Mottl —thoroughbred musicians—are, without doubt, able to appreciate Berlioz's genius better and more quickly than we French musicians. But I rather mistrust the kind of appreciation they feel for a spirit so opposed to their own. It is for France and French people to learn to read his thoughts ; they

by a sort of simplicity, and even by a solidity and concise-ness, which one only meets with in Beethoven. . . . One may find here and there harmonies that are commonplace and trivial, and others that are incorrect—at least according to the old rules. In some places his harmonies have a fine effect, and in others their result is vague and indeterminate, or it sounds badly, or is too elaborate and far-fetched. Yet with Berlioz all this somehow takes on a certain distinction. If one attempted to correct it, or even slightly to modify it —for a skilled musician it would be child's play—the music would become dull " (Article on the *Symphonie fantastique*).

But let us leave that " grammatical discussion " as well as what Wagner wrote on " the childish question as to whether it is permitted or not to introduce ' neologisms ' in matters of harmony and melody " (Wagner to Berlioz, 22 February, 1860). As Schumann has said, " Look out for fifths, and then leave us in peace."

are intimately theirs, and one day will give them
their salvation.

.     .     .     .     .     .

Berlioz's other great originality lay in his talent
for music that was suited to the spirit of the common
people, recently raised to sovereignty, and the
young democracy.  In spite of his aristocratic disdain, his soul was with the masses.  M. Hippeau
applies to him Taine's definition of a romantic
artist : " the plebeian of a new race, richly gifted,
and filled with aspirations, who, having attained
for the first time the world's heights, noisily displays
the ferment of his mind and heart."  Berlioz grew
up in the midst of revolutions and stories of Imperial
achievement.  He wrote his cantata for the *Prix de
Rome* in July, 1830, " to the hard, dull noise of
stray bullets, which whizzed above the roofs, and
came to flatten themselves against the wall near
his window."[1]  When he had finished this cantata,
he went, " pistol in hand, to play the blackguard
in Paris with the *sainte canaille*."  He sang the
*Marseillaise*, and made " all who had a voice and
heart and blood in their veins "[2] sing it too.  On
his journey to Italy he travelled from Marseilles
to Livourne with Mazzinian conspirators, who were
going to take part in the insurrection of Modena
and Bologna.  Whether he was conscious of it or
not, he was the musician of revolutions ; his

[1] *Mémoires*, I, 155.
[2] These words are taken from Berlioz's directions on the
score of his arrangement of the *Marseillaise* for full orchestra
and double choir.

sympathies were with the people. Not only did he fill his scenes in the theatre with swarming and riotous crowds, like those of the Roman Carnival in the second act of *Benvenuto* (anticipating by thirty years the crowds of *Die Meistersinger*), but ⸌he created a music of the masses and a colossal style.

His model here was Beethoven ; Beethoven of the Eroica, of the C minor, of the A, and, above all, of the Ninth Symphony. He was Beethoven's follower in this as well as other things, and the apostle who carried on his work.[1] And with his understanding of material effects and sonorous matter, he built edifices, as he says, that were "Babylonian and Ninevitish,"[2] "music after Michelangelo,"[3] " on an immense scale."[4] It was the *Symphonie funèbre et triomphale* for two orchestras

[1] " From Beethoven," says Berlioz, " dates the advent in art of colossal forms " (*Mémoires*, II, 112). But Berlioz forgot one of Beethoven's models—Handel. One must also take into account the musicians of the French revolution : Mehul, Gossec, Cherubini, and Lesueur, whose works, though they may not equal their intentions, are not without grandeur, and often disclose the intuition of a new and noble and popular art.

[2] Letter to Morel, 1855. Berlioz thus describes the *Tibi omnes* and the *Judex* of his *Te Deum*. Compare Heine's judgment : " Berlioz's music makes me think of gigantic kinds of extinct animals, of fabulous empires. . . . Babylon, the hanging gardens of Semiramis, the wonders of Nineveh, the daring buildings of Mizraïm."

[3] *Mémoires*, I, 17.

[4] Letter to an unknown person, written probably about 1855, in the collection of Siegfried Ochs, and published in the *Geschichte der französischen Musik* of Alfred Bruneau, 1904. That letter contains a rather curious analytical catalogue of Berlioz's works, drawn up by himself. He notes there his predilection for compositions of a " colossal nature," such as the *Requiem*, the *Symphonie funèbre et triomphale*, and the *Te Deum*, or those of " an immense style," such as the *Impériale*.

and a choir, and the *Te Deum* for orchestra, organ,
and three choirs, which Berlioz loved (whose finale
*Judex crederis* seemed to him the most effective
thing he had ever written[1]), as well as the *Impériale*,
for two orchestras and two choirs, and the famous
*Requiem*, with its "four orchestras of brass instruments, placed round the main orchestra and the
mass of voices, but separated and answering one
another at a distance." Like the *Requiem*, these
compositions are often crude in style and of rather
commonplace sentiment, but their grandeur is
overwhelming. This is not due only to the hugeness
of the means employed, but also to " the breadth of
the style and to the formidable slowness of some
of the progressions—whose final aim one cannot
guess—which gives these compositions a strangely
gigantic character."[2] Berlioz has left in these
compositions striking examples of the beauty that
may reveal itself in a crude mass of music. Like
the towering Alps, they move one by their very
immensity. A German critic says : " In these
Cyclopean works the composer lets the elemental
and brute forces of sound and pure rhythm have
their fling."[3] It is scarcely music, it is the force of
Nature herself. Berlioz himself calls his *Requiem*
" a musical cataclysm."[4]

These hurricanes are let loose in order to speak to
the people, to stir and rouse the dull ocean of

[1] *Mémoires*, II, 364. See also the letter quoted above.
[2] *Mémoires*, II, 363. See also II, 163, and the description of
the great festival of 1844, with its 1,022 performers.
[3] Hermann Kretzschmar, *Führer durch den Konzertsaal*.
[4] *Mémoires*, I, 312.

humanity. The *Requiem* is a Last Judgment, not meant, like that of the Sixtine Chapel (which Berlioz did not care for at all) for great aristocracies, but for a crowd, a surging, excited, and rather savage crowd. The *Marche de Rakoczy* is less an Hungarian march than the music for a revolutionary fight; it sounds the charge; and Berlioz tells us it might bear Virgil's verses for a motto :—

"... Furor iraque mentes
Praecipitant, pulchrumque mori succurrit in armis."[1]

When Wagner heard the *Symphonie funèbre et triomphale* he was forced to admit Berlioz's " skill in writing compositions that were popular in the best sense of the word."

" In listening to that symphony I had a lively impression that any little street boy in a blue blouse and red bonnet would understand it perfectly. I have no hesitation in giving precedence to that work over Berlioz's other works; it is big and noble from the first note to the last; a fine and eager patriotism rises from its first

[1] Letter to some young Hungarians, 14 February, 1861. See the *Mémoires*, II, 212, for the incredible emotion which the *Marche de Rakoczy* roused in the audience at Budapest, and, above all, for the astonishing scene at the end :—

" I saw a man enter unexpectedly. He was miserably clad, but his face shone with a strange rapture. When he saw me, he threw himself upon me and embraced me with fervour; his eyes filled with tears, and he was hardly able to get out the words, ' Ah, monsieur, monsieur! moi Hongrois . . . pauvre diable . . . pas parler Français . . . un poco Italiano. Pardonnez mon extase. . . . Ah! ai compris votre canon. . . . Oui, oui, la grande bataille. . . . Allemands chiens ! ' And then striking his breast violently : ' Dans le cœur, moi . . . je vous porte. . . . *Ah ! Français . . . révolutionnaire . . . savoir faire la musique des révolutions !* ' "

expression of compassion to the final glory of the apotheosis, and keeps it from any unwholesome exaggeration. I want gladly to express my conviction that that symphony will fire men's courage and will live as long as a nation bears the name of France."[1]

How do such works come to be neglected by our Republic ? How is it they have not a place in our public life ? Why are they not part of our great ceremonies ? That is what one would wonderingly ask oneself if one had not seen, for the last century, the indifference of the State to Art. What might not Berlioz have done if the means had been given him, or if his works had found a place in the fêtes of the Revolution ? Unhappily, one must add that here again his character was the enemy of his genius. As this apostle of musical freedom, in the second part of his life, became afraid of himself and recoiled before the results of his own principles, and returned to classicism, so this revolutionary fell to sullenly disparaging the people and revolutions ; and he talks about " the republican cholera," " the dirty and stupid republic," " the republic of street-porters and rag-gatherers," " the filthy rabble of humanity a hundred times more stupid and animal in its twitchings and revolutionary grimacings than the baboons and orang-outangs of Borneo."[2] What

---

[1] Written 5 May, 1841.
[2] Berlioz never ceased to inveigh against the Revolution of 1848—which should have had his sympathies. Instead of finding material, like Wagner, in the excitement of that time for impassioned compositions, he worked at *L'Enfance du Christ*. He

ingratitude ! He owed to these revolutions, to
these democratic storms, to these human tempests,
the best of all his genius—and he disowned it all.
This musician of a new era took refuge in the past.

.　　.　　.　　.　　.　　.

Well, what did it matter ? Whether he wished it
or not, he opened out some magnificent roads for
Art. He has shown the music of France the way in
which her genius should tread ; he has shown her
possibilities she had never before dreamed of. He
has given us a musical utterance at once truthful
and expressive, free from foreign traditions, coming
from the depths of our being, and reflecting our
spirit ; an utterance which responded to his imagination, to his instinct for what was picturesque,
to his fleeting impressions, and his delicate shades
of feeling. He has laid the strong foundation of a
national and popular music for the greatest republic
in Europe.

These are shining qualities. If Berlioz had had
Wagner's reasoning power and had made the
utmost use of his intuitions, if he had had Wagner's
will and had shaped the inspirations of his genius
and welded them into a solid whole, I venture to
say that he would have made a revolution in music
greater than Wagner's own ; for Wagner, though
stronger and more master of himself, was less
original and, at bottom, but the close of a glorious
past.

affected absolute indifference—he who was so little made for
indifference. He approved the State's action, and despised its
visionary hopes,

Will that revolution still be accomplished?
Perhaps; but it has suffered half a century's
delay. Berlioz bitterly calculated that people would
begin to understand him about the year 1940.[1]

After all, why be astonished that his mighty
mission was too much for him? He was so alone.[2]
As people forsook him, his loneliness stood out in
greater relief. He was alone in the age of Wagner,
Liszt, Schumann, and Franck; alone, yet containing a whole world in himself, of which his
enemies, his friends, his admirers, and he himself,
were not quite conscious; alone, and tortured by
his loneliness. Alone—the word is repeated by the
music of his youth and his old age, by the *Symphonie fantastique* and *Les Troyens*. It is the word
I read in the portrait before me as I write these
lines—the beautiful portrait of the *Mémoires*,
where his face looks out in sad and stern reproach
on the age that so misunderstood him.

[1] " My musical career would finish very pleasingly if only I
could live for a hundred and forty years " (*Mémoires*, II, 390).
[2] This solitude struck Wagner. " Berlioz's loneliness is not
only one of external circumstances; its origin is in his temperament. Though he is a Frenchman, with quick sympathies and
interests like those of his fellow-citizens, yet he is none the less
alone. He sees no one before him who will hold out a helping
hand, there is no one by his side on whom he may lean "
(Article written 5 May, 1841). As one reads these words, one
feels it was Wagner's lack of sympathy and not his intelligence
that prevented him from understanding Berlioz. In his heart I
do not doubt that he knew well who was his great rival. But he
never said anything about it—unless perhaps one counts an odd
document, certainly not intended for publication, where he (even
he) compares him to Beethoven and to Bonaparte (Manuscript
in the collection of Alfred Bovet, published by Mottl in German
magazines, and by M. Georges de Massougnes in the *Revue d'art
dramatique*, 1 January, 1902).

# WAGNER

## " SIEGFRIED "

THERE is nothing so thrilling as first impressions.
I remember when, as a child, I heard fragments of
Wagner's music for the first time at one of old
Pasdeloup's concerts in the Cirque d'Hiver. I was
taken there one dull and foggy Sunday afternoon;
and as we left the yellow fog outside and entered
the hall we were met by an overpowering warmth,
a dazzling blaze of light, and the murmuring voice
of the crowd. My eyes were blinded, I breathed
with difficulty, and my limbs soon became cramped ;
for we sat on wooden benches, crushed in a narrow
space between solid walls of human beings. But
with the first note of the music all was forgotten,
and one fell into a state of painful yet delicious
torpor. Perhaps one's very discomfort made the
pleasure keener. Those who know the intoxication
of climbing a mountain know also how closely it is
associated with the discomforts of the climb—with
fatigue and the blinding light of the sun, with out-
of-breathness, and all the other sensations that
rouse and stimulate life and make the body tingle,
so that the remembrance of it all is carved indelibly
on the mind. The comfort of a playhouse adds

nothing to the illusion of a play ; and it may even be due to the entire inconvenience of the old concert-rooms that I owe my vivid recollection of my first meeting with Wagner's work.

How mysterious it was, and what a strange agitation it filled me with ! There were new effects of orchestration, new timbres, new rhythms, and new subjects ; it held the wild poetry of the far-away Middle Ages and old legends, it throbbed with the fever of our hidden sorrows and desires. I did not understand it very well. How should I ? The music was taken from works quite unknown to me. It was almost impossible to seize the connection of the ideas on account of the poor acoustics of the room, the bad arrangement of the orchestra, and the unskilled players—all of which served to break up the musical design and spoil the harmony of its colouring. Passages that should have been made prominent were slurred over, and others were distorted by faulty time or want of precision. Even to-day, when our orchestras are seasoned by years of study, I should often be unable to follow Wagner's thought throughout a whole scene if I did not happen to know the score, for the outline of a melody is often smothered by the accompaniment, and so its sentiment is lost. If we still find obscurity of meaning in Wagner's works you can imagine how much worse it was then. But what did it matter ? I used to feel myself stirred with passions that were not human : some magnetic influence seemed to thrill me with both pleasure and pain, and I felt invigorated and happy, for it brought me strength.

It seemed as if my child's heart were torn from me and the heart of a hero put in its place.

Nor was I alone in the experience. On the faces of the people round about me I saw the reflection of my own emotions. What was the meaning of it ? The audience consisted chiefly of poor and commonplace people, whose faces were lined with the wear and tear of a life without interest or ideals; their minds were dull and heavy, and yet here they responded to the divine spirit of the music. There is no more impressive sight than that of thousands of people held spellbound by a melody ; it is by turns sublime, grotesque, and touching.

What a place in my life those Sunday concerts held ! All the week I lived for those two hours ; and when they were over I thought about them until the following Sunday. The fascination of Wagner's music for youth has often troubled people ; they think it poisons the thoughts and dulls the activities. But the generation that was then intoxicated by Wagner does not seem to have shown signs of demoralisation since. Why do not people understand that if we had need of that music it was not because it was death to us, but life. Cramped by the artificiality of a town, far from action, or nature, or any strong or real life, we expanded under the influence of this noble music— music which flowed from a heart filled with understanding of the world and the breath of Nature. In *Die Meistersinger*, in *Tristan*, and in *Siegfried*, we went to find the joy, the love, and the vigour that we so lacked.

At the time when I was feeling Wagner's seductiveness so strongly there were always some carping people among my elders ready to quench my admiration and say with a superior smile : " That is nothing. One can't judge Wagner at a concert. You must hear him in the opera-house at Bayreuth." Since then I have been several times to Bayreuth ; I have seen Wagner's works performed in Berlin, in Dresden, in Munich, and in other German towns, but I have never again felt the old intoxication. People are wrong to pretend that closer acquaintance with a fine work adds to one's enjoyment of it. It may throw light upon it, but it nips one's imagination and dispels the mystery. The puzzling fragments one hears at concerts will take on splendid proportions on account of all the mind adds to them. That epic poem of the *Niebelungen* was once like a forest in our dreams, where strange and awful beings flashed before our vision and then vanished. Later on, when we had explored all its paths, we discovered that order and reason reigned in the midst of this apparent jungle ; and when we came to know the least wrinkle on the faces of its inhabitants, the confusion and emotion of other days no longer filled us.

But this may be the result of growing older ; and if I do not recognise the Wagner of other days, it is perhaps because I do not recognise my former self. A work of art, and above all a work of musical art, changes with ourselves. *Siegfried*, for example, is for me no longer full of mystery. The qualities in it that strike me to-day are its cheerful vigour, its clearness of form, its virile force and freedom, and the extraordinary healthiness of the hero, and, indeed, of the whole work.

I sometimes think of poor Nietzsche and his passion for destroying the things he loved, and how he sought in others the decadence that was really in himself. He tried to embody this decadence in Wagner, and, led away by his flights of fancy and his mania for paradox (which would be laughable if one did not remember that his whims were not hatched in hours of happiness), he denied Wagner his most obvious qualities—his vigour, his determination, his unity, his logic, and his power of progress. He amused himself by comparing Wagner's style with that of Goncourt, by making him—with amusing irony—a great miniaturist painter, a poet of half-tones, a musician of affectations and melancholy, so delicate and effeminate in style that " after him all other musicians seemed too robust."[1] He has painted Wagner and his time delightfully. We all enjoy these little pictures of the Tetralogy, delicately drawn and worked up by the aid of a magnifying-glass—pictures of Wagner, languishing and beautiful, in a mournful salon, and pictures of the athletic meetings of the other musicians, who were " too robust " ! The amusing part is that this piece of wit has been taken seriously by certain arbiters of elegance, who are only too happy to be able to run counter to any current opinion, whatever it may be.

I do not say that there may not be a decadent

[1] F. Nietzsche, *Der Fall Wagner.*

side in Wagner, revealing super-sensitiveness or even hysteria and other modern nervous affections. And if this side was lacking he would not be representative of his time, and that is what every great artist ought to be. But there is certainly something more in him than decadence; and if women and young men cannot see anything beyond it, it only proves their inability to get outside themselves. A long time ago Wagner himself complained to Liszt that neither the public nor artists knew how to listen to or understand any side of his music but the effeminate side: "They do not grasp its strength," he said. "My supposed successes," he also tells us, "are founded on misunderstanding. My public reputation isn't worth a walnut-shell." And it is true he has been applauded, patronised, and monopolised for a quarter of a century by all the decadents of art and literature. Scarcely anyone has seen in him a vigorous musician and a classic writer, or has recognised him as Beethoven's direct successor, the inheritor of his heroic and pastoral genius, of his epic inspirations and battle-field rhythms, of his Napoleonic phrases and atmosphere of stirring trumpet-calls.

Nowhere is Wagner nearer to Beethoven than in *Siegfried*. In *Die Walküre* certain characters, certain phrases of Wotan, of Brünnhilde, and, especially, of Siegmund, bear a close relationship to Beethoven's symphonies and sonatas. I can never play the recitative *con espressione e semplice* of the seventeenth sonata for the piano (Op. 31, No. 2) without being reminded of the forests of *Die Walküre* and the fugitive hero. But in *Siegfried* I find, not only a likeness to Beethoven in details, but the same spirit running through the work—both the poem and the music. I cannot help thinking that Beethoven would perhaps have disliked *Tristan*, but would have loved *Siegfried;* for the latter is a perfect incarnation of the spirit of old Germany, virginal and gross, sincere and malicious, full of humour and sentiment, of deep feeling, of dreams of bloody and joyous battles, of the shade of great oak-trees and the song of birds.

.    .    .    .    .    .

In my opinion, *Siegfried*, in spirit and in form, stands alone in Wagner's work. It breathes perfect health and happiness, and it overflows with gladness. Only *Die Meistersinger* rivals it in merriment, though even there one does not find such a nice balance of poetry and music.

And *Siegfried* rouses one's admiration the more when one thinks that it was the offspring of sickness and suffering. The time at which Wagner wrote it was one of the saddest in his life. It often happens so in art. One goes astray in trying to interpret an artist's life by his work, for it is exceptional to find one a counterpart of the other. It is more likely that an artist's work will express the opposite of his life—the things that he did not experience. The object of art is to fill up what is missing in the artist's experience : " Art begins where life leaves off," said Wagner. A man of action is rarely pleased with stimulating works of art. Borgia and Sforza

patronised Leonardo.  The strong, full-blooded men
of the seventeenth century ;  the apoplectic court
at Versailles (where Fagon's lancet played so necessary a part) ;  the generals and ministers who
harassed the Protestants and burned the Palatinate
—all these loved pastorales.  Napoleon wept at a
reading of *Paul et Virginie*, and delighted in the
pallid music of Paesiello.  A man wearied by an
over-active life seeks repose in art ;  a man who
lives a narrow, commonplace life seeks energy in
art.  A great artist writes a gay work when he is
sad, and a sad work when he is gay, almost in spite
of himself.  Beethoven's symphony *To Joy* is the
offspring of his misery ;  and Wagner's *Meistersinger*
was composed immediately after the failure of
*Tannhäuser* in Paris.  People try to find in *Tristan*
the trace of some love-story of Wagner's, but
Wagner himself says :  " As in all my life I have
never truly tasted the happiness of love, I will
raise a monument to a beautiful dream of it :  I have
the idea of *Tristan und Isolde* in my head."  And so
it was with his creation of the happy and heedless
*Siegfried*.

.     .     .     .     .     .

The first ideas of *Siegfried* were contemporary
with the Revolution of 1848, which Wagner took
part in with the same enthusiasm he put into everything else.  His recognised biographer, Herr Houston
Stewart Chamberlain—who, with M. Henri Lichtenberger, has succeeded best in unravelling Wagner's
complex soul, though he is not without certain

prejudices—has been at great pains to prove that
Wagner was always a patriot and a German
monarchist. Well, he may have been so later on,
but it was not, I think, the last phase of his evolution. His actions speak for themselves. On 14 June,
1848, in a famous speech to the National Democratic Association, Wagner violently attacked the
organisation of society itself, and demanded both
the abolition of money and the extinction of what
was left of the aristocracy. In *Das Kunstwerk der
Zukunft* (1849) he showed that beyond the " local
nationalism " were signs of a " supernational univer-
salism." And all this was not merely talk, for he
risked his life for his ideas. Herr Chamberlain himself quotes the account of a witness who saw him,
in May, 1849, distributing revolutionary pamphlets
to the troops who were besieging Dresden. It was
a miracle that he was not arrested and shot. We
know that after Dresden was taken a warrant was
out against him, and he fled to Switzerland, with a
passport on which was a borrowed name. If it be
true that Wagner later declared that he had been
" involved in error and led away by his feelings "
it matters little to the history of that time   Errors
and enthusiasms are an integral part of life, and
one must not ignore them in a man's biography
under the pretext that he regretted them twenty
or thirty years later, for they have, nevertheless,
helped to guide his actions and impressed his
imagination. It was out of the Revolution itself
that *Siegfried* directly sprang.

In 1848, Wagner was not yet thinking of a

Tetralogy, but of an heroic opera in three acts
called *Siegfried's Tod*, in which the fatal power of
gold was to be symbolised in the treasure of the
Niebelungen ; and Siegfried was to represent " a
socialist redeemer come down to earth to abolish
the reign of Capital." As the rough draft developed,
Wagner went up the stream of his hero's life. He
dreamed of his childhood, of his conquest of the
treasure, of the awakening of Brünnhilde ; and in
1851 he wrote the poem of *Der Junge Siegfried*.
Siegfried and Brünnhilde represent the humanity
of the future, the new era that should be realised
when the earth was set free from the yoke of gold.
Then Wagner went farther back still, to the sources of
the legend itself, and Wotan appeared, the symbol of
our time, a man such as you or I—in contrast to Siegfried, man as he ought to be, and one day will be. On
this subject Wagner says, in a letter to Roeckel :
" Look well at Wotan ; he is the unmistakable likeness of ourselves, and the sum of the present-day
spirit, while Siegfried is the man we wait and wish for
—the future man whom we cannot create, but who
will create himself by our annihilation—the most
perfect man I can imagine." Finally Wagner conceived the Twilight of the Gods, the fall of the
Valhalla—our present system of society—and the
birth of a regenerated humanity. Wagner wrote
to Uhlig in 1851 that the complete work was to be
played after the great Revolution.

The opera public would probably be very astonished to learn that in *Siegfried* they applaud a revolutionary work, expressly directed by Wagner against

this detested Capital, whose downfall would have been so dear to him. And he never doubted that he was expressing grief in all these pages of shining joy.

Wagner went to Zurich after a stay in Paris, where he felt " so much distrust for the artistic world and horror for the restraint that he was forced to put upon himself " that he was seized with a nervous malady which nearly killed him. He returned to work at *Der Junge Siegfried*, and he says it brought him great joy.

" But I am unhappy in not being able to apply myself to anything but music. I know I am feeding on an illusion, and that reality is the only thing worth having. My health is not good, and my nerves are in a state of increasing weakness. My life, lived entirely in the imagination and without sufficient action, tires me so, that I can only work with frequent breaks and long intervals of rest; otherwise I pay the penalty with long and painful suffering. . . . I am very lonely. I often wish for death.

" While I work I forget my troubles; but the moment I rest they come flocking about me, and I am very miserable. What a splendid life is an artist's! Look at it! How willingly would I part with it for a week of real life.

" I can't understand how a really happy man could think of serving art. If we enjoyed life, we should have no need of art. When the present has nothing more to offer us we cry out our needs by means of art. To have my youth again and my health, to enjoy nature, to have a wife who would love me devotedly, and fine children—for this I would give up *all my art*. Now I have said it—give me what is left."

Thus the poem of the Tetralogy was written with doubts, as he said, as to whether he should abandon art and all belonging to it and become a healthy, normal man—a son of nature. He began to compose the music of the poem while in a state of suffering, which every day became more acute.

" My nights are often sleepless ; I get out of bed, wretched and, exhausted, with the thought of a long day before me, which will not bring me a single joy. The society of others tortures me, and I avoid it only to torture myself. Everything I do fills me with disgust. It can't go on for ever. I can't stand such a life any longer. I will kill myself rather than live like this. . . . I don't believe in anything, and I have only one desire—to sleep so soundly that human misery will exist no more for me. I ought to be able to get such a sleep somehow ; it should not be really difficult."

For distraction he went to Italy ; Turin, Genoa, Spezia, and Nice. But there, in a strange world, his loneliness seemed so frightful that he became very depressed, and made all haste back to Zurich. It was there he wrote the happy music of *Das Rheingold*. He began the score of *Die Walküre* at a time when his normal condition was one of suffering.

Then he discovered Schopenhauer, whose philosophy only helped to confirm and crystallise his instinctive pessimism. In the spring of 1855 he went to London to give concerts; but he was ill there, and this fresh contact with the world only served to annoy him further. He had some difficulty in again taking up *Die Walküre*; but he finished it at last in spite of frequent attacks of facial erysipelas, for which he afterwards had to undergo a hydropathic cure at Geneva. He began the score of *Siegfried* towards the end of 1856, while the thought of Tristan was stirring within him. In *Tristan* he wished to depict love as " a dreadful anguish "; and this idea obsessed him so completely that he could not finish *Siegfried*. He seemed to be consumed by a burning fever; and, abandoning *Siegfried* in the middle of the second act, he threw himself madly into *Tristan*. "I want to gratify my desire for love," he says, "until it is completely satiated; and in the folds of the black flag that floats over its consummation I wish to wrap myself and die." [1] *Siegfried* was not finished until 5 February, 1871, at the end of the Franco-Prussian war—that is fourteen years later, after several interruptions.

Such is, in a few words, the history of this heroic idyll. It is perhaps as well to remind the public now and then that the hours of distraction they enjoy by means of art may represent years of suffering for the artist.

. . . . . .

[1] The quotations from Wagner are taken from his letters to Roeckel, Uhlig, and Liszt, between 1851 and 1856.

Do you know the amusing account Tolstoy gave of a performance of *Siegfried ?* I will quote it from his book, *What is Art ?*—

"When I arrived, an actor in tight-fitting breeches was seated before an object that was meant to represent an anvil. He wore a wig and false beard ; his white and manicured hands had nothing of the workman about them ; and his easy air, prominent belly, and flabby muscles readily betrayed the actor. With an absurd hammer he struck—as no one else would ever strike—a fantastic-looking sword-blade. One guessed he was a dwarf, because when he walked he bent his legs at the knees. He cried out a great deal, and opened his mouth in a queer fashion. The orchestra also emitted peculiar noises like several beginnings that had nothing to do with one another. Then another actor appeared with a horn in his belt, leading a man dressed up as a bear, who walked on all-fours. He let loose the bear on the dwarf, who ran away, but forgot to bend his knees this time. The actor with the human face represented the hero, Siegfried. He cried out for a long time, and the dwarf replied in the same way. Then a traveller arrived —the god Wotan. He had a wig, too ; and, settling himself down with his spear, in a silly attitude, he told Mimi all about things he already knew, but of which the audience was ignorant. Then Siegfried seized some bits that were supposed to represent pieces of a sword, and sang :

Heaho, heaho, hoho ! Hoho, hoho, hoho, hoho ! Hoheo, haho, haheo, hoho!' And that was the end of the first act. It was all so artificial and stupid that I had great difficulty in sitting it out. But my friends begged me to stay, and assured me that the second act would be better.

"The next scene represented a forest. Wotan was waking up the dragon. At first the dragon said, ' I want to go to sleep ' ; but eventually he came out of his grotto. The dragon was represented by two men clothed in a green skin with some scales stuck about it. At one end of the skin they wagged a tail, and at the other end they opened a crocodile's mouth, out of which came fire. The dragon, which ought to have been a frightful beast—and perhaps he would have frightened children about five years old—said a few words in a bass voice. It was so childish and feeble that one was astonished to see grown-up people present ; even thousands of so-called cultured people looked on and listened attentively, and went into raptures. Then Siegfried arrived with his horn. He lay down during a pause, which is reputed to be very beautiful ; and sometimes he talked to himself, and sometimes he was quite silent. He wanted to imitate the song of the birds, and cut a rush with his horn, and made a flute out of it. But he played the flute badly, and so he began to blow his horn. The scene is intolerable, and there is not the least trace of music in it. I was annoyed to see three thousand people round about me, listening submissively to this absurdity and dutifully admiring it.

" With some courage I managed to wait for the next scene—Siegfried's fight with the dragon. There were roarings and flames of fire and brandishings of the sword. But I could not stand it any longer ; and I fled out of the theatre with a feeling of disgust that I have not yet forgotten."

I admit I cannot read this delightful criticism without laughing ; and it does not affect me painfully like Nietzsche's pernicious and morbid irony. It used to be a grief to me that two men whom I loved with an equal affection, and whom I reverenced as the finest spirits in Europe, remained strangers and hostile to each other. I could not bear the thought that a genius, hopelessly misunderstood by the crowd, should be bent on making his solitude more bitter and narrow by refusing, with a sort of jealous waywardness, to be reconciled to his equals, or to offer them the hand of friendship. But now I think that perhaps it was better so. The first virtue of genius is sincerity. If Nietzsche had to go out of his way *not* to understand Wagner, it is natural, on the other hand, that Wagner should be a closed book to Tolstoy ; it would be almost surprising if it were otherwise. Each one has his own part to play, and has no need to change it. Wagner's wonderful dreams and magic intuition of the inner life are not less valuable to us than Tolstoy's pitiless truth, in which he exposes modern society and tears away the veil of hypocrisy with which she covers

herself. So I admire *Siegfried*, and at the same time
enjoy Tolstoy's satire ; for I like the latter's sturdy
humour, which is one of the most striking features
of his realism, and which, as he himself noticed,
makes him closely resemble Rousseau. Both
men show us an ultra-refined civilisation, and
both are uncompromising apostles of a return to
nature.

Tolstoy's rough banter recalls Rousseau's sarcasm
about an opera of Rameau's. In the *Nouvelle
Heloïse*, he rails in a similar fashion against the
sadly fantastic performances at the theatre. It was,
even then, a question of monsters, " of dragons
animated by a blockhead of a Savoyard, who had
not enough spirit for the beast."

" They assured me that they had a tremendous
lot of machinery to make all this movement,
and they offered several times to show it to me ;
but I felt no curiosity about little effects achieved
by great efforts. . . . The sky is represented by
some blue rags suspended from sticks and cords,
like a laundry display. . . . The chariots of the
gods and goddesses are made of four joists in a
frame, suspended by a thick rope, as a swing
might be. Then a plank is stuck across the joists,
and on this is seated a god. In front of him hangs
a piece of daubed cloth, which serves as a cloud
upon which his splendid chariot may rest. . . .
The theatre is furnished with little square trap-
doors which, opening as occasion requires, show
that the demons can be let loose from the cellars.

G

When the demons have to fly in the air, dummies
of brown cloth are substituted, or sometimes real
chimney-sweeps, who swing in the air, suspended
by cords, until they are gloriously lost in the rag
sky. . . .

" But you can have no idea of the dreadful cries
and roarings with which the theatre resounds. . . .
What is so extraordinary is that these howlings are
almost the only things that the audience applaud.
By the way they clap their hands one would take
them to be a lot of deaf creatures, who were so
delighted to catch a few piercing sounds now and
then that they wanted the actors to do them all
over again.  I am quite sure that people applaud
the bawling of an actress at the opera as they
would a mountebank's feats of skill at a fair—
one suffers while they are going on, but one is
so delighted to see them finish without an accident
that one willingly demonstrates one's pleasure.
. . . With these beautiful sounds, as true as they
are sweet, those of the orchestra blend very
worthily.  Imagine an unending clatter of instruments without any melody ; a lingering and endless groaning among the bass parts ; and the
whole the most mournful and boring thing that
I ever heard in my life.  I could not put up with it
for half an hour without getting a violent headache.

" All this forms a sort of psalmody, possessing
neither tune nor time.  But if by any chance a
lively air is played, there is a general stamping ;
the audience is set in motion, and follows, with a

great deal of trouble and noise, some performer
in the orchestra. Delighted to feel for a few
moments the rhythm that is so lacking, they
torment the ear, the voice, the arms, the legs, and
all the body, to chase after a tune that is ever
ready to escape them. . . .

I have quoted this rather long passage to show
how the impression made by one of Rameau's
operas on his contemporaries resembled that
made by Wagner on his enemies. It was not
without reason that Rameau was said to be
Wagner's forerunner, as Rousseau was Tolstoy's
forerunner.

In reality, it was not against *Siegfried* itself that
Tolstoy's criticism was directed ; and Tolstoy was
closer than he thought to the spirit of this drama.
Is not Siegfried the heroic incarnation of a free
and healthy man, sprung directly from Nature ?
In a sketch of *Siegfried*, written in 1848, Wagner
says :

> " To follow the impulses of my heart is my
> supreme law ; what I can accomplish by obeying
> my instincts is what I ought to do. Is that
> voice of instinct cursed or blessed ? I do not
> know ; but I yield to it, and never force myself
> to run counter to my inclination."

Wagner fought against civilisation by quite other
methods than those employed by Tolstoy ; and
if the efforts of the two were equally great, the
practical result is—one must really say it—as poor
on one side as on the other,

What Tolstoy's raillery is really aimed at is not
Wagner's work, but the way in which his work was
represented. The splendours of the setting do not
hide the childishness of the ideas behind them : the
dragon Fafna, Fricka's rams, the bear, the serpent,
and all the Valhalla menagerie have always been
ridiculous. I will only add that the dragon's
failure to be terrifying was not Wagner's fault, for
he never attempted to depict a terrifying dragon.
He gave it quite clearly, and of his own choice, a
comic character. Both the text and the music make
Fafner a sort of ogre, a simple creature, but, above
all, a grotesque one.

Besides, I cannot help feeling that scenic reality
takes away rather than adds to the effect of these
great philosophical fairylands. Malwida von Meysenbug told me that at the Bayreuth festival of
1876, while she was following one of the *Ring* scenes
very attentively with her opera-glasses, two hands
were laid over her eyes, and she heard Wagner's
voice say impatiently : " Don't look so much at
what is going on. Listen ! " It was good counsel.
There are dilettanti who pretend that at a concert
the best way to enjoy Beethoven's last works—
where the sonority is defective—is to stop the ears
and read the score. One might say with less of a
paradox that the best way to follow a performance
of Wagner's operas is to listen with the eyes shut.
So perfect is the music, so powerful its hold on the
imagination, that it leaves nothing to be desired ;
what it suggests to the mind is infinitely finer than
what the eyes may see. I have never shared the

opinion that Wagner's works may be best appreciated in the theatre. His works are epic symphonies. As a frame for them I should like temples; as scenery, the illimitable land of thought; as actors, our dreams.

．　　．　　．　　．　　．　　．

The first act of *Siegfried* is one of the most dramatic in the Tetralogy. Nothing satisfied me more completely at Bayreuth, both as regards the actors and the dramatic effects. Fantastic creatures like Alberich and Mimi, who seem to be out of their element in France, are rooted deep down in German imaginations. The Bayreuth actors surpassed themselves in making them startlingly lifelike, with a trembling and grimacing realism. Burgstaller, who was then making his debut in *Siegfried*, acted with an impetuous awkwardness which accorded well with the part. I remember with what zest—which seemed in no way affected—he played the hero smith, labouring like a true workman, blowing the fire and making the blade glow, dipping it in the steaming water, and working it on the anvil; and then, in a burst of Homeric gaiety, singing that fine hymn at the end of the first act, which sounds like an air by Bach or Handel.

But in spite of all this, I felt how much better it was to dream, or to hear this poem of a youthful soul at a concert. It is then that the magic murmurs of the forest in the second act speak more directly to the heart. However beautiful the scenery of glades

and woods, however cleverly the light is made to
change and dance among the trees—and it is
manipulated now like a set of organ stops—it still
seems almost wrong to listen with open eyes to
music that, unaided, can show us a glorious summer's
day, and make us see the swaying of the tree-tops,
and hear the brush of the wind against the leaves.
Through the music alone the hum and murmur of a
thousand little voices is about us, the glorious song
of the birds floats into the depths of a blue sky ; or
comes a silence, vibrating with invisible life, when
Nature, with her mysterious smile, opens her arms
and hushes all things in a divine sleep.

.    .    .    .    .    .

Wagner left *Siegfried* asleep in the forest in order
to embark on the funereal vessel of *Tristan und
Isolde*. But he left Siegfried with some anguish of
heart. When writing to Liszt in 1857, he says :

" I have taken young Siegfried into the depths
of a lonely forest ; there I have left him under a
lime-tree, and said good-bye to him with tears in
my eyes. It has torn my heart to bury him alive,
and I had a hard and painful fight with myself
before I could do it. . . . Shall I ever go back to
him ? No, it is all finished. Don't let us speak
of it again."

Wagner had reason to be sad. He knew well that
he would never find his young Siegfried again. He

roused him up ten years later. But all was changed That splendid third act has not the freshness of the first two. Wotan has become an important figure, and brought reason and pessimism with him into the drama. Wagner's later conceptions were perhaps loftier, and his genius was more master of itself (think of the classic dignity in the awakening of Brünnhilde) ; but the ardour and happy expression of youth is gone. I know that this is not the opinion of most of Wagner's admirers ; but, with the exception of a few pages of sublime beauty, I have never altogether liked the love scenes at the end of *Siegfried* and at the beginning of *Götterdämmerung*. I find their style rather pompous and declamatory ; and their almost excessive refinement makes them border upon dulness. The form of the duet, too, seems cut and dried, and there are signs of weariness in it. The heaviness of the last pages of *Siegfried* recalls *Die Meistersinger*, which is also of that period. It is no longer the same joy nor the same quality of joy that is found in the earlier acts.

Yet it does not really matter, for joy is there, nevertheless ; and so splendid was the first inspiration of the work that the years have not dimmed its brilliancy. One would like to end with *Siegfried*, and escape the gloomy *Götterdämmerung*. For those who have sensitive feelings the fourth day of the Tetralogy has a depressing effect. I remember the tears I have seen shed at the end of the *Ring*, and the words of a friend, as we left the theatre at Bayreuth and descended the hill at night : " I feel as

though I were coming away from the burial of someone I dearly loved." It was truly a time of mourn-
ing. Perhaps there was something incongruous in
building such a structure when it had universal
death for its conclusion—or at least in making the
whole an object of show and instruction. *Tristan*
achieves the same end with much more power, as the
action is swifter. Besides that, the end of *Tristan*
is not without comfort, for life there is terrible.
But it is not the same in *Götterdämmerung* ; for in
spite of the absurdity of the spell which is set upon
the love of Siegfried and Brünnhilde, life with them
is happy and desirable, since they are beings capable
of love, and death appears to be a splendid but
awful catastrophe. And one cannot say the *Ring*
breathes a spirit of renunciation and sacrifice like
*Parsifal ;* renunciation and sacrifice are only talked
about in the *Ring ;* and, in spite of the last transports which impel Brünnhilde to the funeral pyre,
they are neither an inspiration nor a delight. One
has the impression of a great gulf yawning at one's
feet, and the anguish of seeing those one loves fall
into it.

I have often regretted that Wagner's first conception of *Siegfried* changed in the course of years ;
and in spite of the magnificent *dénouement* of
*Götterdämmerung* (which is really more effective in
a concert room, for the real tragedy ends with
Siegfried's death), I cannot help thinking with
regret how fine a more optimistic poem from this
revolutionary of '48 might have been. People tell
me that it would then have been less true to life.

But why should it be truthful to depict life only as a bad thing ? Life is neither good nor bad   it is just what we make it, and the result of the way in which we look at it.   Joy is as real as sorrow, and a very fertile source of action.   What inspiration there is in the laugh of a great man   Let us welcome, therefore, the sparkling if transient gaiety of *Siegfried*.

Wagner wrote to Malwida von Meysenbug : " I have, by chance, just been reading Plutarch's life of Timoleon.   That life ended very happily—a rare and unheard-of thing, especially in history.   It does one good to think that such a thing is possible.   It moved me profoundly."

I feel the same when I hear *Siegfried*.   We are rarely allowed to contemplate happiness in great tragic art ;  but when we may, how splendid it is, and how good for one !

## " TRISTAN "

Tristan towers like a mountain above all other
love poems, as Wagner above all other artists of his
century.  It is the outcome of a sublime conception,
though the work as a whole is far from perfect.  Of
perfect works there is none where Wagner is concerned.  The effort necessary for the creation of
them was too great to be long sustained ; for a single
work might means years of toil.  And the tense
emotions of a whole drama cannot be expressed by
a series of sudden inspirations put into form the
moment they are conceived.  Long and arduous
labour is necessary.  These giants, fashioned like
Michelangelo's, these concentrated tempests of
heroic force and decadent complexity, are not
arrested, like the work of a sculptor or painter, in
one moment of their action ; they live and go on
living in endless detail of sensation.  To expect
sustained inspiration is to expect what is not human.
Genius may reveal what is divine ; it may call up
and catch a glimpse of *die Mütter*, but it cannot always
breathe in the exhausted air of this world.  So will
must sometimes take the place of inspiration ;
though the will is uncertain and often stumbles in
its task.  That is why we encounter things that jar
and jolt in the greatest works—they are the marks
of human weakness.  Well, perhaps there is less

weakness in *Tristan* than in Wagner's other dramas
—*Götterdämmerung*, for instance—for nowhere else
is the effort of his genius more strenuous or its flight
more dizzy. Wagner himself knew it well. His
letters show the despair of a soul wrestling with its
familiar spirit, which it clutches and holds, only to
lose again. And we seem to hear cries of pain, and
feel his anger and despair.

> " I can never tell you what a really wretched
> musician I am. In my inmost heart I know I am
> a bungler and an absolute failure. You should
> see me when I say to myself, ' It ought to go now,'
> and sit down to the piano and put together some
> miserable rubbish, which I fling away again like
> an idiot. I know quite well the kind of musical
> trash I produce. . . . Believe me, it is no good
> expecting me to do anything decent. Sometimes
> I really think it was Reissiger who inspired me to
> write *Tannhäuser* and *Lohengrin*."

This is how Wagner wrote to Liszt when he was
finishing this amazing work of art. In the same
way Michelangelo wrote to his father in 1509 : " I
am in agony. I have not dared to ask the Pope for
anything, because my work does not make sufficient
progress to merit any remuneration. The work is
too difficult, and indeed it is not my profession. I
am wasting my time to no purpose. Heaven help
me ! " For a year he had been working at the
ceiling of the Sixtine chapel.

This is something more than a burst of modesty.

No one had more pride than Michelangelo or Wagner;
but both felt the defects of their work like a sharp
wound.  And although those defects do not prevent
their works from being the glory of the human
spirit, they are there just the same.

I do not want to dwell upon the inherent imperfections of Wagner's dramas; they are really
dramatic or epic symphonies, impossible to act, and
gaining nothing from representation.  This is
especially true of *Tristan*, where the disparity
between the storm of sentiment depicted, and the
cold convention and enforced timidity of action on
the stage, is such that at certain moments—in the
second act, for example—it pains and shocks one,
and seems almost grotesque.

But while admitting that *Tristan* is a symphony
that is not suitable for representation, one also
recognises its blemishes and, above all, its uneven-
ness.  The orchestration in the first act is often
rather thin, and the plot lacks solidity.  There are
gaps and unaccountable holes, and melodious lines
left suspended in space.  From beginning to end,
lyrical bursts of melody are broken by declamations,
or, what is worse, by dissertations.  Frenzied
whirlwinds of passion stop suddenly to give place
to recitatives of explanation or argument.  And
although these recitatives are nearly always a great
relief, although these metaphysical reveries have a
character of barbarous cunning that one relishes,
yet the superior beauty of the movements of pure
poetry, emotion, and music is so evident, that this
musical and philosophical drama serves to give one

a distaste for philosophy and drama and everything else that cramps and confines music.

But the musical part of *Tristan* is not free either
from the faults of the work as a whole, for it, too,
lacks unity. Wagner's music is made up of very
diverse styles : one finds in it Italianisms and Ger-
manisms and even Gallicisms of every kind ; there
are some that are sublime, some that are commonplace ; and at times one feels the awkwardness of
their union and the imperfections of their form.
Then again, perhaps two ideas of equal originality
come together and spoil each other by making too
strong a contrast. The fine lamentation of King
Mark—that personification of a knight of the Grail
—is treated with such moderation and with so
noble a scorn for outward show, that its pure, cold
light is entirely lost after the glowing fire of the
duet.

The work suffers everywhere from a lack of
balance. It is an almost inevitable defect, arising
from its very grandeur. A mediocre work may
quite easily be perfect of its kind ; but it is rarely
that a work of lofty aim attains perfection. A landscape of little dells and smiling meadows is brought
more readily into pleasing harmony than a landscape of dazzling Alps, torrents, glaciers, and tempests ; for the heights may sometimes overwhelm
the picture and spoil the effect. And so it is with
certain great pages of *Tristan*. We may take for
example the verses which tell of excruciating expectation—in the second act, Isolde's expectation on
the night filled with desire ; and, in the third act,

Tristan's expectation, as he lies wounded and delirious, waiting for the vessel that brings Isolde and death—or we may take the Prelude, that expression of eternal desire that is like a restless sea for ever moaning and beating itself upon the shore.

.       .       .       .       .       .

The quality that touches me most deeply in *Tristan* is the evidence of honesty and sincerity in a man who was treated by his enemies as a charlatan that used superficial and grossly material means to arrest and amaze the public eye.  What drama is more sober or more disdainful of exterior effect than *Tristan ?*  Its restraint is almost carried to excess.  Wagner rejected any picturesque episode in it that was irrelevant to his subject.  The man who carried all Nature in his imagination, who at his will made the storms of the *Walküre* rage, or the soft light of Good Friday shine, would not even depict a bit of the sea round the vessel in the first act.  Believe me, that must have been a sacrifice, though he wished it so.  It pleased him to enclose this terrible drama within the four walls of a chamber of tragedy.  There are hardly any choruses ;  there is nothing to distract one's attention from the mystery of human souls ; there are only two real parts—those of the lovers; and if there is a third, it belongs to Destiny, into whose hands the victims are delivered.  What a fine seriousness there is in this love play.  Its passion remains sombre and stern ;  there is no laughter in it, only a belief which is almost religious, more

religious perhaps in its sincerity than that of
*Parsifal.*

It is a lesson for dramatists to see a man supress-
ing all frivolous trifling and empty episodes in order
to concentrate his subject entirely on the inner life
of two living souls. In that Wagner is our master,
a better, stronger, and more profitable master to
follow, in spite of his mistakes, than all the other
literary and dramatic authors of his time.

.    .    .    .    .    .

I see that criticism has filled a larger place in
these notes than I meant it to do. But in spite of
that, I love *Tristan ;* for me and for others of my
time it has long been an intoxicating draught. And
it has never lost anything of its grandeur ; the
years have left its beauty untouched, and it is for
me the highest point of art reached by anyone since
Beethoven's death.

But as I was listening to it the other evening I
could not help thinking : Ah, Wagner, you will one
day go too, and join Gluck and Bach and Monteverde and Palestrina and all the great souls whose
names still live among men, but whose thoughts are
only felt by a handful of the initiated, who try in
vain to revive the past. You, also, are already of
the past, though you were the steady light of our
youth, the strong source of life and death, of desire
and renouncement, whence we drew our moral force
and our power of resistance against the world. And
the world, ever greedy for new sensations, goes on
its way amid the unceasing ebb and flow of its

desires. Already its thoughts have changed, and new musicians are making new songs for the future. But it is the voice of a century of tempest that passes with you.

# CAMILLE SAINT-SAËNS

M. SAINT-SAËNS has had the rare honour of becoming a classic during his lifetime. His name, though it was long unrecognised, now commands universal respect, not less by his worth of character than by the perfection of his art. No artist has troubled so little about the public, or been more indifferent to criticism whether popular or expert. As a child he had a sort of physical repulsion for outward success :

> " De l'applaudissement
> J'entends encor le bruit qui, chose assez étrange,
> Pour ma pudeur d'enfant était comme une fange
> Dont le flot me venait toucher ; je redoutais
> Son contact, et parfois, malin, je l'évitais,
> Affectant la raideur." [1]

Later on, he achieved success by a long and painful struggle, in which he had to fight against the kind of stupid criticism that condemned him " to listen to one of Beethoven's symphonies as a penance

[1] Of applause
I still hear the noise ; and, strangely enough,
In my childish shyness it seemed like mire
About to spot me ; I feared
Its touch, and secretly shunned it,
Affecting obstinacy.

These verses were read by M. Saint-Saëns at a concert given on 10 June, 1896, in the Salle Pleyel, to celebrate the fiftieth anniversary of his *début*, which he made in 1846. It was in this same Salle Pleyel that he gave his first concert.

likely to give him the most excruciating torture." [1]
And yet after this, and after his admission to the
Academy, after *Henry VIII* and the *Symphonie
avec orgue*, he still remained aloof from praise or
blame, and judged his triumphs with sad severity :

> "Tu connaîtras les yeux menteurs, l'hypocrisie
>     Des serrements de mains,
> Le masque d'amitié cachant la jalousie,
>     Les pâles lendemains

> "De ces jours de triomphe où le troupeau vulgaire
>     Qui pèse au même poids
> L'histrion ridicule et le génie austère
>     Vous mets sur le pavois." [2]

M. Saint-Saëns has now grown old, and his fame
has spread abroad, but he has not capitulated.   Not
many years ago he wrote to a German journalist :
"I take very little notice of either praise or censure,
not because I have an exalted idea of my own
merits (which would be foolish), but because in
doing my work, and fulfilling the function of my
nature, as an apple-tree grows apples, I have no
need to trouble myself with other people's views." [3]

---

[1] C. Saint-Saëns, *Harmonie et Mélodie*, 1885.

[2] C. Saint-Saëns, *Rimes familières*, 1890.

> You will know the lying eyes, the insincerity
> Of pressures of the hand,
> The mask of friendship that hides jealousy,
> The tame to-morrows

> Of these days of triumph, when the vulgar herd
> Crowns you with honour ;
> Judging rare genius to be
> Equal in merit to the wit of clowns.

[3] Letter written to M. Levin, the correspondent of the
*Boersen-Courier* of Berlin, 9 September, 1901.

Such independence is rare at any time ; but it is very rare in our day, when the power of public opinion is tyrannical ; and it is rarest of all in France, where artists are perhaps more sociable than in other countries.  Of all qualities in an artist it is the most precious ; for it forms the foundation of his character, and is the guarantee of his conscience and innate strength.  So we must not hide it under a bushel.

.     .     .     .     .     .

The significance of M. Saint-Saëns in art is a double one, for one must judge him from the inside as well as the outside of France.  He stands for something exceptional in French music, something which was almost unique until just lately : that is, a great classical spirit and a fine breadth of musical culture—German culture, we must say, since the foundation of all modern art rests on the German classics.  French music of the nineteenth century is rich in clever artists, imaginative writers of melody, and skilful dramatists ; but it is poor in true musicians, and in good and solid workmanship. Apart from two or three splendid exceptions, our composers have too much the character of gifted amateurs who compose music as a pastime, and regard it, not as a special form of thought, but as a sort of dress for literary ideas.  Our musical education is superficial : it may be got for a few years, in a formal way, at a Conservatoire, but it is not within reach of all ; the child does not breathe music as, in a way, he breathes the atmosphere of

literature and oratory ; and although nearly everyone in France has an instinctive feeling for beautiful
writing, only a very few people care for beautiful
music. From this arise the common faults and
failings in our music. It has remained a luxurious
art ; it has not become, like German music, the
poetical expression of the people's thought.

To bring this about we should need a combination
of conditions that are very rare in France ; though
such conditions went to the making of Camille
Saint-Saëns. He had not only remarkable natural
talent, but came of a family of ardent musicians,
who devoted themselves to his education. At five
years of age he was nourished on the orchestral
score of *Don Juan ;*[1] as a little boy

"De dix ans, délicat, frêle, le teint jaunet,
    Mais confiant, naïf, plein d'ardeur et de joie,"[2]

he "measured himself against Beethoven and
Mozart" by playing in a public concert ; at sixteen
years of age he wrote his *Première Symphonie.* As
he grew older he soaked himself in the music of Bach
and Handel, and was able to compose at will after
the manner of Rossini, Verdi, Schumann, and
Wagner.[3] He has written excellent music in all
styles—the Grecian style, and that of the sixteenth,
seventeenth, and eighteenth centuries. His compositions are of every kind : masses, grand operas,

[1] C. Saint-Saëns, *Charles Gounod et le Don Juan de Mozart,*
1894.

[2] But ten years old, slightly built and pale,
    Yet full of simple confidence and joy (*Rimes familières*).

[3] Charles Gounod, *Mémoires d'un Artiste,* 1896.

light operas, cantatas, symphonies, symphonic
poems ; music for the orchestra, the organ, the
piano, the voice, and chamber music. He is the
learned editor of Gluck and Rameau ; and is thus
not only an artist, but an artist who can talk about
his art. He is an unusual figure in France—one
would have thought rather to find his home in
Germany.

In Germany, however, they make no mistake
about him. There, the name of Camille Saint-Saëns
stands for the French classical spirit, and is thought
worthiest to represent us in music from the time of
Berlioz until the appearance of the young school of
César Franck—though Franck himself is as yet
little known in Germany. M. Saint-Saëns possesses,
indeed, some of the best qualities of a French artist,
and among them the most important quality of all
—perfect clearness of conception. It is remarkable
how little this learned artist is bothered by his
learning, and how free he is from all pedantry.
Pedantry is the plague of German art, and the
greatest men have not escaped it. I am not speaking
of Brahms, who was ravaged with it, but of delightful geniuses like Schumann, or of powerful ones like
Bach. " This unnatural art wearies one like the
sanctimonious salon of some little provincial town ;
it stifles one, it is enough to kill one." [1] " Saint-
Saëns is not a pedant," wrote Gounod ; " he has

[1] Quoted from Saint-Saëns by Edmond Hippeau in *Henry
VIII et L'Opéra français*, 1883. M. Saint-Saëns speaks elsewhere of " these works, well written, but heavy and unattractive,
and reflecting in a tiresome way the narrow and pedantic spirit
of certain little towns in Germany " (*Harmonie et Mélodie*).

remained too much of a child and become too clever
for that." Besides, he has always been too much of
a Frenchman.

Sometimes Saint-Saëns reminds me of one of our
eighteenth-century writers. Not a writer of the
*Encyclopédie,* nor one of Rousseau's camp, but rather
of Voltaire's school. He has a clearness of thought,
an elegance and precision of expression, and a quality
of mind that make his music " not only noble, but
very noble, as coming of a fine race and distinguished
family." [1]

He has also excellent discernment, of an un-
emotional kind ; and he is " calm in spirit, restrained in imagination, and keeps his self-control
even in the midst of the most disturbing emotions." [2]
This discernment is the enemy of anything approach-
ing obscurity of thought or mysticism ; and its
outcome was that curious book, *Problèmes et
Mystères*—a misleading title, for the spirit of reason
reigns there and makes an appeal to young people
to protect " the light of a menaced world " against
"the mists of the North, Scandinavian gods, Indian
divinities, Catholic miracles, Lourdes, spiritualism,
occultism, and obscurantism." [3]

His love and need of liberty is also of the eighteenth century. One may say that liberty is his
only passion. " I am passionately fond of liberty,"
he wrote. [4] And he has proved it by the absolute

---

[1] Charles Gounod, " *Ascanio* " *de Saint-Saëns,* 1890.
[2] *Id., ibid.*
[3] C. Saint-Saëns, *Problèmes et Mystères,* 1894.
[4] *Harmonie et Mélodie.*

fearlessness of his judgments on art ; for not only
has he reasoned soundly against Wagner, but dared
to criticise the weaknesses of Gluck and Mozart,
the errors of Weber and Berlioz, and the accepted
opinions about Gounod ; and this classicist, who
was nourished on Bach, goes so far as to say : " The
performance of works by Bach and Handel to-day
is an idle amusement," and that those who wish to
revive their art are like " people who would live in
an old mansion that has been uninhabited for centuries." [1]  He went even further ; he criticised his
own work and contradicted his own opinions.  His
love of liberty made him form, at different periods,
different opinions of the same work.  He thought
that people had a right to change their opinions, as
sometimes they deceived themselves.  It seemed to
him better boldly to admit an error than to be the
slave of consistency.  And this same feeling showed
itself in other matters besides art : in ethics, as is
shown by some verses which he addressed to a
young friend, urging him not to be bound by a too
rigid austerity :

> " Je sens qu'une triste chimère
> A toujours assombri ton âme : la Vertu. . . ." [2]

and in metaphysics also, where he judges religions,
faith, and the Gospels with a quiet freedom of
thought, seeking in Nature alone the basis of morals
and society.

---

[1] C. Saint-Saëns, *Portraits et Souvenirs*, 1900.

[2] I know that a vain dream of virtue
Has always cast a shadow on your soul (*Rimes familières*).

Here are some of his opinions, taken at random from *Problèmes et Mystères* :

" As science advances, God recedes."

" The soul is only a medium for the expression of thought."

" The discouragement of work, the weakening of character, the sharing of one's goods under pain of death—this is the Gospel teaching on the foundation of society."

" The Christian virtues are not social virtues."

" Nature is without aim : she is an endless circle, and leads us nowhere."

His thoughts are unfettered and full of love for humanity and a sense of the responsibility of the individual. He called Beethoven " the greatest, the only really great artist," because he upheld the idea of universal brotherhood. His mind is so comprehensive that he has written books on philosophy, on the theatre, on classical painting,[1] as well as scientific essays,[2] volumes of verse, and even plays.[3] He has been able to take up all sorts of things, I will not say with equal skill, but with discernment and undeniable ability. He shows a type of mind rare among artists and, above all, among musicians. The two principles that he enunciates and himself

[1] C. Saint-Saëns, *Note sur les décors de théâtre dans l'antiquité romaine*, 1880, where he discusses the mural paintings of Pompeii.

[2] Lecture on the Phenomena of Mirages, given to the Astronomical Society of France in 1905.

[3] C. Saint-Saëns, *La Crampe des Écrivains*, a comedy in one act, 1892.

follows out are : " Keep free from all exaggeration "
and " Preserve the soundness of your mind's
health." [1] They are certainly not the principles of
a Beethoven or a Wagner, and it would be rather
difficult to find a noted musician of the last century
who had applied them. They tell us, without need
of comment, what is distinctive about M. Saint-
Saëns, and what is defective in him. He is not
troubled by any sort of passion. Nothing disturbs
the clearness of his reason. " He has no prejudices ;
he takes no side " [2]—one might add, not even his
own, since he is not afraid to change his views—
" he does not pose as a reformer of anything " ; he
is altogether independent, perhaps almost too much
so. He seems sometimes as if he did not know what
to do with his liberty. Goethe would have said, I
think, that he needed a little more of the devil in
him.

His most characteristic mental trait seems to be
a languid melancholy, which has its source in a
rather bitter feeling of the futility of life; [3] and this
is accompanied by fits of weariness which are not
altogether healthy, followed by capricious moods
and nervous gaiety, and a freakish liking for bur-
lesque and mimicry. It is his eager, restless spirit
that makes him rush about the world writing Breton
and Auvergnian rhapsodies, Persian songs, Algerian
suites, Portuguese barcarolles, Danish, Russian, or
Arabian caprices, souvenirs of Italy, African fan-

---

[1] *Harmonie et Mélodie.*
[2] Charles Gounod, *Mémoires d'un Artiste.*
[3] *Les Heures ; Mors ; Modestie (Rimes familières).*

tasias, and Egyptian concertos ; and, in the same
way, he roams through the ages, writing Greek
tragedies, dance music of the sixteenth and seventeenth centuries, and preludes and fugues of the
eighteenth.  But in all these exotic and archaic
reflections of times and countries through which his
fancy wanders, one recognises the gay, intelligent
countenance of a Frenchman on his travels, who
idly follows his inclinations, and does not trouble
to enter very deeply into the spirit of the people
he meets, but gleans all he can, and then reproduces
it with a French complexion—after the manner of
Montaigne in Italy, who compared Verona to
Poitiers, and Padua to Bordeaux, and who, when
he was in Florence, paid much less attention to
Michelangelo than to "a very strangely shaped
sheep, and an animal the size of a large mastiff,
shaped like a cat and striped with black and white,
which they called a tiger."

From a purely musical point of view there is some
resemblance between M. Saint-Saëns and Mendelssohn.  In both of them we find the same intellectual
restraint, the same balance preserved among the
heterogeneous elements of their work.  These elements are not common to both of them, because the
time, the country, and the surroundings in which
they lived are not the same ; and there is also a
great difference in their characters.  Mendelssohn
is more ingenuous and religious ; M. Saint-Saëns is
more of a dilettante and more sensuous.  They are
not so much kindred spirits by their science as good
company by a common purity of taste, a sense of

rhythm, and a genius for method, which gave all they wrote a neo-classic character.

As for the things that directly influenced M. Saint-Saëns, they are so numerous that it would be difficult and rather bold of me to pretend to be able to pick them out. His remarkable capacity for assimilation has often moved him to write in the style of Wagner or Berlioz, of Handel or Rameau, of Lulli or Charpentier, or even of some English harpsichord or clavichord player of the sixteenth century, like William Byrd—whose airs are introduced quite naturally in the music of *Henry VIII;* but we must remember that these are deliberate imitations, the amusements of a virtuoso, about which M. Saint-Saëns never deceives himself. His memory serves him as he pleases, but he is never troubled by it.

As far as one can judge, M. Saint-Saëns' musical ideas are infused with the spirit of the great classics belonging to the end of the eighteenth century— far more, whatever people may say, with the spirit of Beethoven, Haydn, and Mozart, than with the spirit of Bach. Schumann's seductiveness also left its mark upon him, and he has felt the influence of Gounod, Bizet, and Wagner. But a stronger influence was that of Berlioz, his friend and master,[1] and, above all, that of Liszt. We must stop at this last name.

M. Saint-Saëns has good reason for liking Liszt, for Liszt was also a lover of freedom, and had shaken off traditions and pedantry, and scorned German

[1] " Thanks to Berlioz, all my generation has been shaped and well shaped " (*Portraits et Souvenirs*).

routine; and he liked him, too, because his music
was a reaction from the stiff school of Brahms.[1] He
was enthusiastic about Liszt's work, and was one
of the earliest and most ardent champions of that
new music of which Liszt was the leading spirit—
of that "programme" music which Wagner's
triumph seemed to have nipped in the bud, but
which has suddenly and gloriously burst into life
again in the works of Richard Strauss. "Liszt is
one of the great composers of our time," wrote
M. Saint-Saëns; "he has dared more than either
Weber, or Mendelssohn, or Schubert, or Schumann.
He has created the symphonic poem. He is the
deliverer of instrumental music. . . . He has proclaimed the reign of free music."[2] This was not
said impulsively in a moment of enthusiasm;
M. Saint-Saëns has always held this opinion. All
his life he has remained faithful to his admiration
of Liszt—since 1858, when he dedicated a *Veni
Creator* to "the Abbé Liszt," until 1886, when, a
few months after Liszt's death, he dedicated his
masterpiece, the *Symphonie avec orgue*, "To the
memory of Franz Liszt."[3] "People have not
hesitated to scoff at what they call my weakness

---

[1] "I like Liszt's music so much, because he does not bother
about other people's opinions; he says what he wants to say;
and the only thing that he troubles about is to say it as well as
he possibly can" (Quoted by Hippeau).

[2] The quotations are taken from *Harmonie et Mélodie* and
*Portraits et Souvenirs*.

[3] In *Harmonie et Mélodie* M. Saint-Saëns tells us that he
organised and directed a concert in the Théâtre-Italien where
only Liszt's compositions were played. But all his efforts to
make the French musical public appreciate Liszt were a failure.

for Liszt's works. But even if the feelings of affection and gratitude that he inspired in me did come like a prism and interpose themselves between my eyes and his face, I do not see anything greatly to be regretted in it.[1] I had not yet felt the charm of his personal fascination, I had neither heard nor seen him, and I did not owe him anything at all, when my interest was gripped in reading his first symphonic poems ; and when later they pointed the way which was to lead to *La Danse macabre, Le Rouet d'Omphale*, and other works of the same nature, I am sure that my judgment was not biassed by any prejudice in his favour, and that I alone was responsible for what I did." [2]

This influence seems to me to explain some of M. Saint-Saëns' work. Not only is this influence evident in his symphonic poems—some of his best work—but it is to be found in his suites for orchestra, his fantasias, and his rhapsodies, where the descriptive and narrative element is strong. " Music should charm unaided," said M. Saint-Saëns; "but its effect is much finer when we use our imagination and let it flow in some particular channel, thus

---

[1] The admiration was mutual. M. Saint-Saëns even said that without Liszt he could not have written *Samson et Dalila*. " Not only did Liszt have *Samson et Dalila* performed at Weimar, but without him that work would never have come into being. My suggestions on the subject had met with such hostility that I had given up the idea of writing it ; and all that existed were some illegible notes. . . . Then at Weimar one day I spoke to Liszt about it, and he said to me, quite trustingly and without having heard a note, ' Finish your work ; I will have it performed here.' The events of 1870 delayed its performance for several years " (*Revue Musicale*, 8 November, 1901).

[2] *Portraits et Souvenirs.*

imaging the music.  It is then that all the faculties
of the soul are brought into play for the same end.
What art gains from this is not greater beauty, but
a wider field for its scope—that is, a greater variety
of form and a larger liberty." [1]

.    .    .    .    .    .    .

And so we find that M. Saint-Saëns has taken part
in the vigorous attempt of modern German symphony
writers to bring into music some of the power of the
other arts :  poetry, painting, philosophy, romance,
drama—the whole of life.  But what a gulf divides
them and him !  A gulf made up, not only of diversi-
ties of style, but of the difference between two races
and two worlds.  Beside the frenzied outpourings of
Richard Strauss, who flounders uncertainly between
mud and debris and genius, the Latin art of Saint-
Saëns rises up calm and ironical.  His delicacy of
touch, his careful moderation, his happy grace,
" which enters the soul by a thousand little paths," [2]
bring with them the pleasures of beautiful speech
and honest thought ;  and we cannot but feel their
charm.  Compared with the restless and troubled
art of to-day, his music strikes us by its calm, its
tranquil harmonies, its velvety modulations, its
crystal clearness, its smooth and flowing style, and
an elegance that cannot be put into words.  Even
his classic coldness does us good by its reaction
against the exaggerations, sincere as they are, of
the new school.  At times one feels oneself carried

[1] *Harmonie et Mélodie.*
[2] C. Saint-Saëns, *Portraits et Souvenirs.*

back to Mendelssohn, even to Spontini and the school of Gluck. One seems to be travelling in a country that one knows and loves; and yet in M. Saint-Saëns' works one does not find any direct resemblance to the works of other composers; for with no one are reminiscences rarer than with this master who carries all the old masters in his mind— it is his spirit that is akin to theirs. And that is the secret of his personality and his value to us; he brings to our artistic unrest a little of the light and sweetness of other times. His compositions are like fragments of another world.

"From time to time," he said, in speaking of *Don Giovanni*, " in the sacred earth of Hellene we find a fragment, an arm, the debris of a torso, scratched and damaged by the ravages of time; it is only the shadow of the god that the sculptor's chisel once created; but the charm is somehow still there, the sublime style is radiant in spite of everything."[1]

And so with this music. It is sometimes a little pale, a little too restrained; but in a phrase, in a few harmonies, there will shine out a clear vision of the past.

[1] *Portraits et Souvenirs.*

# VINCENT D'INDY

" I CONSIDER that criticism is useless, I would
even say that it is harmful. . . . Criticism generally means the opinion some man or other holds
about another person's work. How can that
opinion help forward the growth of art ? It is
interesting to know the ideas, even the erroneous
ideas, of geniuses and men of great talent, such
as Goethe, Schumann, Wagner, Sainte-Beuve,
and Michelet, when they wish to indulge in criticism ; but it is of no interest at all to know
whether Mr. So-and-so likes, or does not like,
such-and-such dramatic or musical work."[1]

So writes M. Vincent d'Indy.

After such an expression of opinion one imagines
that a critic ought to feel some embarrassment in
writing about M. Vincent d'Indy. And I myself
ought to be the more concerned in the matter, for
in the number of the review where the above
was written the only other opinions expressed with
equal conviction belonged to the author of this
book. There is only one thing to be done—to copy
M. d'Indy's example ; for that forsworn enemy of
criticism is himself a keen critic.

[1] *Révue d'Art dramatique*, 5 February, 1899.

It is not altogether on M. d'Indy's musical gifts that I want to dwell. It is known that in Europe to-day he is one of the masters of dramatic musical expression, of orchestral colouring, and of the science of style. But that is not the end of his attainments ; he has artistic originality, which springs from something deeper still. When an artist has some worth, you will find it not only in his work but in his being. So we will endeavour to explore M. d'Indy's being.

M. d'Indy's personality is not a mysterious one. On the contrary, it is open and clear as daylight ; and we see this in his musical work, in his artistic activities, and in his writings. To his own writings we may apply the exception of his rule about criticism in favour of a small number of men whose thoughts are interesting even when they are erroneous. It would be a pity indeed not to know M. d'Indy's thoughts—even the erroneous ones ; for they let us catch a glimpse, not only of the ideas of an eminent artist, but of certain surprising characteristics of the thought of our time. M. d'Indy has closely studied the history of his art ; but the chief interest of his writings lies rather in their unconscious expression of the spirit of modern art than in what they tell us about the past.

M. d'Indy is not a man hedged in by the boundaries of his art ; his mind is open and well fertilised. Musicians nowadays are no longer entirely absorbed in their notes, but let their minds go out to other interests. And it is not one of the least interesting phenomena of French music to-day that gives us these learned and thoughtful composers, who are

I

conscious of what they create, and bring to their
art a keen critical faculty, like that of M. Saint-Saëns,
M. Dukas, or M. d'Indy. From M. d'Indy we have
had scholarly editions of Rameau, Destouches, and
Salomon de Rossi. Even in the middle of rehearsals
of *L'Étranger* at Brussels he was working at a recon-
struction of Monteverde's *Orfeo*. He has published
selections of folksongs with critical notes, essays on
Beethoven's predecessors, a history of Musical
Composition, and debates and lectures. This fine
intellectual culture is not, however, the most
remarkable of M. d'Indy's characteristics, though
it may have been the most remarked. Other
musicians share this culture with him ; and his real
distinction lies in his moral and almost religious
qualities, and it is this side of him that gives him
an unusual interest for us among other contemporary artists.

.     .     .     .     .     .

" Maneant in vobis Fides, Spes, Caritas.
Tria haec : major autem horum est Caritas.

" An artist must have at least Faith, faith in
God and faith in his art ; for it is Faith that dis-
poses him to *learn*, and by his learning to raise
himself higher and higher on the ladder of Being,
up to his goal, which is God.

" An artist should practise Hope ; for he can
expect nothing from the present ; he knows that
his mission is to *serve*, and to give his work for
the life and teaching of the generations that shall
come after him.

" An artist should be inspired by a splendid
Charity—' the greatest of these.' To *love* should
be his aim in life ; for the moving principle of all
creation is divine and charitable Love."

Who speaks like this ?   Is it the monk Denys in
his cell at Mount Athos ?   Or Cennini, who spread
the pious teaching of the Giotteschi ?   Or one of
the old painters of Sienna, who in their profession
of faith called themselves " by the grace of God,
those who manifest marvellous things to common
and illiterate men, by the virtue of the holy faith,
and to its glory " ?

No ; it was the director of the *Schola Cantorum*,
addressing the students in an inaugural speech, or
giving them a lecture on Composition.[1]

We must consider a little this singular book,
where a living science and a Gothic spirit are
closely intermingled (I use the word " Gothic " in
its best sense ; I know it is the highest praise one
can give M. d'Indy).   This work has not received
the attention it deserves.   It is a record of the
spirit of contemporary art ; and if it stands rather
apart from other writings, it should not be allowed
to pass unnoticed on that account.

In this book, Faith is shown to be everything—
the beginning and the end.   We learn how it fans
the flame of genius, nourishes thought, directs work,

[1] Vincent d'Indy : *Cours de Composition musicale*, Book I,
drawn up from notes taken in Composition classes at the *Schola
Cantorum*, 1897–1898, p. 16 (Durand, 1902).   See also the
inaugural speech given at the school, and published by the
*Tribune de Saint-Gervais*, November, 1900.

and governs even the modulations and the style of
a musician. There is a passage in it that one would
think was of the thirteenth century ; it is curious,
but not without dignity :

" One should have an aim in the progressive
march of modulations, as one has in the different
stages of life. The reason, instincts, and faith
that guide a man in the troubles of his life also
guide the musician in his choice of modulations.
Thus useless and contradictory modulations, an
undecided balance between light and shade, produce a painful and confusing impression on the
hearer, comparable to that which a poor human
being inspires when he is feeble and inconsistent,
buffeted between the East and the West in the
course of his unhappy life, without an aim and
without belief." [1]

This book seems to be of the Middle Ages by
reason of a sort of scholastic spirit of abstraction
and classification.

" In artistic creation, seven faculties are called
into play by the soul : the Imagination, the
Affections, the Understanding, the Intelligence,
the Memory, the Will, and the Conscience." [2]

And again its mediæval spirit is shown by an
extraordinary symbolism, which discovers in every-

---

[1] Vincent d'Indy, *Cours de Composition musicale*, p. 132.
[2] *Id., ibid.*, p. 13.

thing (as far as I understand it) the imprint of divine mysteries, and the mark of God in Three Persons in such things as the beating of the heart and ternary rhythms—" an admirable application of the principle of the Unity of the Trinity " ! [1]

From these remote times comes also M. d'Indy's method of writing history, not by tracing facts back to laws, but by deducing, on the contrary, facts from certain great general ideas, which have once been admitted, but not proved by frequent recurrence, such as : " The origin of art is in religion " [2]—a fact which is anything but certain. From this reasoning it follows that folksongs are derived from Gregorian chants, and not the Gregorian chants from the folksongs—as I would sooner believe. The history of art may thus become a sort of history of the world in moral achievement. One could divide it into two parts : the world before the coming of Pride, and after it.

" Subdued by the Christian faith, that formidable enemy of man, Pride, rarely showed itself in the soul of an artist in the Middle Ages. But with the weakening of religious belief, with the spirit of the Reformation applying itself almost at the same time to every branch of human learning, we see Pride reappear, and watch its veritable Renaissance." [3]

[1] *Id.*, *ibid.*, p. 25. In the thirteenth century, Philippe de Vitry, Bishop of Meaux, called triple time " perfect," because " it hath its name from the Trinity, that is to say, from the Father, the Son, and the Holy Ghost, in whom is divine perfection."

[2] *Id.*, *ibid.*, pp. 66, 83, and *passim*.          [3] *Id.*, *ibid.*

Finally, this Gothic spirit shows itself—in a less original way, it is true—in M. d'Indy's religious antipathies, which, in spite of the author's goodness of heart and great personal tolerance, constantly break out against the two faiths that are rivals to his own ; and to them he attributes all the faults of art and all the vices of humanity. Each has its offence. Protestantism is made responsible for the extremes of individualism ; [1] and Judaism, for the absurdities of its customs and the weakness of its moral sense. [2]   I do not know which of the two is the more soundly belaboured ; the second has the privilege of being so, not only in writing, but in pictures. [3]  The worst of it is, these antipathies are apt to spoil the fairness of M. d'Indy's artistic judgment. It goes without saying that the Jewish musicians are treated with scant consideration ; and even the great Protestant musicians, giants in their art, do not escape rebuke. If Goudimel is mentioned, it is because he was Palestrina's master, and his achievement of " turning the Calvinist psalms into chorales " is dismissed as being of little importance. [4]  Handel's oratorios are spoken of as

[1] " Make war against Particularism, that unwholesome fruit of the Protestant heresy ! " (Speech to the *Schola*, taken from the *Tribune de Saint-Gervais*, November, 1900.)

[2] At least Judaism has the honour of giving its name to a whole period of art, the " Judaic period." " The modern style is the last phase of the Judaic school. . . ." etc.

[3] In the *Cours de Composition musicale* M. d'Indy speaks of " the admirable initial T in the *Rouleau mortuaire* of Saint-Vital (twelfth century), which represents Satan vomiting two Jews . . . an expressive and symbolic work of art, if ever there was one." I should not mention this but for the fact that there are only two illustrations in the whole book.

[4] *Cours de Composition musicale*, p. 160.

"chilling, and, frankly speaking, tedious." [1] Bach himself escapes with this qualification: "If he is great, it is not because of, but in spite of the dogmatic and parching spirit of the Reformation." [2]

I will not try to play the part of judge ; for a man is sufficiently judged by his own writings. And, after all, it is rather interesting to meet people who are sincere and not afraid to speak their minds. I will admit that I rather enjoy—a little perversely, perhaps—some of these extreme opinions, where the writer's personality stands strongly revealed.

So the old Gothic spirit still lives among us, and informs the mind of one of our best-known artists, and also, without doubt, the minds of hundreds of those who listen to him and admire him. M. Louis Laloy has shown the persistence of certain forms of plain-song in M. Debussy's *Pelléas ;* and in a dim sense of far-away kinship he finds the cause of the mysterious charm that such music holds for some of us. [3] This learned paradox is possible. Why not ? The mixtures of race and the vicissitudes of history have given us so full and complex a soul that we may very well find its beginnings there, if it pleases us—or the beginnings of quite other things. Of beginnings there is no end ; the choice is quite

[1] *L'Oratorio moderne* (*Tribune de Saint-Gervais*, March, 1899).
[2] *Ibid.* As much as to say he was a Catholic without knowing it. And that is what a friend of the *Schola*, M. Edgar Tinel, declares : " Bach is a truly Christian artist and, without doubt, *a Protestant by mistake*, since in his immortal *Credo* he confesses his faith in one holy, catholic, and apostolic Church " (*Tribune de Saint-Gervais*, August–September, 1902). M. Edgar Tinel was, as you know, one of the principal masters of Belgian oratorio.
[3] *Révue musicale*, November, 1902.

embarrassing, and I imagine one's inclination has
as much to do with the matter as one's temperament.

However that may be, M. d'Indy hails from the
Middle Ages, and not from antiquity (which does
not exist for him [1]), or from the Renaissance, which
he confounds with the Reformation (though the
two sisters are enemies) in order to crush it the
better.[2]  " Let us take for models," he says, " the
fine workers in art of the Middle Ages." [3]

.     .     .     .     .     .

In this return to the Gothic spirit, in this awakening of faith, there is a name—a modern one this
time—that they are fond of quoting at the *Schola ;*
it is that of César Franck, under whose direction
the little Conservatoire in the Rue Saint-Jacques
was placed.  And indeed they could quote no better
name than that of this simple-hearted man.  Nearly
all who came into contact with him felt his irresistible
charm—a charm that has perhaps a great deal to do
with the influence that his works still have on French
music to-day.  None has felt Franck's power, both
morally and musically, more than M. Vincent d'Indy;
and none holds a more profound reverence for the
man whose pupil he was for so long.

The first time I saw M. d'Indy was at a concert

---

[1] " The only documents extant on ancient music are either
criticisms or appreciations, and not musical texts " (*Cours de
Composition*).

[2] " The influence of the Renaissance, with its pretension and
vanity, caused a check in all the arts—the effect of which we
are still feeling " (*Traité de Composition*, p. 89.  See also the
passage quoted before on Pride).

[3] *Tribune de Saint-Gervais*, November, 1900.

of the *Société nationale*, in the Salle Pleyel, in 1888. They were playing several of Franck's works; among others, for the first time, his admirable *Thème, fugue, et variation*, for the harmonium and pianoforte, a composition in which the spirit of Bach is mingled with a quite modern tenderness. Franck was conducting, and M. d'Indy was at the pianoforte. I shall always remember his reverential manner towards the old musician, and how careful he was to follow his directions; one would have said he was a diligent and obedient pupil. It was a touching homage from one who had already proved himself a master by works like *Le Chant de la cloche, Wallensiein, La Symphonie sur un thème montagnard*, and who was perhaps at that time better known and more popular than César Franck himself. Since then twenty years have passed, and I still see M. d'Indy as I saw him that evening; and, whatever may happen in the future, his memory for me will be always associated with that of the grand old artist, presiding with his fatherly smile over the little gathering of the faithful.

Of all the characteristics of Franck's fine moral nature, the most remarkable was his religious faith. It must have astonished the artists of his time, who were even more destitute of such a thing than they are now. It made itself felt in some of his followers, especially in those who were near the master's heart, as M. d'Indy was. The religious thought of the latter reflects in some degree the thought of his master; though the shape of that thought may have undergone unconscious alteration. I do not

know if Franck altogether fits the conception people
have of him to-day. I do not want to introduce
personal memories of him here. I knew him well
enough to love him, and to catch a glimpse of the
beauty and sincerity of his soul ; but I did not know
him well enough to discover the secrets of his mind.
Those who had the happiness of being his intimate
friends seem always to represent him as a mystic
who shut himself away from the spirit of his time.
I hope at some future date one of his friends will
publish some of the conversations that he had with
him, of which I have heard. But this man who had
so strong a faith was also very independent. In
his religion he had no doubts : it was the mainspring
of his life ; though faith with him was much more
a matter of feeling than a matter of doctrine. But
all was feeling with Franck, and reason made little
appeal to him. His religious faith did not disturb
his mind, for he did not measure men and their works
by its rules ; and he would have been incapable of
putting together a history of art according to the
Bible. This great Catholic had at times a very pagan
soul ; and he could enjoy without a qualm the
musical dilettantism of Renan and the sonorous
nihilism of Leconte de Lisle. There were no limits
to his vast sympathies. He did not attempt to
criticise the thing he loved—understanding was
already in his heart. Perhaps he was right ; and
perhaps there was more trouble in the depths of his
heart than the valiant serenity of its surface would
lead us to believe.

His faith too. . . . I know how dangerous it is to

interpret a musician's feelings by his music ; but how can we do otherwise when we are told by Franck's followers that the expression of the soul is the only end and aim of music ? Do we find his faith, as expressed through his music, always full of peace and calm ? [1] I ask those who love that music because they find some of their own sadness reflected there. Who has not felt the secret tragedies that some of his musical passages enfold—those short, characteristically abrupt phrases which seem to rise in supplication to God, and often fall back in sadness and in tears ? It is not all light in that soul ; but the light that is there does not affect us less because it shines from afar,

" Dans un écartement de nuages, qui laisse
  Voir au-dessus des mers la céleste allégresse. . . ." [2]

And so Franck seems to me to differ from M. d'Indy in that he has not the latter's urgent desire for clearness.

\   .   .   .   .   .   .

Clearness is the distinguishing quality of M. d'Indy's mind. There are no shadows about him. His ideas and his art are as clear as the look that gives so much youth to his face. For him to examine,

---

[1] I speak of the passages where he expresses himself freely, and is not interpreting a dramatic situation necessary to his subject, as in that fine symphonic part of the *Rédemption*, where he describes the triumph of Christ. But even there we find traces of sadness and suffering.

[2] Through a break in the clouds, revealing
Celestial joy shining above the deeps.

to arrange, to classify, to combine, is a necessity.
No one is more French in spirit. He has sometimes
been taxed with Wagnerism, and it is true that he
has felt Wagner's influence very strongly. But even
when this influence is most apparent it is only
superficial : his true spirit is remote from Wagner's.
You may find in *Fervaal* a few trees like those in
*Siegfried's* forest ; but the forest itself is not the
same ; broad avenues have been cut in it, and daylight fills the caverns of the Niebelungs.

This love of clearness is the ruling factor of M.
d'Indy's artistic nature. And this is the more
remarkable, for his nature is far from being a simple
one. By his wide musical education and his constant thirst for knowledge he has acquired a very
varied and almost contradictory learning. It must
be remembered that M. d'Indy is a musician familiar
with the music of other countries and other times ;
all kinds of musical forms are floating in his mind ;
and he seems sometimes to hesitate between them.
He has arranged these forms into three principal
classes, which seem to him to be models of musical
art : the decorative art of the singers of plain-song,
the architectural art of Palestrina and his followers,
and the expressive art of the great Italians of the
seventeenth century.[1] But in doing this is not his
eclecticism trying to reconcile arts that are naturally
disunited ? Again, we must remember that M.
d'Indy has had direct or indirect contact with some
of the greatest musical personalities of our time :
with Wagner, Liszt, Brahms, and César Franck.

[1] *Tribune de Saint-Gervais*, November, 1900.

And he has been readily attracted by them ; for he is
not one of those egotistic geniuses whose thoughts
are fixed on his own interests, nor has he one of
those carnivorous minds that sees nothing, looks
for nothing, and relishes nothing, unless it may be
afterwards useful to it. His sympathies are readily
with others, he is happy in giving homage to their
greatness, and quick to appreciate their charm. He
speaks somewhere of the " irresistible need of trans-
formation " that every artist feels.[1] But in order
to escape being overwhelmed by conflicting elements
and interests, one should have great force of feeling
or will, in order to be able to eliminate what is not
necessary, and choose out and transform what is.
M. d'Indy eliminates hardly anything ; he makes
use of it. In his music he exercises the qualities of
an army general : understanding of his purpose and
the patience to attain it, a perfect knowledge of the
means at his disposal, the spirit of order, and command over his work and himself. Despite the
variety of the materials he employs, the whole is
always clear. One might almost reproach him
with being too clear ; he seems to simplify too
much.

Nothing helps one to grasp the essence of M.
d'Indy's personality more than his last dramatic
work. His personality shows itself plainly in all
his compositions, but nowhere is it more evident
than in *L'Étranger*.[2]

[1] *Id.*, September, 1899.
[2] *L'Étranger*, " action musicale " in two acts. Poem and
music by M. Vincent d'Indy. Played for the first time at
Brussels in the Théâtre de la Monnaie, 7 January, 1903. The

The scene of *L'Étranger* is laid in France, by the
sea, whose murmuring calm we hear in a symphonic
introduction. The fishermen are coming back to
port ; the fishing has been bad. But one among
them, " a man about forty years old, with a sad and
dignified air," has been more fortunate than the
others. The fishermen envy him, and vaguely
suspect him of sorcery. He tries to enter into
friendly conversation with them, and offers his
catch to a poor family. But in vain ; his advances
are repulsed and his generosity is eyed with sus-
picion. He is a stranger—the Stranger.[1] Evening
falls, and the angelus rings. Some work-girls come
trooping out of their workshop, singing a merry
folksong.[2] One of the young girls, Vita, goes up to
the Stranger and speaks to him, for she alone, of all
the village, is his friend. The two feel themselves
drawn together by a secret sympathy. Vita con-
fides artlessly in the unknown man ; they love each
other though they do not admit it. The Stranger
tries to repress his feelings ; for Vita is young and
already affianced, and he thinks that he has no right
to claim her. But Vita, offended by his coldness,

quotations from the drama, whose poetry is not as good as its
music, are taken from the score.

[1] There is a certain likeness in the subject to Herr Richard
Strauss's *Feuersnot*. There, too, the hero is a stranger who
is persecuted, and treated as a sorcerer in the very town to which
he has brought honour. But the *dénouement* is not the same ;
and the fundamental difference of temperament between the
two artists is strongly marked. M. d'Indy finishes with the
renouncement of a Christian, and Herr Richard Strauss by a
proud and joyous affirmation of independence.

[2] Found by M. d'Indy in his own province, as he tells us in
his *Chansons populaires du Vivarais.*

seeks to wound him, and succeeds. In the end he
betrays himself. " Yes, he loves her, and she knew
it well. But now that he has told her so, he will
never see her again ; and he bids her good-bye."

That is the first act. Up to this point we seem to
be witnessing a very human and realistic drama—
the ordinary story of the man who tries to do good
and receives ingratitude, and the sad tragedy of
old age that comes to a heart still young and unable
to resign itself to growing old. But the music puts
us on our guard. We had heard its religious tone
when the Stranger was speaking, and it seemed to
us that we recognised a liturgical melody in the
principal theme. What secret is being hidden from
us ? Are we not in France ? Yet, in spite of the
folksong and a passing breath of the sea, the atmosphere of the Church and César Franck is evident.
Who is this Stranger ?

He tells us in the second act.

" My name ? I have none. I am He who
dreams ; I am He who loves. I have passed
through many countries, and sailed on many
seas, loving the poor and needy, dreaming of the
happiness of the brotherhood of man."

" Where have I seen you ?—for I know you."

" Where ? you ask. But everywhere : under
the warm sun of the East, by the white oceans of
the Pole. . . . I have found you everywhere, for
you are Beauty itself, you are immortal Love ! "

The music is not without a certain nobility, and

bears the imprint of the calm, strong spirit of belief. But I was sorry that the story was only about a mere entity when I had been getting interested in a man. I can never understand the attraction of this kind of symbolism. Unless it is allied to sublime powers of creation in metaphysics or morals—such as that possessed by a Goethe or an Ibsen—I do not see what such symbolism can add to life, though I see very well what it takes away from it. But it is, after all, a matter of taste; and, anyway, there is nothing in this story to astonish us greatly. This transition from realism to symbolism is something in opera with which we have grown only too familiar since the time of Wagner.

But the story does not stop there ; for we leave symbolic abstractions to enter a still more extraordinary domain, which is removed even farther still from realities.

There had been some talk at the beginning of an emerald that sparkled in the Stranger's cap ; and this emerald now takes its turn in the action of the piece. " It had sparkled formerly in the bows of the boat that carried the body of Lazarus, the friend of our Master, Jesus ; and the boat had safely reached the port of the Phoceans—without a helm or sails or oars. For by this miraculous stone a clean and upright heart could command the sea and the winds." But now that the Stranger has done amiss, by falling a victim to passion, its power is gone ; so he gives it to Vita.

Then follows a real scene in fairyland Vita stands before the sea and invokes it in an incan-

tation full of weird and beautiful vocal music :
" O sea ! Sinister sea with your angry charm,
gentle sea with your kiss of death, hear me ! " And
the sea replies in a song. Voices mingle with the
orchestra in a symphony of increasing anger. Vita
swears she will give herself to no one but the Stranger.
She lifts the emerald above her head, and it shines
with a lurid light. " ' Receive, O sea, as a token of
my oath, the sacred stone, the holy emerald ! Then
may its power be no longer invoked, and none may
know again its protecting virtue. Jealous sea, take
back your own, the last offering of a betrothed ! '
With an impressive gesture she throws the emerald
into the waves, and a dark green light suddenly
shines out against the black sky. This supernatural
light slowly spreads over the water until it reaches
the horizon, and the sea begins to roll in great
billows." Then the sea takes up its song in an
angrier tone ; the orchestra thunders, and the
storm bursts.

The boats put hurriedly back to land, and one of
them seems likely to be dashed to pieces on the
shore. The whole village turns out to watch the
disaster ; but the men refuse to risk their lives in
aid of the shipwrecked crew. Then the Stranger gets
into a boat, and Vita jumps in after him. The
squall redoubles in violence. A wave of enormous
height breaks on the jetty, flooding the scene with
a dazzling green light. The crowd recoil in fear.
There is a silence ; and an old fisherman takes
off his woollen cap and intones the *De Profundis*.
The villagers take up the chant. . . .

K

One may see by this short account what a heterogeneous work it is.  Two or three quite different
worlds are brought into it :  the realism of the
bourgeois characters of Vita's mother and lover is
mixed up with symbolisms of Christianity, represented by the Stranger, and with the fairy-tale of the
magic emerald and the voices of the ocean.  This
complexity, which is evident enough in the poem,
is even more evident in the music, where a union
of different arts and different ideas is attempted.
We get the art of the folksong, religious art, the art
of Wagner, the art of Franck, as well as a note of
familiar realism (which is something akin to the
Italian *opéra-bouffe*) and descriptions of sensation
that are quite personal.  As there are only two
short acts, the rapidity of the action only serves to
accentuate this impression.  The changes are very
abrupt :  we are hurried from a world of human
beings to a world of abstract ideas, and then taken
from an atmosphere of religion to a land of fairies.
The work is, however, clear enough from a musical
point of view.  The more complex the elements that
M. d'Indy gathers round him the more anxious he
is to bring them into harmony.  It is a difficult task,
and is only possible when the different elements are
reduced to their simplest expression and brought
down to their fundamental qualities—thus depriving
them of the spice of their individuality.  M. d'Indy
puts different styles and ideas on the anvil, and
then forges them vigorously.  It is natural that here
and there we should see the mark of the hammer,
the imprint of his determination ;  but it is only by

his determination that he welded the work into a solid whole.

Perhaps it is determination that brings unity now and then into M. d'Indy's spirit. With reference to this, I will dwell upon one point only, since it is curious, and seems to me to be of general artistic interest. M. d'Indy writes his own poems for his " *actions musicales* "—Wagner's example, it seems, has been catching. We have seen how the harmony of a work may suffer through the dual gifts of its author ; though he may have thought to perfect his composition by writing both words and music. But an artist's poetical and musical gifts are not necessarily of the same order. A man has not always the same kind of talent in other arts that he has in the art which he has made his own—I am speaking not only of his technical skill, but of his temperament as well. Delacroix was of the Romantic school in painting, but in literature his style was Classic. We have all known artists who were revolutionaries in their own sphere, but conservative and behind the times in their opinions about other branches of art. The double gift of poetry and music is in M. d'Indy up to a certain point. But is his reason always in agreement with his heart ? [1] Of course his nature

[1] In his criticisms his heart is not always in agreement with his mind. His mind denounces the Renaissance, but his instinct obliges him to appreciate the great Florentine painters of the Renaissance and the musicians of the sixteenth century. He only gets out of the difficulty by the most extraordinary compromises, by saying that Ghirlandajo and Filippo Lippi were Gothic, or by stating that the Renaissance in music did not begin till the seventeenth century ! (*Cours de Composition*, pp. 214 and 216.)

is too dignified to let the quarrel be shown openly.
His heart obeys the commands of his reason, or
compromises with it, and by seeming respectful of
authority saves appearances. His reason, represented here by the poet, likes simple, realistic, and
relevant action, together with moral or even religious
teaching. His heart, represented by the musician,
is romantic ; and if he followed it altogether he
would wander off to any subject that enabled him
to indulge in his love of the picturesque, such as the
descriptive symphony, or even the old form of opera.

For myself, I am in sympathy with his heart ;
and I find his heart is in the right, and his reason
in the wrong. There is nothing that M. d'Indy has
made more his own than the art of painting landscapes in music. There is one page in *Fervaal* at
the beginning of Act II which calls up misty mountain tops covered with pine forests ; there is another
page in *L'Étranger* where one sees strange lights
glimmering on the sea while a storm is brooding.[1]
I should like to see M. d'Indy give himself up freely,
in spite of all theories, to this descriptive lyricism,
in which he so excels ; or I wish at least he would
seek inspiration in a subject where both his religious
beliefs and his imagination could find satisfaction :
a subject such as one of the beautiful episodes of
the Golden Legend, or the one which *L'Étranger*
itself recalls—the romantic voyage of the Magdalen
in Provence. But it is foolish to wish an artist to

---

[1] Act III, scene 3. The power of that evocation is so strong
that it carries the poet along with it. It would seem that part
of the action had only been conceived with a view to the final
effect of the sudden colouring of the waves.

do anything but the thing he likes ; he is the best
judge of what pleases him.

.        .        .        .        .        .

In this sketchy portrait I must not forget one of
the finest of this composer's gifts—his talent as a
teacher of music. Everything has fitted M. d'Indy
for this part. By his knowledge and his precise,
orderly mind he must be a perfect teacher of composition. If I submit some question of harmony
or melodic phrasing to his analysis, the result is the
essence of clear, logical reasoning ; and if the reasoning is a little dry and simplifies the thing almost too
much, it is still very illuminating and from the hand
of a master of French prose. And in this I find him
exercising the same consistent instinct of good
sense and sincerity, the same art of development,
the same seventeenth and eighteenth century principles of classic rhetoric that he applies to his music.
In truth, M. d'Indy could write a musical *Discourse
on Style*, if he wished.

But, above all, he is gifted with the moral qualities
of a teacher—the vocation for teaching, first of all.
He has a firm belief in the absolute duty of giving
instruction in art, and, what is rarer still, in the
efficacious virtue of that teaching. He readily
shares Tolstoy's scorn, which he sometimes quotes,
of the foolishness of art for art's sake.

" At the bottom of art is this essential condition—teaching. The aim of art is neither gain
nor glory ; the true aim of art is to teach, to

elevate gradually the spirit of humanity ; in a word, to serve in the highest sense—' *dienen* ' as Wagner says by the mouth of the repentant Kundry, in the third act of Parsifal." [1]

There is in this a mixture of Christian humility and aristocratic pride.  M. d'Indy has a sincere desire for the welfare of humanity, and he loves the people ;  but he treats them with an affectionate kindness, at once protective and tolerant ;  he regards them as children that must be led. [2]

The popular art that he extols is not an art belonging to the people, but that of an aristocracy interested in the people.  He wishes to enlighten them, to mould them, to direct them, by means of art.  Art is the source of life ;  it is the spirit of progress ;  it gives the most precious of possessions to the soul—liberty.  And no one enjoys this liberty more than the artist.  In a lecture to the *Schola* he said :

" What makes the name of ' artist ' so splendid is that the artist is free—absolutely free.  Look about you, and tell me if from this point of view there is any career finer than that of an artist who is conscious of his mission ?  The Army ? The Law ?  The University ?  Politics ? "

And then follows a rather cold appreciation of these different careers.

[1] *Cours de Composition*, and *Tribune de Saint-Gervais*.
[2] *Cours de Composition*.

" There is no need to mention the excessive bureaucracy and officialism which is the crying evil of this country. We find everywhere submission to rules and servitude to the State. But what government, pope, emperor, or president could oblige an artist to think and write against his will ? Liberty—that is the true wealth and the most precious inheritance of the artist, the liberty to think, and the liberty that no one has the power to take away from us—that of doing our work according to the dictates of our conscience."

Who does not feel the infectious warmth and beauty of these spirited words ? How this force of enthusiasm and sincerity must grip all young and eager hearts. " There are two qualities," says M. d'Indy, on the last page of *Cours de Composition*, " which a master should try to encourage and develop in the spirit of the pupil, for without them science is useless ; these qualities are an unselfish love of art and enthusiasm for good work." And these two virtues radiate from M. d'Indy's personality as they do from his writings ; that is his power.

But the best of his teaching lies in his life. One can never speak too highly of his disinterested devotion for the good of art. As if it were not enough to put all his might into his own creations, M. d'Indy gives his time and the results of his study unsparingly to others. Franck gave lessons in order to be able to live ; M. d'Indy gives them for the pleasure of instructing, and to serve his art and aid artists. He directs schools, and accepts and almost seeks out the most thankless, though the most necessary, kinds of teaching. Or he will apply himself devoutly to the study of the past and the resuscitation of some old master. And he seems to take so much pleasure in training young minds to appreciate music, or in repairing the injustices of history to some fine but forgotten musician, that he almost forgets about himself. To what work or to what worker, worthy of interest, or seeming to be so, has he ever refused his advice and help? I have known his kindness personally, and I shall always be sincerely grateful for it.

His devotion and his faith have not been in vain. The name of M. d'Indy will be associated in history, not only with fine works, but with great works: with the *Société Nationale de Musique*, of which he is president; with the *Schola Cantorum*, which he founded with Charles Bordes, and which he directs; with the young French school of music, a group of skilful artists and innovators, to whom he is a kind of elder brother, giving them encouragement by his example and helping them through the first hard years of struggle; and, lastly, with an awakening of music in Europe, with a movement which, after the death of Wagner and Franck, attracted the interest of the world by its revival of the art of the Middle Ages and the Renaissance. M. d'Indy has been the chief representative of all this artistic evolution in France. By his deeds, by his example, and by his spirit, he was among the first to stir up interest in the musical education of France to-day.

He has done more for the advancement of our music
than the entire official teaching of the Conservatoires.
A day will come when, by the force of things and in
spite of all resistance, such a man will take the
place that belongs to him at the head of the organisation of music in France.

.    .    .    .    .    .

I have tried to unearth M. d'Indy's strongest
characteristics, and I think I have found them in
his faith and in his activity.  I am only too aware
of the pitfalls that have beset me in this attempt ;
it is always difficult to criticise a man's personality,
and it is most difficult when he is alive and still in
the midst of his development.  Every man is a
mystery, not only to others, but to himself.  There
is something very presumptuous about pretending
to know anyone who does not quite know himself.
And yet one cannot live without forming opinions ;
it is a necessity of life.  The people we see and know
(or say we know), our friends, and those we love,
are never what we think them.  Often they are not
at all like the portrait we conjure up ; for we walk
among the phantoms of our hearts.  But still one
must go on having opinions, and go on constructing
and creating things, if we do not want to become
impotent through inertia.  Error is better than
doubt, provided we err in good faith ; and the main
thing is to speak out the thing that one really feels
and believes.  I hope M. d'Indy will forgive me if I
have gone far wrong, and that he will see in these
pages a sincere effort to understand him and a keen

sympathy with himself, and even with his ideas, though I do not always share them. But I have always thought that in life a man's opinions go for very little, and that the only thing that matters is the man himself. Freedom of spirit is the greatest happiness one can know; one must be sorry for those who have not got it. And there is a secret pleasure in rendering homage to another's splendid creed, even though it is one that we do not ourselves profess.

# RICHARD STRAUSS

THE composer of *Heldenleben* is no longer unknown to Parisians. Every year at Colonne's or Chevillard's we see his tall, thin silhouette reappear in the conductor's desk. There he is with his abrupt and imperious gestures, his wan and anxious face, his wonderfully clear eyes, restless and penetrating at the same time, his mouth shaped like a child's, a moustache so fair that it is nearly white, and curly hair growing like a crown above his high round forehead.

I should like to try to sketch here the strange and arresting personality of the man who in Germany is considered the inheritor of Wagner's genius— the man who has had the audacity to write, after Beethoven, an Heroic Symphony, and to imagine himself the hero.

   .     .     .     .     .     .

Richard Strauss is thirty-four years old.[1] He was born in Munich on 11 June, 1864. His father, a well-known virtuoso, was first horn in the Royal orchestra, and his mother was a daughter of the brewer Pschorr. He was brought up among musical surroundings. At four years old he played the piano, and at six he composed little dances,

---

[1] This essay was written in 1899.

*Lieder*, sonatas, and even overtures for the orchestra. Perhaps this extreme artistic precocity has had something to do with the feverish character of his talents, by keeping his nerves in a state of tension and unduly exciting his mind. At school he composed choruses for some of Sophocles' tragedies. In 1881, Hermann Levi had one of the young collegian's symphonies performed by his orchestra. At the University he spent his time in writing instrumental music. Then Bülow and Radecke made him play in Berlin ; and Bülow, who became very fond of him, had him brought to Meiningen as *Musikdirector*. From 1886 to 1889 he held the same post at the *Hoftheater* in Munich. From 1889 to 1894 he was *Kapellmeister* at the *Hoftheater* in Weimar. He returned to Munich in 1894 as *Hofkapellmeister*, and in 1897 succeeded Hermann Levi. Finally, he left Munich for Berlin, where at present he conducts the orchestra of the Royal Opera.

Two things should be particularly noted in his life : the influence of Alexander Ritter—to whom he has shown much gratitude—and his travels in the south of Europe. He made Ritter's acquaintance in 1885. This musician was a nephew of Wagner's, and died some years ago. His music is practically unknown in France, though he wrote two well-known operas, *Fauler Hans* and *Wem die Krone ?* and was the first composer, according to Strauss, to introduce Wagnerian methods into the *Lied*. He is often discussed in Bülow's and Liszt's letters. " Before I met him," says Strauss, " I had been brought up on strictly classical lines ; I had lived

entirely on Haydn, Mozart, and Beethoven, and
had just been studying Mendelssohn, Chopin,
Schumann, and Brahms.  It is to Ritter alone I am
indebted for my knowledge of Liszt and Wagner ;
it was he who showed me the importance of the
writings and works of these two masters in the
history of art.  It was he who by years of lessons
and kindly counsel made me a musician of the
future (*Zukunftsmusiker*), and set my feet on a road
where now I can walk unaided and alone.  It was
he also who initiated me in Schopenhauer's philosophy."

The second influence, that of the South, dates
from April, 1886, and seems to have left an indelible
impression upon Strauss.  He visited Rome and
Naples for the first time, and came back with a
symphonic fantasia called *Aus Italien*.  In the
spring of 1892, after a sharp attack of pneumonia,
he travelled for a year and a half in Greece, Egypt,
and Sicily.  The tranquillity of these favoured
countries filled him with never-ending regret.  The
North has depressed him since then, " the eternal
grey of the North and its phantom shadows without
a sun."[1]  When I saw him at Charlottenburg, one
chilly April day, he told me with a sigh that he
could compose nothing in winter, and that he
longed for the warmth and light of Italy.  His music
is infected by that longing ; and it makes one feel
how his spirit suffers in the gloom of Germany, and
ever yearns for the colours, the laughter, and the
joy of the South.  Like the musician that Nietzsche

[1] Nietzsche.

dreamed of,[1] he seems "to hear ringing in his ears
the prelude of a deeper, stronger music, perhaps a
more wayward and mysterious music ; a music that
is super-German, which, unlike other music, would
not die away, nor pale, nor grow dull beside the blue
and wanton sea and the clear Mediterranean sky ;
a music super-European, which would hold its own
even by the dark sunsets of the desert ; a music
whose soul is akin to the palm trees ; a music that
knows how to live and move among great beasts of
prey, beautiful and solitary ; a music whose
supreme charm is its ignorance of good and evil.
Only from time to time perhaps there would flit
over it the longing of the sailor for home, golden
shadows, and gentle weaknesses ; and towards it
would come flying from afar the thousand tints of
the setting of a moral world that men no longer
understood ; and to these belated fugitives it would
extend its hospitality and sympathy." But it is
always the North, the melancholy of the North,
and " all the sadness of mankind," mental anguish,
the thought of death, and the tyranny of life, that
come and weigh down afresh his spirit hungering
for light, and force it into feverish speculation and
bitter argument. Perhaps it is better so.

. . . . . .

Richard Strauss is both a poet and a musician.
These two natures live together in him, and each

---

[1] *Beyond Good and Evil*, 1886. I hope I may be excused for
introducing Nietzsche here, but his thoughts seem constantly to
be reflected in Strauss, and to throw much light on the soul of
modern Germany.

RICHARD STRAUSS                143

strives to get the better of the other. The balance
is not always well maintained ; but when he does
succeed in keeping it by sheer force of will the
union of these two talents, directed to the same end,
produces an effect more powerful than any known
since Wagner's time. Both natures have their
source in a mind filled with heroic thoughts—a
rarer possession, I consider, than a talent for either
music or poetry. There are other great musicians
in Europe ; but Strauss is something more than a
great musician, for he is able to create a hero.

When one talks of heroes one is thinking of drama.
Dramatic art is everywhere in Strauss's music, even
in works that seem least adapted to it, such as
his *Lieder* and compositions of pure music. It is
most evident in his symphonic poems, which are
the most important part of his work. These poems
are : *Wanderers Sturmlied* (1885), *Aus Italien* (1886),
*Macbeth* (1887), *Don Juan* (1888), *Tod und Verklärung* (1889), *Guntram* (1892–93), *Till Eulenspiegel*
(1894), *Also sprach Zarathustra* (1895), *Don Quixote*
(1897), and *Heldenleben* (1898).[1]

I shall not say much about the four first works,
where the mind and manner of the artist is taking
shape. The *Wanderers Sturmlied* (the song of a
traveller during a storm, op. 14) is a vocal sextette
with an orchestral accompaniment, whose subject
is taken from a poem of Goethe's. It was written
before Strauss met Ritter, and its construction is

---

[1] This article was written in 1899. Since then the *Sinfonia
Domestica* has been produced, and will be noticed in the essay
*French and German Music.*

after the manner of Brahms, and shows a rather affected thought and style. *Aus Italien* (op. 16) is an exuberant picture of impressions of his tour in Italy, of the ruins at Rome, the seashore at Sorrento, and the life of the Italian people. *Macbeth* (op. 23) gives us a rather undistinguished series of musical interpretations of poetical subjects. *Don Juan* (op. 20) is much finer, and translates Lenau's poem into music with bombastic vigour, showing us the hero who dreams of grasping all the joy of the world, and how he fails, and dies after he has lost faith in everything.

*Tod und Verklärung* ("Death and Transfiguration," op. 24[1]) marks considerable progress in Strauss's thought and style. It is still one of the most stirring of Strauss's works, and the one that is conceived with the most perfect unity. It was inspired by a poem of Alexander Ritter's, and I will give you an idea of its subject.

In a wretched room, lit only by a nightlight, a sick man lies in bed. Death draws near him in the midst of awe-inspiring silence. The unhappy man seems to wander in his mind at times, and to find comfort in past memories. His life passes before his eyes : his innocent childhood, his happy youth, the struggles of middle age, and his efforts to attain the splendid goal of his desires, which always eludes him. He had been striving all his life for this goal, and at last thought it was within reach, when Death, in a voice of thunder, cries, suddenly, "Stop!" And

---

[1] Composed in 1889, and performed for the first time at Eisenach in 1890.

even now in his agony he struggles desperately, being set upon realising his dream ; but the hand of Death is crushing life out of his body, and night is creeping on. Then resounds in the heavens the promise of that happiness which he had vainly sought for on earth—Redemption and Transfiguration.

Richard Strauss's friends protested vigorously against this orthodox ending; and Seidl,[1] Jorisenne,[2] and Wilhelm Mauke[3] pretended that the subject was something loftier, that it was the eternal struggle of the soul against its lower self and its deliverance by means of art. I shall not enter into that discussion, though I think that such a cold and commonplace symbolism is much less interesting than the struggle with death, which one feels in every note of the composition. It is a classical work, comparatively speaking; broad and majestic and almost like Beethoven in style. The realism of the subject in the hallucinations of the dying man, the shiverings of fever, the throbbing of the veins, and the despairing agony, is transfigured by the purity of the form in which it is cast. It is realism after the manner of the symphony in C minor, where Beethoven argues with Destiny. If all suggestion of a programme is taken away, the symphony still remains intelligible and impressive by its harmonious expression of feeling. Many German musicians think that Strauss has reached the

---

[1] *Richard Strauss, eine Charakterskizze,* 1896, Prague.
[2] *R. Strauss, Essai critique et biologique,* 1898, Brussels.
[3] *Der Musikführer : Tod und Verklärung,* Frankfort.

L

highest point of his work in *Tod und Verklärung*.
But I am far from agreeing with them, and believe
myself that his art has developed enormously as
the result of it. It is true it is the summit of
one period of his life, containing the essence of all
that is best in it ; but *Heldenleben* marks the second
period, and is its corner-stone. How the force and
fulness of his feeling has grown since that first
period ! But he has never re-found the delicate and
melodious purity of soul and youthful grace of his
earlier work, which still shines out in *Guntram*,
and is then effaced.

　　·　　　·　　　·　　　·　　　·　　　·

Strauss has directed Wagner's dramas at Weimar
since 1889. While breathing their atmosphere he
turned his attention to the theatre, and wrote the
libretto of his opera *Guntram*. Illness interrupted
his work, and he was in Egypt when he took it up
again. The music of the first act was written
between December, 1892, and February, 1893,
while travelling between Cairo and Luxor ; the
second act was finished in June, 1893, in Sicily; and
the third act early in September, 1893, in Bavaria.
There is, however, no trace of an oriental atmosphere in this music. We find rather the melodies of
Italy, the reflection of a mellow light, and a resigned
calm. I feel in it the languid mind of the convalescent, almost the heart of a young girl whose tears
are ready to flow, though she is smiling a little at
her own sad dreams. It seems to me that Strauss
must have a secret affection for this work, which

owes its inspiration to the undefinable impressions of convalescence. His fever fell asleep in it, and certain passages are full of the caressing touch of nature, and recall Berlioz's *Les Troyens*. But too often the music is superficial and conventional, and the tyranny of Wagner makes itself felt—a rare enough occurrence in Strauss's other works. The poem is interesting ; Strauss has put much of himself into it, and one is conscious of the crisis that unsettled his broad-minded but often self-satisfied and inconsistent ideas.

Strauss had been reading an historical study of an order of *Minnesänger* and mystics, which was founded in Austria in the Middle Ages to fight against the corruption of art, and to save souls by the beauty of song. They called themselves *Streiter der Liebe* ("Warriors of Love"). Strauss, who was imbued at that time with neo-Christian ideas and the influence of Wagner and Tolstoy, was carried away by the subject, and took Guntram from the *Streiter der Liebe*, and made him his hero.

The action takes place in the thirteenth century, in Germany. The first act gives us a glade near a little lake. The country people are in revolt against the nobles, and have just been repulsed. Guntram and his master Friedhold distribute alms among them, and the band of defeated men then take fligh' into the woods. Left alone, Guntram begins to muse on the delights of springtime and the innocent awakening of Nature. But the thought of the misery that its beauty hides weighs upon him. He thinks of men's evil doing, of human suffering, and of civil war. He gives thanks to Christ for having led him to this unhappy country, kisses the cross, and decides to go to the court of the tyrant who is the cause of all the trouble, and make known to him the Divine revelation. At that moment Freihild appears. She is the wife of Duke Robert, who is the cruellest of all the nobles, and she is horrified by all that is happening around her ; life seems hateful to her, and she wishes to drown herself. But Guntram prevents her ; and the pity that her beauty and trouble had at first aroused changes unconsciously into love when he recognises her as the beloved princess and sole benefactress of the unhappy people. He tells her that God has sent him to her for her salvation. Then he goes to the castle, where he believes himself to be sent on the double mission of saving the people—and Freihild.

In the second act, the princes celebrate their victory in the Duke's castle. After some pompous talk on the part of the official *Minnesänger*, Guntram is invited to sing. Discouraged beforehand by the wickedness of his audience, and feeling that he can sing to no purpose, he hesitates and is on the point of leaving them. But Freihild's sadness holds him back, and for her sake he sings. His song is at first calm and measured, and expresses the melancholy that fills him in the midst of a feast which celebrates triumphant power. He then loses himself in dreams, and sees the gentle figure of Peace moving among the company. He describes her lovingly and with youthful tenderness, which approaches ecstasy as he draws a picture of the

ideal life of humanity made free. Then he paints
War and Death, and the disorder and darkness that
they spread over the world. He addresses himself
directly to the Prince ; he shows him his duty, and
how the love of his people would be his recompense ;
he threatens him with the hate of the unhappy who
are driven to despair ; and, finally, he urges the
nobles to rebuild the towns, to liberate their prisoners,
and to come to the aid of their subjects. His song
is ended amid the profound emotion of his audience.
Duke Robert, feeling the danger of these outspoken
words, orders his men to seize the singer ; but the
vassals side with Guntram. At this juncture news
is brought that the peasants have renewed the
attack. Robert calls his men to arms, but Guntram,
who feels that he will be supported by those around
him, orders Robert's arrest. The Duke draws his
sword, but Guntram kills him. Then a sudden
change comes over Guntram's spirit, which is
explained in the third act. In the scene that follows
he speaks no word, his sword falls from his hand,
and he lets his enemies again assume their authority
over the crowd ; he allows himself to be bound and
taken to prison, while the band of nobles noisily
disperses to fight against the rebels. But Freihild
is full of an unaffected and almost savage joy at her
deliverance by Guntram's sword. Love for Guntram fills her heart, and her one desire is to save
him.

The third act takes place in the prison of the
château ; and it is a surprising, uncertain, and very
curious act. It is not a logical result of the action

that has preceded it. One feels a sudden commotion
in the poet's ideas, a crisis of feeling which disturbed
him even as he wrote, and a difficulty which he did
not succeed in solving. The new light towards
which he was beginning to move appears very
clearly. Strauss was too advanced in the composition of his work to escape the neo-Christian renouncement which had to finish the drama ; he could only
have avoided that by completely remodelling his
characters. So Guntram rejects Freihild's love.
He sees he has fallen, even as the others, under the
curse of sin. He had preached charity to others
when he himself was full of egoism ; he had killed
Robert rather to satisfy his instinctive and animal
jealousy than to deliver the people from a tyrant.
So he renounces his desires, and expiates the sin
of being alive by retirement from the world. But
the interest of the act does not lie in this anticipated
*dénouement*, which since *Parsifal* has become rather
common ; it lies in another scene, which has
evidently been inserted at the last moment, and
which is uncomfortably out of tune with the action,
though in a singularly grand way. This scene gives
us a dialogue between Guntram and his former
companion, Friedhold.[1] Friedhold had initiated him
in former days, and he now comes to reproach him
for his crime, and to bring him before the Order, who
will judge him. In the original version of the poem
Guntram complies, and sacrifices his passion to his
vow. But while Strauss had been travelling in the

[1] Some people have tried to see Alexander Ritter's thoughts
in Friedhold, as they have seen Strauss's thoughts in Guntram.

East he had conceived a sudden horror for this Christian annihilation of will, and Guntram revolts along with him, and refuses to submit to the rules of his Order. He breaks his lute—a symbol of false hope in the redemption of humanity through faith—and rouses himself from the glorious dreams in which he used to believe, for he sees they are shadows that are scattered by the light of real life. He does not abjure his former vows ; but he is not the same man he was when he made them. While his experience was immature he was able to believe that a man ought to submit himself to rules, and that life should be governed by laws. A single hour has enlightened him. Now he is free and alone— alone with his spirit. " I alone can lessen my suffering ; I alone can expiate my crime. Through myself alone God speaks to me ; to me alone God speaks. *Ewig einsam.*" It is the proud awakening of individualism, the powerful pessimism of the Super-man. Such an expression of feeling gives the character of action to renouncement and even to negation itself, for it is a strong affirmation of the will.

I have dwelt rather at length on this drama on account of the real value of its thought and, above all, on account of what one may call its autobiographical interest. It was at this time that Strauss's mind began to take more definite form. His further experience will develop that form still more, but without making any important change in it.

*Guntram* was the cause of bitter disappointment to its author. He did not succeed in getting it produced at Munich, for the orchestra and singers declared that the music could not be performed. It is even said that they got an eminent critic to draw up a formal document, which they sent to Strauss, certifying that *Guntram* was not meant to be sung. The chief difficulty was the length of the principal part, which took up by itself, in its musings and discourses, the equivalent of an act and a half. Some of its monologues, like the song in the second act, last half an hour on end. Nevertheless, *Guntram* was performed at Weimar on 16 May, 1894. A little while afterwards Strauss married the singer who played Freihild, Pauline de Ahna, who had also created Elizabeth in *Tannhäuser* at Bayreuth, and who has since devoted herself to the interpretation of her husband's *Lieder*.

.     .     .     .     .     .

But the rancour of his failure at the theatre still remained with Strauss, and he turned his attention again to the symphonic poem, in which he showed more and more marked dramatic tendencies, and a soul which grew daily prouder and more scornful. You should hear him speak in cold disdain of the theatre-going public—" that collection of bankers and tradespeople and miserable seekers after pleasure "—to know the sore that this triumphant artist hides. For not only was the theatre long closed to him, but, by an additional irony, he was obliged to conduct musical rubbish at the opera in Berlin, on account of the poor taste in music—really of Royal origin—that prevailed there.

The first great symphony of this new period was *Till Eulenspiegel's lustige Streiche, nach alter Schelmenweise, in Rondeauform* ("Till Eulenspiegel's Merry Pranks, according to an old legend, in rondeau form"), op. 28.[1] Here his disdain is as yet only expressed by witty bantering, which scoffs at the world's conventions. This figure of Till, this devil of a joker, the legendary hero of Germany and Flanders, is little known with us in France. And so Strauss's music loses much of its point, for it claims to recall a series of adventures which we know nothing about —Till crossing the market place and smacking his whip at the good women there; Till in priestly attire delivering a homely sermon; Till making love to a young woman who rebuffs him; Till making a fool of the pedants; Till tried and hung. Strauss's liking to present, by musical pictures, sometimes a character, sometimes a dialogue, or a situation, or a landscape, or an idea—that is to say, the most volatile and varied impressions of his capricious spirit—is very marked here. It is true that he falls back on several popular subjects, whose meaning would be very easily grasped in Germany; and that he develops them, not quite in the strict form of a rondeau, as he pretends, but still with a certain method, so that apart from a few frolics, which are unintelligible without a programme, the whole has real musical unity. This symphony, which is a great favourite in Germany, seems to me less original than some of his other compositions. It sounds rather

[1] Composed in 1894–95, and played for the first time at Cologne in 1895.

like a refined piece of Mendelssohn's, with curious harmonies and very complicated instrumentation.

There is much more grandeur and originality in his *Also sprach Zarathustra, Tondichtung frei, nach Nietzsche* ("Thus spake Zarathustra, a free Tone-poem, after Nietzsche"), op. 30.[1] Its sentiments are more broadly human, and the programme that Strauss has followed never loses itself in picturesque or anecdotic details, but is planned on expressive and noble lines. Strauss protests his own liberty in the face of Nietzsche's. He wishes to represent the different stages of development that a free spirit passes through in order to arrive at that of Super-man. These ideas are purely personal, and are not part of some system of philosophy. The sub-titles of the work are: *Von den Hinterweltern* ("Of Religious Ideas"), *Von der grossen Sehnsucht* ("Of Supreme Aspiration"), *Von den Freuden und Leidenschaften* ("Of Joys and Passions"), *Das Grablied* ("The Grave Song"), *Von der Wissenschaft* ("Of Knowledge"), *Der Genesende* ("The Convalescent"—the soul delivered of its desires), *Das Tanzlied* ("Dancing Song"), *Nachtlied* ("Night Song"). We are shown a man who, worn out by trying to solve the riddle of the universe, seeks refuge in religion. Then he revolts against ascetic ideas, and gives way madly to his passions. But he is quickly sated and disgusted and, weary to death, he tries science, but rejects it again, and succeeds in ridding himself of the uneasiness its knowledge

---

[1] Composed in 1895–96, and performed for the first time at Frankfort-on-Main in November, 1896.

brings by laughter—the master of the universe—
and the merry dance, that dance of the universe
where all the human sentiments enter hand-in-hand
—religious beliefs, unsatisfied desires, passions,
disgust, and joy. " Lift up your hearts on high,
my brothers ! Higher still ! And mind you don't
forget your legs ! I have canonised laughter. You
super-men, learn to laugh!" [1] And the dance dies
away and is lost in ethereal regions, and Zarathustra
is lost to sight while dancing in distant worlds. But
if he has solved the riddle of the universe for himself,
he has not solved it for other men ; and so, in contrast to the confident knowledge which fills the
music, we get the sad note of interrogation at the
end.

There are few subjects that offer richer material
for musical expression. Strauss has treated it with
power and dexterity ; he has preserved unity in
this chaos of passions, by contrasting the *Sehnsucht*
of man with the impassive strength of Nature. As
for the boldness of his conceptions, I need hardly
remind those who heard the poem at the Cirque
d'Été of the intricate " Fugue of Knowledge," the
trills of the wood wind and the trumpets that voice
Zarathustra's laugh, the dance of the universe, and
the audacity of the conclusion which, in the key of
B major, finishes up with a note of interrogation,
in C natural, repeated three times.

I am far from thinking that the symphony is
without a fault. The themes are of unequal value :
some are quite commonplace ; and, in a general way,

[1] Nietzsche.

the working up of the composition is superior to its underlying thought. I shall come back later on to certain faults in Strauss's music ; here I only want to consider the overflowing life and feverish joy that set these worlds spinning.

*Zarathustra* shows the progress of scornful individualism in Strauss—" the spirit that hates the dogs of the populace and all that abortive and gloomy breed; the spirit of wild laughter that dances like a tempest as gaily on marshes and sadness as it does in fields." [1] That spirit laughs at itself and at its idealism in the *Don Quixote* of 1897, *fantastische Variationen über ein Thema ritterlichen Charakters* (" Don Quixote, fantastic variations on a theme of knightly character "), op. 35 ; and that symphony marks, I think, the extreme point to which programme music may be carried. In no other work does Strauss give better proof of his prodigious cleverness, intelligence, and wit ; and I say sincerely that there is not a work where so much force is expended with so great a loss for the sake of a game and a musical joke which lasts forty-five minutes, and has given the author, the executants, and the public a good deal of tiring work. These symphonic poems are most difficult to play on account of the complexity, the independence, and the fantastic caprices of the different parts. Judge for yourself what the author expects to get out of the music by these few extracts from the programme :—

The introduction represents Don Quixote buried

[1] Nietzsche, *Zarathustra.*

in books of chivalrous romance ; and we have to see in the music, as we do in little Flemish and Dutch pictures, not only Don Quixote's features, but the words of the books he reads.  Sometimes it is the story of a knight who is fighting a giant, sometimes the adventures of a knight-errant who has dedicated himself to the services of a lady, sometimes it is a nobleman who has given his life in fulfilment of a vow to atone for his sins.  Don Quixote's mind becomes confused (and our own with it) over all these stories ; he is quite distracted. He leaves home in company with his squire.  The two figures are drawn with great spirit ; the one is an old Spaniard, stiff, languishing, distrustful, a bit of a poet, rather undecided in his opinions but obstinate when his mind is once made up ; the other is a fat, jovial peasant, a cunning fellow, given to repeating himself in a waggish way and quoting droll proverbs—translated in the music by short-winded phrases that always return to the point they started from.  The adventures begin.  Here are the windmills (trills from the violins and wood wind), and the bleating army of the grand emperor, Alifanfaron (tremolos from the wood wind) ; and here, in the third variation, is a dialogue between the knight and his squire, from which we are to guess that Sancho questions his master on the advantages of a chivalrous life, for they seem to him doubtful.  Don Quixote talks to him of glory and honour ; but Sancho has no thought for it.  In reply to these grand words he urges the superiority of sure profits, fat meals, and sounding money.

Then the adventures begin again. The two companions fly through the air on wooden horses ; and the illusion of this giddy voyage is given by chromatic passages on the flutes, harps, kettledrums, and a " windmachine," while " the tremolo of the double basses on the key-note shows that the horses have never left the earth." [1]

But I must stop. I have said enough to show the fun the author is indulging in. When one hears the work one cannot help admiring the composer's technical knowledge, skill in orchestration, and sense of humour. And one is all the more surprised that he confines himself to the illustration of texts [2] when he is so capable of creating comic and dramatic matter without it. Although *Don Quixote* is a marvel of skill and a very wonderful work, in which Strauss has developed a suppler and richer style, it marks, to my mind, a progress in his technique and a backward step in his mind, for he seems to have adopted the decadent conceptions of an art suited to playthings and trinkets to please a frivolous and affected society.

In *Heldenleben* ("The Life of a Hero"), op. 40, [3] he recovers himself, and with a stroke of his wings reaches the summits. Here there is no foreign text for the music to study or illustrate or transcribe. Instead, there is lofty passion and an heroic will

---

[1] Arthur Hahn, *Der Musikführer : Don Quixote*, Frankfort.

[2] At the head of each variation Strauss has marked on the score the chapter of " Don Quixote " that he is interpreting.

[3] Finished in December, 1898. Performed for the first time at Frankfort-on-Main on 3 March, 1899. Published by Leuckart, Leipzic.

gradually developing itself and breaking down all
obstacles.  Without doubt Strauss had a programme
in his mind, but he said to me himself: "You have
no need to read it.  It is enough to know that the
hero is there fighting against his enemies."  I do
not know how far that is true, or if parts of the
symphony would not be rather obscure to anyone
who followed it without the text ; but this speech
seems to prove that he has understood the dangers
of the literary symphony, and that he is striving
for pure music.

*Heldenleben* is divided into six chapters :  The
Hero, The Hero's Adversaries, The Hero's Companion, The Field of Battle, The Peaceful Labours
of the Hero, The Hero's Retirement from the World,
and the Achievement of His Ideal.  It is an extraordinary work, drunken with heroism, colossal, half
barbaric, trivial, and sublime.  An Homeric hero
struggles among the sneers of a stupid crowd, a herd
of brawling and hobbling ninnies.  A violin solo, in
a sort of concerto, describes the seductions, the
coquetry, and the degraded wickedness of woman.
Then strident trumpet-blasts sound the attack ;
and it is beyond me to give an idea of the terrible
charge of cavalry that follows, which makes the
earth tremble and our hearts leap ; nor can I
describe how an iron determination leads to the
storming of towns, and all the tumultuous din and
uproar of battle—the most splendid battle that has
ever been painted in music.  At its first performance
in Germany I saw people tremble as they listened
to it, and some rose up suddenly and made violent

gestures quite unconsciously. I myself had a strange feeling of giddiness, as if an ocean had been upheaved, and I thought that for the first time for thirty years Germany had found a poet of Victory.

*Heldenleben* would be in every way one of the masterpieces of musical composition if a literary error had not suddenly cut short the soaring flight of its most impassioned pages, at the supreme point of interest in the movement, in order to follow the programme ; though, besides this, a certain coldness, perhaps weariness, creeps in towards the end. The victorious hero perceives that he has conquered in vain : the baseness and stupidity of men have remained unaltered. He stifles his anger, and scornfully accepts the situation. Then he seeks refuge in the peace of Nature. The creative force within him flows out in imaginative works ; and here Richard Strauss, with a daring warranted only by his genius, represents these works by reminiscences of his own compositions, and *Don Juan, Macbeth, Tod und Verklärung, Till, Zarathustra, Don Quixote, Guntram,* and even his *Lieder,* associate themselves with the hero whose story he is telling. At times a storm will remind this hero of his combats ; but he also remembers his moments of love and happiness, and his soul is quieted. Then the music unfolds itself serenely, and rises with calm strength to the closing chord of triumph, which is placed like a crown of glory on the hero's head.

There is no doubt that Beethoven's ideas have often inspired, stimulated, and guided Strauss's own ideas. One feels an indescribable reflection of

the first *Heroic* and of the *Ode to Joy* in the key of
the first part (E flat) ; and the last part recalls, even
more forcibly, certain of Beethoven's *Lieder*. But
the heroes of the two composers are very different :
Beethoven's hero is more classical and more rebel-
lious ; and Strauss's hero is more concerned with
the exterior world and his enemies, his conquests
are achieved with greater difficulty, and his triumph
is wilder in consequence. If that good Oulibicheff
pretends to see the burning of Moscow in a dis-
cord in the first *Heroic*, what would he find here ?
What scenes of burning towns, what battlefields !
Besides that there is cutting scorn and a mis-
chievous laughter in *Heldenleben* that is never
heard in Beethoven. There is, in fact, little
kindness in Strauss's work ; it is the work of a
disdainful hero.

.    .    .    .    .    .

In considering Strauss's music as a whole, one is
at first struck by the diversity of his style. The
North and the South mingle ; and in his melodies
one feels the attraction of the sun. Something
Italian had crept into *Tristan ;* but how much
more of Italy there is in the work of this disciple of
Nietzsche. The phrases are often Italian and their
harmonies ultra-Germanic. Perhaps one of the
greatest charms of Strauss's art is that we are able
to watch the rent in the dark clouds of German
polyphony, and see shining through it the smiling
line of an Italian coast and the gay dancers on its
shore. This is not merely a vague analogy. It

M

would be easy, if idle, to notice unmistakable reminiscences of France and Italy even in Strauss's most advanced works, such as *Zarathustra* and *Heldenleben*. Mendelssohn, Gounod, Wagner, Rossini, and Mascagni elbow one another strangely. But these disparate elements have a softer outline when the work is taken as a whole, for they have been absorbed and controlled by the composer's imagination.

His orchestra is not less composite. It is not a compact and serried mass like Wagner's Macedonian phalanxes; it is parcelled out and as divided as possible. Each part aims at independence and works as it thinks best, without apparently troubling about the other parts. Sometimes it seems, as it did when reading Berlioz, that the execution must result in incoherence, and weaken the effect. But somehow the result is very satisfying. " Now doesn't that sound well ? " said Strauss to me with a smile, just after he had finished conducting *Heldenleben*.[1]

But it is especially in Strauss's subjects that caprice and a disordered imagination, the enemy of all reason, seem to reign. We have seen that these

---

[1] The composition of the orchestra in Strauss's later works is as follows : In *Zarathustra :* one piccolo, three flutes, three oboes, one English horn, one clarinet in E flat, two clarinets in B, one bass-clarinet in B, three bassoons, one double-bassoon, six horns in F, four trumpets in C, three trombones, three bass-tuba, kettledrums, big drum, cymbals, triangle, chime of bells, bell in E, organ, two harps, and strings. In *Heldenleben :* eight horns instead of six, five trumpets instead of four (two in E flat, three in B) ; and, in addition, military drums.

poems try to express in turn, or even simultaneously, literary texts, pictures, anecdotes, philosophical ideas, and the personal sentiments of the composer. What unity is there in the adventures of Don Quixote or Till Eulenspiegel ? And yet unity is there, not in the subjects, but in the mind that deals with them. And these descriptive symphonies with their very diffuse literary life are vindicated by their musical life, which is much more logical and concentrated. The caprices of the poet are held in rein by the musician. The whimsical Till disports himself " after the old form of rondeau," and the folly of Don Quixote is told in " ten variations on a chivalrous theme, with an introduction and finale." In this way, Strauss's art, one of the most literary and descriptive in existence, is strongly distinguished from others of the same kind by the solidarity of its musical fabric, in which one feels the true musician—a musician brought up on the great masters, and a classic in spite of everything.

And so throughout that music a strong unity is felt among the unruly and often incongruous elements. It is the reflection, so it seems to me, of the soul of the composer. Its unity is not a matter of what he feels, but a matter of what he wishes. His emotion is much less interesting to him than his will, and it is less intense, and often quite devoid of any personal character. His restlessness seems to come from Schumann, his religious feeling from Mendelssohn, his voluptuousness from Gounod or the Italian masters, his passion from

Wagner.[1] But his will is heroic, dominating, eager, and powerful to a sublime degree. And that is why Richard Strauss is noble and, at present, quite unique. One feels in him a force that has dominion over men.

. . . . . .

It is through this heroic side that he may be considered as an inheritor of some of Beethoven's and Wagner's thought. It is this heroic side which makes him a poet—one of the greatest perhaps in modern Germany, who sees herself reflected in him and in his hero. Let us consider this hero.

He is an idealist with unbounded faith in the power of the mind and the liberating virtue of art. This idealism is at first religious, as in *Tod und Verklärung*, and tender and compassionate as a woman, and full of youthful illusions, as in *Guntram*. Then it becomes vexed and indignant with the baseness of the world and the difficulties it encounters. Its scorn increases, and becomes sarcastic (*Till Eulenspiegel*); it is exasperated with years of conflict, and, in increasing bitterness, develops into a contemptuous heroism. How Strauss's laugh whips and stings us in *Zarathustra*! How his will bruises and cuts us in *Heldenleben*! Now that he has proved his power by victory, his pride knows no limit; he is elated and is unable to see that his lofty visions have become realities. But the people

---

[1] In *Guntram* one could even believe that he had made up his mind to use a phrase in *Tristan*, as if he could not find anything better to express passionate desire.

whose spirit he reflects see it. There are germs of
morbidity in Germany to-day, a frenzy of pride, a
belief in self, and a scorn for others that recalls
France in the seventeenth century. *"Dem Deutschen
gehört die Welt"* ("Germany possesses the world")
calmly say the prints displayed in the shop windows
in Berlin. But when one arrives at this point the
mind becomes delirious. All genius is raving mad
if it comes to that ; but Beethoven's madness concentrated itself in himself, and imagined things for
his own enjoyment. The genius of many contemporary German artists is an aggressive thing, and is
characterised by its destructive antagonism. The
idealist who "possesses the world" is liable to
dizziness. He was made to rule over an interior
world. The splendour of the exterior images that
he is called upon to govern dazzles him ; and, like
Cæsar, he goes astray. Germany had hardly attained
the position of empire of the world when she found
Nietzsche's voice and that of the deluded artists of
the *Deutsches Theater* and the *Secession.* Now there
is the grandiose music of Richard Strauss.

. What is all this fury leading to ? What does this
heroism aspire to ? This force of will, bitter and
strained, grows faint when it has reached its goal,
or even before that. It does not know what to do
with its victory. It disdains it, does not believe in
it, or grows tired of it.[1]

Like Michelangelo's *Victory*, it has set its knee on

---

[1] "The German spirit, which but a little while back had the
will to dominate Europe, the force to govern Europe, has finally
made up its mind to abandon it."—Nietzsche.

the captive's back, and seems ready to despatch him. But suddenly it stops, hesitates, and looks about with uncertain eyes, and its expression is one of languid disgust, as though weariness had seized it.

And this is how the work of Richard Strauss appears to me up to the present. Guntram kills Duke Robert, and immediately lets fall his sword. The frenzied laugh of Zarathustra ends in an avowal of discouraged impotence. The delirious passion of Don Juan dies away in nothingness. Don Quixote when dying forswears his illusions. Even the Hero himself admits the futility of his work, and seeks oblivion in an indifferent Nature. Nietzsche, speaking of the artists of our time, laughs at " those Tantaluses of the will, rebels and enemies of laws, who come, broken in spirit, and fall at the foot of the cross of Christ." Whether it is for the sake of the Cross or Nothingness, these heroes renounce their victories in disgust and despair, or with a resignation that is sadder still. It was not thus that Beethoven overcame his sorrows. Sad adagios make their lament in the middle of his symphonies, but a note of joy and triumph is always sounded at the end. His work is the triumph of a conquered hero ; that of Strauss is the defeat of a conquering hero. This irresoluteness of the will can be still more clearly seen in contemporary German literature, and in particular in the author of *Die versunkene Glocke*. But it is more striking in Strauss, because he is more heroic. And so we get all this display of superhuman will, and the end is only " My desire is gone ! "

In this lies the undying worm of German thought

—I am speaking of the thought of the choice few who enlighten the present and anticipate the future. I see an heroic people, intoxicated by its triumphs, by its great riches, by its numbers, by its force, which clasps the world in its great arms and subjugates it, and then stops, fatigued by its conquest, and asks: " Why have I conquered ? "

# HUGO WOLF

THE more one learns of the history of great artists, the more one is struck by the immense amount of sadness their lives enclose. Not only are they subjected to the trials and disappointments of ordinary life—which affect them more cruelly through their greater sensitiveness—but their surroundings are like a desert, because they are twenty, thirty, fifty, or even hundreds of years in advance of their contemporaries; and they are often condemned to despairing efforts, not to conquer the world, but to live.

These highly-strung natures are rarely able to keep up this incessant struggle for very long; and the finest genius may have to reckon with illness and misery and even premature death. And yet there were people like Mozart and Schumann and Weber who were happy in spite of everything, because they had been able to keep their soul's health and the joy of creation until the end; and though their bodies were worn out with fatigue and privation, a light was kept burning which sent its rays far into the darkness of their night. There are worse destinies; and Beethoven, though he was poor, shut up within himself, and deceived in his affections, was far from being the most unhappy of men. In his case, he posse ed nothing but himself;

but he possessed himself truly, and reigned over the world that was within him ; and no other empire could ever be compared with that of his vast imagination, which stretched like a great expanse of sky, where tempests raged. Until his last day the old Prometheus in him, though fettered by a miserable body, preserved his iron force unbroken. When dying during a storm, his last gesture was one of revolt ; and in his agony he raised himself on his bed and shook his fist at the sky. And so he fell, struck down by a single blow in the thick of the fight.

But what shall be said of those who die little by little, who outlive themselves, and watch the slow decay of their souls ?

Such was the fate of Hugo Wolf, whose tragic destiny has assured him a place apart in the hell of great musicians.[1]

. . . . . .

He was born at Windischgratz in Styria, 13 March, 1860. He was the fourth son of a currier—a currier-musician, like old Veit Bach, the baker-musician, and Haydn's father, the wheelwright-musician. Philipp Wolf played the violin, the guitar, and the piano, and used to have little quintet parties at his

---

[1] A large number of works on Hugo Wolf have been published in Germany since his death. The chief is the great biography of Herr Ernst Decsey—*Hugo Wolf* (Berlin, 1903-4). I have found this book of great service ; it is a work full of knowledge and sympathy. I have also consulted Herr Paul Müller's excellent little pamphlet, *Hugo Wolf* (*Moderne essays*, Berlin, 1904), and the collections of Wolf's letters, in particular his letters to Oskar Grohe, Emil Kaufmann, and Hugo Faisst.

house, in which he played the first violin, Hugo
the second violin, Hugo's brother the violoncello,
an uncle the horn, and a friend the tenor violin.
The musical taste of the country was not properly
German. Wolf was a Catholic ; and his taste was
not formed, like that of most German musicians,
by books of chorales. Besides that, in Styria they
were fond of playing the old Italian operas of
Rossini, Bellini, and Donizetti. Later on, Wolf used
to like to think that he had a few drops of Latin
blood in his veins ; and all his life he had a predilection for the great French musicians.

His term of apprenticeship was not marked by
anything brilliant. He went from one school to
another without being kept long anywhere. And
yet he was not a worthless lad ; but he was always
very reserved, little caring to be intimate with
others, and passionately devoted to music. His
father naturally did not want him to take up music
as a profession ; and he had the same struggles that
Berlioz had. Finally he succeeded in getting per-
mission from his family to go to Vienna, and he
entered the Conservatoire there in 1875. But he
was not any the happier for it, and at the end of two
years he was sent away for being unruly.

What was to be done ? His family was ruined,
for a fire had demolished their little possessions. He
felt the silent reproaches of his father already
weighing upon him—for he loved his father dearly,
and remembered the sacrifices he had made for
him. He did not wish to return to his own province ;
indeed he could not return—that would have been

death. It was necessary that this boy of seventeen should find some means of earning a livelihood and be able to instruct himself at the same time. After his expulsion from the Conservatoire he attended no other school ; he taught himself. And he taught himself wonderfully ; but at what a cost ! The suffering he went through from that time until he was thirty, the enormous amount of energy he had to expend in order to live and cultivate the fine spirit of poetry that was within him—all this effort and toil was, without doubt, the cause of his unhappy death. He had a burning thirst for knowledge and a fever for work which made him sometimes forget the necessity for eating and drinking.

He had a great admiration for Goethe, and was infatuated by Heinrich von Kleist, whom he rather resembles both in his gifts and in his life ; he was an enthusiast about Grillparzer and Hebbel at a time when they were but little appreciated ; and he was one of the first Germans to discover the worth of Mörike, whom, later on, he made popular in Germany. Besides this, he read English and French writers. He liked Rabelais, and was very partial to Claude Tillier, the French novelist of the provinces, whose *Oncle Benjamin* has given pleasure to so many German provincial families, by bringing before them, as Wolf said, the vision of their own little world, and helping them by his own jovial good humour to bear their troubles with a smiling face. And so little Wolf, with hardly enough to eat, found the means of learning both French and English, in order better to appreciate the thoughts of foreign artists.

In music he learned a great deal from his friend Schalk,[1] a professor at the Vienna Conservatoire ; but, like Berlioz, he got most of his education from the libraries, and spent months in reading the scores of the great masters. Not having a piano, he used to carry Beethoven's sonatas to the Prater Park in Vienna and study them on a bench in the open air. He soaked himself in the classics—in Bach and Beethoven, and the German masters of the *Lied*—Schubert and Schumann. He was one of the young Germans who was passionately fond of Berlioz ; and it is due to Wolf that France was afterwards honoured in the possession of this great artist, whom French critics, whether of the school of Meyerbeer, Wagner, Franck, or Debussy, have never understood. He was also early a friend of old Anton Bruckner, whose music we do not know in France, neither his eight symphonies, nor his *Te Deum*, nor his masses, nor his cantatas, nor anything else of his fertile work. Bruckner had a sweet and modest character, and an endearing, if rather childish, personality. He was rather crushed all his life by the Brahms party ; but, like Franck in France, he gathered round him new and original talent to fight the academic art of his time.

But of all these influences, the strongest was that of Wagner. Wagner came to Vienna in 1875 to

---

[1] Joseph Schalk was one of the founders of the *Wagner-Verein* at Vienna, and devoted his life to propagating the cult of Bruckner (who called him his " *Herr Generalissimus* "), and to fighting for Wolf.

conduct *Tannhäuser* and *Lohengrin*. There was then among the younger people a fever of enthusiasm similar to that which *Werther* had caused a century before. Wolf saw Wagner. He tells us about it in his letters to his parents. I will quote his own words, and though they make one smile, one loves the impulsive devotion of his youth; and they make one feel, too, that a man who inspires such an affection, and who can do so much good by a little sympathy, is to blame when he does not befriend others—above all if he has suffered, like Wagner, from loneliness and the want of a helping hand. You must remember that this letter was written by a boy of fifteen.

"I have been to—guess whom? . . . to the master, Richard Wagner! Now I will tell you all about it, just as it happened. I will copy the words down exactly as I wrote them in my note-book.

"On Thursday, 9 December, at half-past ten, I saw Richard Wagner for the second time at the Hotel Imperial, where I stayed for half an hour on the staircase, awaiting his arrival (I knew that on that day he would conduct the last rehearsal of his *Lohengrin*). At last the master came down from the second floor, and I bowed to him very respectfully while he was yet some distance from me. He thanked me in a very friendly way. As he neared the door I sprang forward and opened it for him, upon which he looked fixedly at me for a few seconds, and then went on his way to

the rehearsal at the Opera. I ran as fast as I
could, and arrived at the Opera sooner than
Richard Wagner did in his cab. I bowed to him
again, and I wanted to open the door of his cab
for him ; but as I could not get it open, the coachman jumped down from his seat and did it for
me. Wagner said something to the coachman—
I think it was about me. I wanted to follow him
into the theatre, but they would not let me pass.

"I often used to wait for him at the Hotel
Imperial ; and on this occasion I made the
acquaintance of the manager of the hotel, who
promised that he would interest himself on my
behalf. Who was more delighted than I when he
told me that on the following Saturday afternoon,
11 December, I was to come and find him, so that
he could introduce me to Mme. Cosima's maid
and Richard Wagner's valet ! I arrived at the
appointed hour. The visit to the lady's maid was
very short. I was advised to come the following
day, Sunday, 12 December, at two o'clock. I
arrived at the right hour, but found the maid and
the valet and the manager still at table. . . .
Then I went with the maid to the master's rooms,
where I waited for about a quarter of an hour
until he came. At last Wagner appeared in company with Cosima and Goldmark. I bowed to
Cosima very respectfully, but she evidently did
not think it worth while to honour me with a
single glance. Wagner was going into his room
without paying any attention to me, when the
maid said to him in a beseeching voice : ' Ah,

Herr Wagner, it is a young musician who wishes to speak to you ; he has been waiting for you a long time.'

" He then came out of his room, looked at me, and said : ' I have seen you before, I think. You are . . .'

" Probably he wanted to say, ' You are a fool.'

" He went in front of me and opened the door of the reception-room, which was furnished in a truly royal style. In the middle of the room was a couch covered in velvet and silk. Wagner himself was wrapped in a long velvet mantle bordered with fur.

" When I was inside the room he asked me what I wanted."

Here Hugo Wolf, to excite the curiosity of his parents, broke off his story and put " To be continued in my next." In his next letter he continues :

"I said to him: ' Highly honoured master, for a long time I have wanted to hear an opinion on my compositions, and it would be . . .'

" Here the master interrupted me and said : ' My dear child, I cannot give you an opinion of your compositions ; I have far too little time ; I can't even get my own letters written. I understand nothing at all about music (*Ich verstehe gar nichts von der Musik*).'

" I asked the master whether I should ever be able really to do anything, and he said to me : ' When I was your age and composing music, no one could tell me then whether I should ever do anything great. You could at most play me your compositions on the piano ; but I have no time to hear them. When you are older, and when you have composed bigger works, and if by chance I return to Vienna, you shall show me what you have done. But that is no use now ; I cannot give you an opinion of them yet.'

" When I told the master that I took the classics as models, he said : ' Good, good. One can't be original at first.' And he laughed, and then said, ' I wish you, dear friend, much happiness in your career. Go on working steadily, and if I come back to Vienna, show me your compositions.'

" Upon that I left the master, profoundly moved and impressed."

Wolf and Wagner did not see each other again. But Wolf fought unceasingly on Wagner's behalf. He went several times to Bayreuth, though he had no personal intercourse with the Wagner family; but he met Liszt, who, with his usual goodness, wrote him a kind letter about a composition that he had sent him, and showed him what alterations to make in it.

Mottl and the composer, Adalbert de Goldschmidt, were the first friends to aid him in his years of misery, by finding him some music pupils. He taught music to little children of seven and eight years old ; but he was a poor teacher, and found giving lessons was a martyrdom. The money he earned hardly served to feed him, and he only ate once a day—Heaven knows how. To comfort himself he read Hebbel's Life ; and for a time he thought of going to America. In 1881 Goldschmidt got him the post of second *Kapellmeister* at the Salzburg theatre. It was his business to rehearse the choruses for the operettas of Strauss and Millöcker. He did his work conscientiously, but in deadly weariness ; and he lacked the necessary power of making his authority felt. He did not stay long in this post, and came back to Vienna.

Since 1875 he had been writing music : *Lieder*, sonatas, symphonies, quartets, etc., and already his *Lieder* held the most important place. He also composed in 1883 a symphonic poem on the *Penthesilea* of his friend Kleist.

In 1884 he succeeded in getting a post as musical critic. But on what a paper ! It was the *Salonblatt*—a mundane journal filled with articles on sport and fashion news. One would have said that this little barbarian was put there for a wager. His articles from 1884 to 1887 are full of life and humour. He upholds the great classic masters in them : Gluck, Mozart, Beethoven, and—Wagner ; he defends Berlioz ; he scourges the modern Italians, whose success at Vienna was simply scandalous ; he breaks lances for Bruckner, and begins a bold campaign against Brahms. It was not that he disliked or had any prejudice against Brahms ; he took a delight in some of his works, especially his chamber music, but he found fault with his symphonies and was shocked by the carelessness of the declamation in his *Lieder* and, in general, could not bear his want

N

of originality and power, and found him lacking in joy and fulness of life. Above all, he struck at him as being the head of a party that was spitefully opposed to Wagner and Bruckner and all innovators. For all that was retrograde in music in Vienna, and all that was the enemy of liberty and progress in art and criticism, was giving Brahms its detestable support by gathering itself about him and spreading his fame abroad ; and though Brahms was really far above his party as an artist and a man, he had not the courage to break away from it.

Brahms read Wolf's articles, but his attacks did not seem to stir his apathy. The " Brahmines," however, never forgave Wolf. One of his bitterest enemies was Hans von Bülow, who found anti-Brahmism " the blasphemy against the Holy Ghost —which shall not be forgiven." [1] Some years later, when Wolf succeeded in getting his own compositions played, he had to submit to criticisms like that of Max Kalbeck, one of the leaders of " Brahmism " at Vienna :

> " Herr Wolf has lately, as a reporter, raised an irresistible laugh in musical circles. So someone suggested he had better devote himself to composition. The last products of his muse show that this well-meant advice was bad. He ought to go back to reporting."

An orchestral society in Vienna gave Wolf's *Penthesilea* a trial reading ; and it was rehearsed,

[1] Letter of H. von Bülow to Detlev von Liliencron.

in disregard of all good taste, amid shouts of laughter. When it was finished, the conductor said: " Gentlemen, I ask your pardon for having allowed this piece to be played to the end ; but I wanted to know what manner of man it is that dares to write such things about the master, Brahms."

W.olf got a little respite from his miseries by going to stay a few weeks in his own country with his brother-in-law, Strasser, an inspector of taxes.[1] He took with him his books, his poets, and began to set them to music.

. . . . . .

He was now twenty-seven years old, and had as yet published nothing. The years of 1887 and 1888 were the most critical ones of his life. In 1887 he lost his father whom he loved so much, and that loss, like so many of his other misfortunes, gave fresh impulse to his energies. The same year, a generous friend called Eckstein published his first collection of *Lieder*. Wolf up to that time had been smothered, but this publication stirred the life in him, and was the means of unloosing his genius. Settled at Perchtoldsdorf, near Vienna, in February, 1888, in absolute peace, he wrote in three months fifty-three *Lieder* to the words of Eduard Mörike, the pastor-poet of Swabia, who died in 1875, and who, misunderstood and laughed at during his lifetime, is now covered with honour, and univer-

---

[1] Wolf's letters to Strasser are of great value in giving us an insight into his artist's eager and unhappy soul.

sally popular in Germany. Wolf composed his songs
in a state of exalted joy and almost fright at the
sudden discovery of his creative power.

In a letter to Dr. Heinrich Werner, he says :

" It is now seven o'clock in the evening, and I
am so happy—oh, happier than the happiest of
kings. Another new *Lied !* If you could hear
what is going on in my heart ! . . . the devil
would carry you away with pleasure ! . . .

" Another two new *Lieder !* There is one that
sounds so horribly strange that it frightens me.
There is nothing like it in existence. Heaven
help the unfortunate people who will one day
hear it ! . . .

" If you could only hear the last *Lied* I have
just composed you would only have one desire
left—to die. . . . Your happy, happy Wolf."

He had hardly finished the *Mörike-Lieder* when
he began a series of *Lieder* on poems of Goethe. In
three months (December, 1888, to February, 1889)
he had written all the *Goethe-Liederbuch*—fifty-one
*Lieder*, some of which are, like *Prometheus*, big
dramatic scenes.

The same year, while still at Perchtoldsdorf, after
having published a volume of Eichendorff *Lieder*,
he became absorbed in a new cycle—the *Spanisches-
Liederbuch*, on Spanish poems translated by Heyse.
He wrote these forty-four songs in the same ecstasy
of gladness :

" What I write now, I write for the future. . . .

Since Schubert and Schumann there has been nothing like it ! ''

In 1890, two months after he had finished the *Spanisches-Liederbuch*, he composed another cycle of *Lieder* on poems called *Alten Weisen*, by the great Swiss writer Gottfried Keller. And lastly, in the same year, he began his *Italienisches-Liederbuch*, on Italian poems, translated by Geibel and Heyse.

And then—then there was silence.

.    .    .    .    .    .

The history of Wolf is one of the most extraordinary in the history of art, and gives one a better glimpse of the mysteries of genius than most histories do.

Let us make a little *résumé*. Wolf at twenty-eight years old had written practically nothing. From 1888 to 1890 he wrote, one after another, in a kind of fever, fifty-three Mörike *Lieder*, fifty-one Goethe *Lieder*, forty-four Spanish *Lieder*, seventeen Eichendorff *Lieder*, a dozen Keller *Lieder*, and the first Italian *Lieder*—that is about two hundred *Lieder*, each one having its own admirable individuality.

And then the music stops. The spring has dried up. Wolf in great anguish wrote despairing letters to his friends. To Oskar Grohe, on 2 May, 1891, he wrote :

"I have given up all idea of composing. Heaven knows how things will finish. Pray for my poor soul."

And to Wette, on 13 August, 1891, he says :

" For the last four months I have been suffering from a sort of mental consumption, which
makes me very seriously think of quitting this
world for ever. . . . Only those who truly live
should live at all.  I have been for some time like
one who is dead.  I only wish it were an apparent
death; but I am really dead and buried; though
the power to control my body gives me a seeming
life.  It is my inmost, my only desire, that the
flesh may quickly follow the spirit that has already
passed.  For the last fifteen days I have been
living at Traunkirchen, the pearl of Traunsee. . . .
All the comforts that a man could wish for are
here to make my life happy—peace, solitude,
beautiful scenery, invigorating air, and everything that could suit the tastes of a hermit like
myself.[1]  And yet—and yet, my friend, I am the
most miserable creature on earth.  Everything
around me breathes peace and happiness, everything throbs with life and fulfils its functions. . . .
I alone, oh God ! . . . I alone live like a beast
that is deaf and senseless.  Even reading hardly
serves to distract me now, though I bury myself
in books in my despair.  As for composition,
that is finished ; I can no longer bring to mind
the meaning of a harmony or a melody, and I
almost begin to doubt if the compositions that
bear my name are really mine.  Good God ! what

---

[1] Wolf was living there with a friend.  He had not a lodging
of his own until 1896, and that was due to the generosity of his
friends.

is the use of all this fame? What is the good of these great aims if misery is all that lies at the end of it? . . .

"*Heaven gives a man complete genius or no genius at all. Hell has given me everything by halves.*

"O unhappy man, how true, how true it is! In the flower of your life you went to hell; into the evil jaws of destiny you threw the delusive present and yourself with it. O Kleist!"

Suddenly, at Döbling, on 29 November, 1891, the stream of Wolf's genius flowed again, and he wrote fifteen Italian *Lieder*, sometimes several in one day. In December it stopped again; and this time for five years. These Italian melodies show, however, no trace of any effort, nor a greater tension of mind than is shown in his preceding works. On the contrary, they have the air of being the simplest and most natural work that Wolf ever did. But the matter is of no real consequence, for when Wolf's genius was not stirring within him he was useless. He wished to write thirty-three Italian *Lieder*, but he had to stop after the twenty-second, and in 1891 he published one volume only of the *Italienisches-Liederbuch.* The second volume was completed in a month, five years later, in 1896.

One may imagine the tortures that this solitary man suffered. His only happiness was in creation, and he saw his life cease, without any apparent cause, for years together, and his genius come and go, and return for an instant, and then go again.

Each time he must have anxiously wondered if it had gone for ever, or how long it would be before it came back again. In letters to Kaufmann on 6 August, 1891, and 26 April, 1893, he says :

"You ask me for news of my opera.[1] Good Heavens ! I should be content if I could write the tiniest little *Liedchen*. And an opera, now ? . . . I firmly believe that it is all over with me. . . . I could as well speak Chinese as compose anything. It is horrible. . . What I suffer from this inaction I cannot tell you. I should like to hang myself."

To Hugo Faisst he wrote on 21 June, 1894 :

"You ask me the cause of my great depression of spirit, and would pour balm on my wounds. Ah yes, if you only could ! But no herb grows that could cure my sickness ; only a god could help me. If you can give me back my inspirations, and wake up the familiar spirit that is asleep in me, and let him possess me anew, I will call you a god and raise altars to your name. My cry is to gods and not to men ; the gods alone are fit to pronounce my fate. But however it may end, even if the worst comes, I will bear it—yes, even if no ray of sunshine lightens my life again. . . . And with that we will, once for all, turn the page and have done with this dark chapter of my life."

---

[1] The writing of an opera was Wolf's great dream and intention for many years.

This letter—and it is not the only one—recalls
the melancholy stoicism of Beethoven's letters, and
shows us sorrows that even the unhappy Beethoven
did not know.  And yet how can we tell ?  Perhaps
Beethoven, too, suffered similar anguish in the sad
days that followed 1815, before the last sonatas, the
*Missa Solemnis*, and the Ninth Symphony had
awaked to life in him.

.     .     .     .     .     .

In March, 1895, Wolf lived once more, and in three
months had written the piano score of *Corregidor*.
For many years he had been attracted towards the
stage, and especially towards light opera.  Enthusiast though he was for Wagner's work, he had
declared openly that it was time for musicians to
free themselves from the Wagnerian *Musik-Drama*.
He knew his own gifts, and did not aspire to take
Wagner's place.  When one of his friends offered
him a subject for an opera, taken from a legend
about Buddha, he declined it, saying that the world
did not yet understand the meaning of Buddha's
doctrines, and that he had no wish to give humanity
a fresh headache.  In a letter to Grohe, on 28 June,
1890, he says :

" Wagner has, by and through his art, accomplished such a mighty work of liberation that we
may rejoice to think that it is quite useless for
us to storm the skies, since he has conquered them
for us.  It is much wiser to seek out a pleasant
nook in this lovely heaven.  I want to find a little

place there for myself, not in a desert with water
and locusts and wild honey, but in a merry company of primitive beings, among the tinkling of
guitars, the sighs of love, the moonlight, and
such-like—in short, in a quite ordinary *opéra-
comique*, without any rescuing spectre of Schopen-
hauerian philosophy in the background."

After having sought the libretto of an opera from
the whole world, from poets ancient and modern,
from Shakespeare, from his friend Liliencron,[1] and
after having tried to write one himself, he finally took
that of Madame Rosa Mayreder, an adaptation of
a Spanish novelette of Don Pedro de Alarcón. This
was *Corregidor*, which, after having been refused by
other theatres, was played in June, 1896, at Mannheim. The work was not a success in spite of its
musical qualities, and the poorness of the libretto
helped on its failure.

But the main thing was that Wolf's creative
genius had returned. In April, 1896, he wrote straight
away the twenty-two songs of the second volume
of the *Italienisches-Liederbuch*. At Christmas his
friend Müller sent him some of Michelangelo's poems,
translated into German by Walter Robert-Tornow ;
and Wolf, deeply moved by their beauty, decided at
once to devote a whole volume of *Lieder* to them.
In 1897 he composed the first three melodies. At
the same time he was also working at a new opera,

[1] Detlev von Liliencron offered him an American subject.
" But in spite of my admiration for Buffalo Bill and his un-
washed crew," said Wolf sarcastically, " I prefer my native soil
and people who appreciate the advantages of soap."

*Manuel Venegas*, a poem by Moritz Hoernes, written after the style of Alarcón. He seemed full of strength and happiness and confidence in his renewed health. Müller was speaking to him of the premature death of Schubert, and Wolf replied, " A man is not taken away before he has said all he has to say."

He worked furiously, " like a steam-engine," as he said, and was so absorbed in the composition of *Manuel Venegas* (September, 1897) that he went without rest, and had hardly time to take necessary food. In a fortnight he had written fifty pages of the pianoforte score, as well as the *motifs* for the whole work, and the music of half the first act.

Then madness came. On 20 September he was seized while he was working at the great recitative of Manuel Venegas in the first act.

He was taken to Dr. Svetlin's private hospital in Vienna, and remained there until January, 1898. Happily he had devoted friends who took care of him and made up for the indifference of the public ; for what he had earned himself would not have enabled him even to die in peace. When Schott, the publisher, sent him in October, 1895, his royalties for the editions of his *Lieder* of Mörike, Goethe, Eichendorff, Keller, Spanish poetry, and the first volume of Italian poetry, their total for five years came to eighty-six marks and thirty-five pfennigs ! And Schott calmly added that he had not expected so good a result. So it was Wolf's friends, and especially Hugo Faisst, who not only saved him from misery by their unobtrusive and often secret

generosity, but spared him the horror of destitution
in his last misfortunes.

He recovered his reason, and was sent in February, 1898, for a voyage to Trieste and Venetia
to complete his cure and prevent him from thinking of work. The precaution was unnecessary; for
he says in a letter to Hugo Faisst, written in the
same month :

"There is no need for you to trouble yourself
or fear that I shall overdo things. A real distaste
for work has taken possession of me, and I believe
I shall never write another note. My unfinished
opera has no more interest for me, and music
altogether is hateful. You see what my kind
friends have done for me ! I cannot think how
I shall be able to exist in this state. . . . Ah,
happy Swabians ! one may well envy you. Greet
your beautiful country for me, and be warmly
greeted yourself by your unhappy and worn-out
friend, Hugo Wolf."

When he returned to Vienna, however, he seemed
to be a little better, and had apparently regained
his health and cheerfulness. But to his own astonish-
ment he had become, as he says in a letter to Faisst,
a quiet, sedate, and silent man, who wished more
and more to be alone. He did not compose anything fresh, but revised his Michelangelo *Lieder*, and
had them published. He made plans for the winter,
and rejoiced in the thought of passing it in the
country near Gmunden, " in perfect quiet, undis-

turbed, and living only for art." In his last letter
to Faisst, 17 September, 1898, he says :

"I am quite well again now, and have no more
need of any cures. You would need them more
than I."

Then came a fresh seizure of madness, and this
time all was finished.

In the autumn of 1898 Wolf was taken to an
asylum at Vienna. At first he was able to receive
a few visits and to enjoy a little music by playing
duets with the director of the establishment, who
was himself a musician and a great admirer of Wolf's
works. He was even able in the spring to take a
few walks out of doors with his friends and an
attendant. But he was beginning not to recognise
things or people or even himself. "Yes," he would
say, sighing, "if only I were Hugo Wolf!" From
the middle of 1899 his malady grew rapidly worse,
and general paralysis followed. At the beginning
of 1900 his speech was affected, and, finally, in
August, 1901, all his body. At the beginning of
1902 all hope was given up by the doctors ; but his
heart was still sound, and the unhappy man dragged
out his life for another year. He died on 16 February,
1903, of peripneumonia.

He was given a magnificent funeral, which was
attended by all the people who had done nothing
for him while he was alive. The Austrian State,
the town of Vienna, his native town Windischgratz,
the Conservatoire that had expelled him, the

*Gesellschaft der Musikfreunde* who had been so long
unfriendly to his works, the Opera that had been
closed to him, the singers that had scorned him, the
critics that had scoffed at him—they were all there.
They sang one of his saddest melodies, *Resignation*,
a setting of a poem of Eichendorff's, and a chorale
by his old friend Bruckner, who had died several
years before him.   His faithful friends, Faisst at the
head of them, took care to have a monument erected
to his memory near those of Beethoven and
Schubert.

.     .     .     .     .     .

Such was his life, cut short at thirty-seven years
of age—for one cannot count the five years of
complete madness.   There are not many examples
in the art world of so terrible a fate.   Nietzsche's
misfortune is nowhere beside this, for Nietzsche's
madness was, to a certain extent, productive, and
caused his genius to flash out in a way that it never
would have done if his mind had been balanced
and his health perfect.   Wolf's madness meant
prostration.   But one may see how, even in the
space of thirty-seven years, his life was strangely
parcelled out.   For he did not really begin his
creative work until he was twenty-seven years old;
and as from 1890 to 1895 he was condemned to
five years' silence, the sum total of his real life,
his productive life, is only four or five years.
But in those few years he got more out of life
than the greater part of artists do in a long career,
and in his work he left the imprint of a person-

ality that no one could forget after once having
known it.

．　　　　．　　　　．　　　　．　　　　．　　　　．

Wolf's work consists chiefly, as we have already
seen, of *Lieder*, and these *Lieder* are characterised
by the application to lyrical music of principles
established by Wagner in the domain of drama.
That does not mean he imitated Wagner. One
finds here and there in Wolf's music Wagnerian
forms, just as elsewhere there are evident reminiscences of Berlioz. It is the inevitable mark of his
time, and each great artist in his turn contributes
his share to the enrichment of the language that
belongs to us all. But the real Wagnerism of Wolf
is not made up of these unconscious resemblances ;
it lies in his determination to make poetry the
inspiration of music. " To show, above all," he
wrote to Humperdinck in 1890, " that poetry is the
true source of my music."

When a man is both a poet and a musician, like
Wagner, it is natural that his poetry and music
should harmonise perfectly. But when it is a
matter of translating the soul of other poets into
music, special gifts of mental subtlety and an
abounding sympathy are needed. These gifts were
possessed by Wolf in a very high degree. No
musician has more keenly savoured and appreciated
the poets. " He was," said one of his critics, G.
Kühl, " Germany's greatest psychologist in music
since Mozart." There was nothing laboured about
his psychology. Wolf was incapable of setting to

music poetry that he did not really love.  He used
to have the poetry he wished to translate read over
to him several times, or in the evening he would
read it aloud to himself.  If he felt very stirred by it
he lived apart with it, and thought about it, and
soaked himself in its atmosphere ; then he went to
sleep, and the next morning he was able to write
the *Lied* straight away.  But some poems seemed
to sleep in him for years, and then would suddenly
awake in him in a musical form.  On these occasions
he would cry out with happiness.  " Do you know ? "
he wrote to Müller, " I simply shouted with joy."
Müller said he was like an old hen after it had laid
an egg.

Wolf never chose commonplace poems for his
music—which is more than can be said of Schubert
or Schumann.  He did not use anything written by
contemporary poets, although he was in sympathy
with some of them, such as Liliencron, who hoped
very much to be translated into music by him.
But he could not do it ; he could not use anything
in the work of a great poet unless he became so
intimate with it that it seemed to be a part of him.

What strikes one also in the *Lieder* is the importance of the pianoforte accompaniment and its
independence of the voice.  Sometimes the voice
and the pianoforte express the contrast that so
often exists between the words and the thought of
the poem ; at other times they express two personalities, as in his setting of Goethe's *Prometheus*,
where the accompaniment represents Zeus sending
out his thunderbolts, and the voice interprets

Titan ; or again, he may depict, as in the setting of Eichendorff's *Serenade*, a student in love in the accompaniment, while the song is the voice of an old man who is listening to it and thinking of his youth. But in whatever he is describing, the pianoforte and the voice have always their own individuality. You cannot take anything away from his *Lieder* without spoiling the whole ; and it is especially so with his instrumental passages, which give us the beginning and end of his emotion, and which circle round it and sum it up. The musical form, following closely the poetic form, is extremely varied. It may sometimes express a fugitive thought, a brief record of a poetic impression or some little action, or it may be a great epic or dramatic picture. Müller remarks that Wolf put more into a poem than the poet himself—as in the *Italienisches-Liederbuch*. It is the worst reproach they can make about him, and it is not an ordinary one. Wolf excelled especially in setting poems which accorded with his own tragic fate, as if he had some presentiment of it. No one has better expressed the anguish of a troubled and despairing soul, such as we find in the old harp-player in *Wilhelm Meister*, or the splendid nihility of certain poems of Michelangelo.

Of all his collections of *Lieder*, the 53 *Gedichte von Eduard Mörike, komponiert für eine Singstimme und Klavier* (1888), the first published, is the most popular. It gained many friends for Wolf, not so much among artists (who are always in the minority) as among those critics who are the best and most disinterested of all—the homely, honest people who

o

do not make a profession of art, but enjoy it as their spiritual daily bread. There are a number of these people in Germany, whose hard lives are beautified by their love of music. Wolf found these friends in all parts, but he found most of them in Swabia. At Stuttgart, at Mannheim, at Darmstadt, and in the country round about these towns he became very popular—the only popular musician since Schubert and Schumann. All classes of society unite in loving him. " His *Lieder*," says Herr Decsey, " are on the pianos of even the poorest houses, by the side of Schubert's *Lieder*." Stuttgart became for Wolf, as he said himself, a second home. He owes this popularity, which is without parallel in Swabia, to the people's passionate love of *Lieder* and, above all, of the poetry of Mörike, the Swabian pastor, who lives again in Wolf's songs. Wolf has set to music a quarter of Mörike's poems, he has brought Mörike into his own, and given him one of the first places among German poets. Such was really his intention, and he said so when he had a portrait of Mörike put on the title-page of the songs. Whether the reading of his poetry acted as a balm to Wolf's unquiet spirit, or whether he became conscious of his genius for the first time when he expressed this poetry in music, I do not know ; but he felt deep gratitude towards it, and wished to show it by beginning the first volume with that fine and rather Beethoven-like song, *Der Genesende an die Hoffnung* (" The Convalescent's Ode to Hope ").

The fifty-one *Lieder* of the *Goethe - Liederbuch* (1888–89) were composed in groups of *Lieder :* the

*Wilhelm Meister Lieder,* the *Divan (Suleika) Lieder,*
etc. Wolf even tried to identify himself with the
poet's line of thought ; and in this we often find him
in rivalry with Schubert. He avoided using the
poems in which he thought Schubert had exactly
conveyed the poet's meaning, as in *Geheimes* and
*An Schwager Kronos ;* but he told Müller that there
were times when Schubert did not understand
Goethe at all, because he concerned himself with
translating their general lyrical thought rather than
with showing the real nature of Goethe's characters.
The peculiar interest of Wolf's *Lieder* is that he
gives each poetic figure its individual character.
The Harpist and Mignon are traced with marvellous insight and restraint ; and in some passages
Wolf shows that he has re-discovered Goethe's art
of presenting a whole world of sadness in a single
word. The serenity of a great soul soars over the
chaos of passions.

The *Spanisches-Liederbuch nach Heyse und Geibel*
(1889–90) had already inspired Schumann, Brahms,
Cornelius, and others. But none had tried to give
it its rough and sensual character. Müller shows
how Schumann, especially, robbed the poems of their
true nature. Not only did he invest them with his
own sentimentalism, but he calmly arranged poems
of the most marked individual character to be sung
by four voices, which makes them quite absurd ;
and, worse than this, he changed the words and
their sense when they stood in his way. Wolf, on
the contrary, steeped himself in this melancholy
and voluptuous world, and would not let anything

draw him from it ; and out of it he produced, as he himself said proudly, some masterpieces. The ten religious songs that come at the beginning of the collection suggest the delusions of mysticism, and weep tears of blood ; they are distressing to the ear and mind alike, for they are the passionate expression of a faith that puts itself on the rack. By the side of them one finds smiling visions of the Holy Family, which recall Murillo. The thirty-four folksongs are brilliant, restless, whimsical, and wonderfully varied in form. Each represents a different subject, a personality drawn with incisive strokes, and the whole collection overflows with life. It is said that the *Spanisches-Liederbuch* is to Wolf's work what *Tristan* is to Wagner's work.

The *Italienisches - Liederbuch* (1890–96) is quite different. The character of the songs is very restrained, and Wolf's genius here approached a classic clearness of form. He was always seeking to simplify his musical language, and said that if he wrote anything more, he wished it to be like Mozart's writings. These *Lieder* contain nothing that is not absolutely essential to their subject ; so the melodies are very short, and are dramatic rather than lyrical. Wolf gave them an important place in his work : " I consider them," he wrote to Kaufmann, " the most original and perfect of my compositions."

As for the *Michelangelo Gedichten* (1897), they were interrupted by the outbreak of his malady, and he had only time to write four, of which he suppressed one. Their associations are pathetic when one remembers the tragic time at which they were composed ; and, by a sort of prophetic instinct, they exhale heaviness of spirit and mournful pride. The second melody is perhaps more beautiful than anything else Wolf wrote ; it is truly his death-song :

> *Alles endet, was entstehet.*
> *Alles, alles rings vergehet.*[1]

And it is a dead man that sings :

> *Menschen waren wir ja auch,*
> *Froh und traurig, so wie Ihr.*
> *Und nun sind wir leblos hier,*
> *Sind nur Erde, wie Ihr sehet.*[2]

At the moment he was writing this song, in the short respite he had from his illness, he himself was nearly a dead man.

. . . . . .

As soon as Wolf was really dead his genius was recognised all over Germany. His sufferings pro-

---

[1] All that is begun must end,
All around will sometime perish.

[2] Once we were also men
Happy or sad like you ;
Now life is taken from us,
We are only of earth, as you see.

> *Chiunque nasce a morte arriva*
> *Nel fuggir del tempo, e'l sole*
> *Niuna cosa lascia viva . . .*
> *Come voi, uomini fummo,*
> *Lieti e tristi, come siete ;*
> *E or siam, come vedete,*
> *Terra al sol, di vita priva.*

(Poems of Michelangelo, **CXXXVI.**)

voked an almost excessive reaction in his favour. *Hugo-Wolf-Vereine* were founded everywhere ; and to-day we have publications, collections of letters, souvenirs, and biographies in abundance. It is a case of who can cry loudest that he always understood the genius of the unhappy artist, and work himself into the greatest fury against his traducers. A little later, and monuments and statues will spring up all over.

I doubt if Wolf with his rough, sincere nature would have found much consolation in this tardy homage if he could have foreseen it. He would have said to his posthumous admirers : " You are hypocrites. It is not for me that you raise those statues ; it is for yourselves. It is that you may make speeches, form committees, and delude yourselves and others that you were my friends. Where were you when I had need of you ? You let me die. Do not play a comedy round my grave. Look rather around you, and see if there are not other Wolfs who are struggling against your hostility or your indifference. As for me, I have come safe to port."

# DON LORENZO PEROSI

THE winter that held Italian thought in its cold clasp is over, and great trees that seemed to be asleep are putting out new life in the sun. Yesterday it was poetry that awaked, and to-day it is music—the sweet music of Italy, calm in its passion and sadness, and artless in its knowledge. Are we really witnessing the return of its spring? Is it the incoming of some great tide of melody, which will wash away the gloom and doubt of our life to-day? As I was reading the oratorios of this young priest of Piedmont, I thought I heard, far away, the song of the children of old Greece: " The swallow has come, has come, bringing the gay seasons and glad years. Ἔαρ ἤδη." I welcome the coming of Don Lorenzo Perosi with great hope.

．　　・　　・　　・　　・　　・　　・

The abbé Perosi, the precentor of St. Mark's chapel at Venice and the director of the Sistine chapel, is twenty-six years old.[1] He is short in stature and of youthful appearance, with a head a little too big for his body, and open and regular features lighted up by intelligent black eyes, his only peculiarity being a projecting underlip. He is

[1] This article was written in 1899, on the occasion of Lorenzo Perosi's coming to Paris to direct his oratorio *La Résurrection*.

simple-hearted and modest, and has a friendly warmth of affection. When he is conducting the orchestra his striking silhouette, his slow and awkward gestures in expressive passages, and his naïve movements of passion at dramatic moments, bring to mind one of Fra Angelico's monks.

For the last eighteen months Don Perosi has been working at a cycle of twelve oratorios descriptive of the life of Christ. In this short time he has finished four : *The Passion, The Transfiguration, The Resurrection of Lazarus, The Resurrection of Christ.* Now he is at work on the fifth—*The Nativity.*

These compositions alone place him in the front rank of contemporary musicians. They abound in faults ; but their qualities are so rare, and his soul shines so clearly through them, and such fine sincerity breathes in them, that I have not the courage to dwell on their weaknesses. So I shall content myself with remarking, in passing, that the orchestration is inadequate and awkward, and that the young musician should strive to make it fuller and more delicate; and though he shows great ease in composition, he is often too impetuous, and should resist this tendency ; and that, lastly, there are sometimes traces of bad taste in the music and reminiscences of the classics—all of which are the sins of youth, which age will certainly cure.

Each of the oratorios is really a descriptive mass, which from beginning to end traces out one dominating thought. Don Perosi said to me : " The mistake of artists to-day is that they attach themselves too much to details and neglect the whole. They begin by carving ornaments, and forget that the most important thing is the unity of their work, its plan and general outline. The outline must first of all be beautiful."

In his own musical architecture one finds well-marked airs, numerous recitatives, Gregorian or Palestrinian choruses, chorales with developments and variations in the old style, and intervening symphonies of some importance.

The whole work is to be preceded by a grand prelude, very carefully worked out, to which Don Perosi atta s particular worth. He wishes, he says, that his building shall have a beautiful door elaborately carved after the fashion of the artists of the Renaissance and Gothic times. And so he means to compose the prelude after the rest of the oratorio is finished, when he is able to think about it in undisturbed peace. He wishes to concentrate a moral atmosphere in it, the very essence of the soul and passions of his sacred drama. He also confided to me that of all he has yet composed there is nothing he likes better than the introductions to *The Trans-figuration* and *The Resurrection of Christ*.

The dramatic tendency of these oratorios is very marked, and it is chiefly on that account that they have conquered Italy. In spite of some passages which have strayed a little in the direction of opera, or even melodrama, the music shows great depth of feeling. The figures of the women especially are drawn with delicacy ; and in the second part of *Lazarus*, Mary's air, " Lord, if Thou hadst been here, my brother had not died," recalls something

of Gluck's *Orfeo* in its heart-broken sadness.    And
again, in the same oratorio, when Jesus gives the
order to raise the stone from the tomb, Martha's
speech, " Domine, jam foetet," is very expressive of
her sadness, fear, and shame, and human horror.
I should like to quote one more passage, the most
moving of all, which is found in the *Resurrection of
Christ*, when Mary Magdalene is beside the tomb
of Christ ; here, in her speech with the angels, in
her touching lamentation, and in the words of the
Evangelist, " And when she had thus said, she
turned herself back, and saw Jesus standing, and
knew not that it was Jesus," we hear a melody filled
with tenderness, and seem to see Christ's eyes shining
as they rest on Mary before she has recognised Him.

It is not, however, Perosi's dramatic genius that
strikes me in his work ; it is rather his peculiar
mournfulness, which is indescribable, his gift of pure
poetry, and the richness of his flowing melody.
·However deep the religious feeling in the music may
be, the music itself is often stronger still, and breaks
in upon the drama that it may express itself freely.
Take, for instance, the fine symphonic passage that
follows the arrival of Jesus and His friends at
Martha and Mary's house, after the death of their
brother (p. 12 *et seq.* of *Lazarus*).  It is true the
orchestra expresses regrets and sighs, the excesses
of sorrow mingled with words of consolation and
faith, in a sort of languishing funeral march that
is feminine and Christian in character.  This,
according to the composer, is a picture he has
painted of the persons in the drama before he makes

them speak. But, in spite of himself, the result is a flood of pure music, and his soul sings its own song of joy and sadness. Sometimes his spirit, in its naïve and delicate charm, recalls that of Mozart ; but his musical visions are always dominated and directed by a religious strength like that of Bach. Even the portions where the dramatic feeling is strongest are really little symphonies, such as the music that describes the miracle in *The Transfiguration*, and the illness of Lazarus. In the latter great depth of suffering is expressed ; indeed, sadness could not have been carried farther even by Bach, and the same serenity of mind runs through its despair.

But what joy there is when these deeds of faith have been performed—when Jesus has cured the possessed man, or when Lazarus has opened his eyes to the light. The heart of the multitude overflows perhaps in rather childish thanksgiving ; and at first it seemed to me expressed in a commonplace way. But did not the joy of all great artists so express itself ?—the joy of Beethoven, Mozart, and Bach, who, when once they had thrown their cares aside, knew how to amuse themselves like the rest of the populace. And the simple phrase at the beginning soon assumes fuller proportions, the harmonies gain in richness, a glowing ardour fills the music, and a chorale blends with the dances in triumphant majesty.

All these works are radiant with a happy ease of expression. *The Passion* was finished in September, 1897, *The Transfiguration* in February, 1898,

*Lazarus* in June, 1898, and *The Resurrection of Christ* in November, 1898. Such an output of work takes us back to eighteenth-century musicians.

But this is not the only resemblance between the young musician and his predecessors. Much of their soul has passed into his. His style is made up of all styles, and ranges from the Gregorian chant to the most modern modulations. All available materials are used in this work. This is an Italian characteristic. Gabriel d'Annunzio threw into his melting-pot the Renaissance, the Italian painters, music, the writers of the North, Tolstoy, Dostoïevsky, Maeterlinck, and our French writers, and out of it he drew his wonderful poems. So Don Perosi, in his compositions, welds together the Gregorian chant, the musical style of the contrapuntists of the fifteenth and sixteenth centuries, Palestrina, Roland, Gabrieli, Carissimi, Schutz, Bach, Händel, Gounod, Wagner—I was going to say César Franck, but Don Perosi told me that he hardly knew this composer at all, though his style bears some resemblance to Franck's.

Time does not exist for Don Perosi. When he courteously wished to praise French musicians, the first name he chose—as if it were that of a contemporary—was that of Josquin, and then that of Roland de Lassus, who seems to him so great and profound a musician that he admires him most of all. And Don Perosi's universality of style is a trait that is Catholic as well as Italian. He expresses his mind quite clearly on the subject. "Great artists formerly," he says, "were more eclectic than ourselves, and less fettered by their nationalities. Josquin's school has peopled all Europe. Roland has lived in Flanders, in Italy, and in Germany. With them the same style expressed the same thought everywhere. We must do as they did. We must try to recreate a universal art in which the resources of all countries and all times are blended."

As a matter of fact, I do not think this is quite correct. I rather doubt if Josquin and Roland were eclectic at all ; for they did not really combine the styles of different countries, but thrust upon other countries the style that the Franco-Flemish school had just created, a style which they themselves were enriching daily. But Don Perosi's idea deserves our appreciation, and one must praise his endeavour to create a universal style. It would be a good thing for music if eclecticism, thus understood, could bring back some of the equilibrium that has been lost since Wagner's death ; it would be a benefit to the human spirit, which might then find in the unity of art a powerful means of bringing about the unity of mind. Our aim should be to efface the differences of race in art, so that it may become a tongue common to all peoples, where the most opposite ideas may be reconciled. We should all join in working to build the cathedral of European art. And the place of the director of the Sistine chapel among the first builders is very plain.

.    .    .    .    .    .

Don Perosi sat down to the piano and played me the *Te Deum* of *The Nativity*, which he had written the day before. He played very sweetly, with youthful gaiety, and sang the choral parts in an undertone. Every now and then he would look at me, not for praise, but to see if we were sharing the same thoughts. He would look me well in the face with his quiet eyes, then turn back to his score, and then look at me again. And I felt a comforting calm radiating from him and his music, from its happy harmony and the full and rhythmic serenity of its spirit. And how pleasant it was after the tempests and convulsions of art in these later days. Can we not tear ourselves away from that romantic suffering in music which was begun by Beethoven ? After a century of battles, of revolutions, and of political and social strife, whose pain has found its reflection in art, let us begin to build a new city of art, where men may gather together in brotherly love for the same ideal. However utopian that hope may sound now, let us think of it as a symptom of new directions of thought, and let us hope that Don Perosi may be one of those who will bring into music that divine peace, that peace which Beethoven craved for in despair at the end of his *Missa Solemnis*, that joy that he sang about but never knew.

# FRENCH AND GERMAN MUSIC

In May, 1905, the first musical festival of Alsace-Lorraine took place at Strasburg. It was an important artistic event, and meant the bringing together of two civilisations that for centuries had been at variance on the soil of Alsace, more anxious for dispute than for mutual understanding.

The official programme of the *fêtes musicales* laid stress on the reconciliatory purpose of its organisers, and I quote these words from the programme book, drawn up by Dr. Max Bendiner, of Strasburg :

" Music may achieve the highest of all missions : she may be a bond between nations, races, and states, who are strangers to one another in many ways ; she may unite what is disunited, and bring peace to what is hostile. . . . No country is more suited for her friendly aid than Alsace-Lorraine, that old meeting-place of people, where from time immemorial the North and South have exchanged their material and their spiritual wealth ; and no place is readier to welcome her than Strasburg, an old town built by the Romans, which has remained to this day a centre of spiritual life. All great intellectual currents have left their mark on the people of Alsace-Lorraine ; and so they have been destined to play the part of mediator between different times and different peoples ; and the East and the West, the past and the present, meet here and join hands. In such festivals as this, it is not a matter of gaining æsthetic victories ; it is a matter of bringing together all that is great and noble and eternal in the art of different times and different nations."

It was a splendid ambition for Alsace—the eternal field of battle—to wish to inaugurate these European Olympian games. But in spite of good intentions, this meeting of nations resulted in a fight, on musical ground, between two civilisations and two arts— French art and German art. For these two arts represent to-day all that is truly alive in European music.

Such jousts are very stirring, and may be of great service to all combatants. But, unhappily, France was very indifferent in the matter. It was the duty of our musicians and critics to attend an international encounter like this, and to see that the conditions of the combat were fair. By that I mean our art should be represented as it ought to be, so that we may learn something from the result. But the French public does nothing at such a time ; it remains absorbed in its concerts at Paris, where everyone knows everyone else so well that they are not able and do not dare to criticise freely. And so our art is withering away in an atmosphere of coteries, instead of seeking the open air and enjoying a vigorous fight with foreign art. For the majority of our critics would rather deny the existence of

foreign art than try to understand it.  Never have
I regretted their indifference more than I did at the
Strasburg festival, where, in spite of the unfavourable conditions in which French art was represented
through our own carelessness, I realised what its
force might have been if we had been interested
spectators in the fight.

.    .    .    .    .    .

Perfect eclecticism had been exercised in the
making up of the programme.  One found mixed
together the names of Mozart, Wagner, and Brahms ;
César Franck and Gustave Charpentier ; Richard
Strauss and Mahler.  There were French singers like
Cazeneuve and Daraux, and French and Italian
virtuosi like Henri Marteau and Ferruccio Busoni,
together with German, Austrian, and Scandinavian
artists.  The orchestra (the *Strassbürger Städtische
Orchester*) and the choir, which was formed of
different *Chorvereine* of Strasburg, were conducted
by Richard Strauss, Gustav Mahler, and Camille
Chevillard.  But the names of these famous *Kapellmeister* must not let us forget the man who was
really the soul of the concerts—Professor Ernst
Münch, of Strasburg, an Alsatian, who conducted
all the rehearsals, and who effaced himself at the
last moment, and left all the honours to the conductors of foreign orchestras.  Professor Münch,
who is also organist at Saint-Guillaume, has done
more than anyone else for music in Strasburg, and
has trained excellent choirs (the " *Chœurs de
Saint-Guillaume* ") there, and organised splendid

P

concerts of Bach's music with the aid of another Alsatian, Albert Schweitzer, whose name is well known to musical historians. The latter is director of the clerical college of St. Thomas (*Thomasstift*), a pastor, an organist, a professor at the University of Strasburg, and the author of interesting works on theology and philosophy. Besides this he has written a now famous book, *Jean-Sébastien Bach*, which is doubly remarkable : first, because it is written in French (though it was published in Leipzig by a professor of the University of Strasburg), and secondly, because it shows an harmonious blend of the French and German spirit, and gives fresh life to the study of Bach and the old classic art. It was very interesting to me to make the acquaintance of these people, born on Alsatian soil, and representing the best Alsatian culture and all that was finest in the two civilisations.

The programme for the three days' festival was as follows :

Saturday, May 20th.

*Oberon Overture :* Weber (conducted by Richard Strauss).

*Les Béatitudes :* César Franck (conducted by Camille Chevillard).

*Impressions d'Italie :* Gustav Charpentier (conducted by Camille Chevillard).

Three songs by Jean Sibelius, Hugo Wolf, Armas Järnefelt (sung by Mme. Järnefelt).

The last scene from *Die Meistersinger :* Wagner (conducted by Richard Strauss).

Sunday, May 21st.

*Cinquième Symphonie :* Gustav Mahler (conducted by Gustav Mahler).

*Rhapsodie,* for contralto, choir, and orchestra :
Johannes Brahms (conducted by Ernst Münch).

*Strasburg Concerto in G major,* for violin (played by
Henri Marteau; conducted by Richard Strauss).

*Sinfonia domestica :* Richard Strauss (conducted
by Richard Strauss).

Monday, May 22nd.

*Coriolan Overture :* Beethoven (conducted by
Gustav Mahler).

*Concerto in G major,* for piano : Beethoven
(played by Ferruccio Busoni).

*Lieder : An die enfernte Geliebte :* Beethoven
(sung by Ludwig Hess).

*Choral Symphony :* Beethoven (conducted by
Gustav Mahler).

.    .    .    .    .    .

M. Chevillard alone represented our French
musicians at the festival ; and they could have made
no better choice of a conductor. But Germany had
delegated her two greatest composers, Strauss and
Mahler, to come to conduct their newest compositions. And I think it would not have been too
much to set up one of our own foremost composers
to combat the glory which these two enjoy in their
own country.

M. Chevillard had been asked to conduct, not one
of the works of our recent masters, like Debussy or

Dukas, whose style he renders to perfection, but Franck's *Les Béatitudes*, a work whose spirit he does not, to my mind, quite understand. The mystic tenderness of Franck escapes him, and he brings out only what is dramatic. And so that performance of *Les Béatitudes*, though in many respects fine, left an imperfect idea of Franck's genius.

But what seemed inconceivable, and what justly annoyed M. Chevillard, was that the whole of *Les Béatitudes* was not given, but only a section of them. And on this subject I shall take the liberty of recommending that French artists who are guests at similar festivals should not in future agree to a programme with their eyes shut, but have their own wishes considered, or refuse their help. If French musicians are to be given a place in German *Musikfeste*, French people must be allowed to choose the works that are to represent them. And, above all, a French conductor must not be brought from Paris, and find on his arrival a mutilated score and an arbitrary choice of a few fragments that are not even whole in themselves. For they played five out of the eight *Béatitudes*, and cuts had been made in the third and eighth *Béatitudes*. That showed a want of respect for art, for works should be given as they are, or not at all.

And it would have been more seemly if in this three-day festival the organisers had had the courteousness to devote the first day to French music, and had set aside one whole concert for it. But, without doubt, they had carefully sandwiched the French works in between German works to weaken their effect, and lessen the probable (and actual) enthusiasm with which French music would be received in the presence of the Statthalter of Alsace-Lorraine by a section of the Alsatian public. In addition to this, and by a choice that neither myself nor anyone else in Strasburg could believe was dictated by musical reasons, the German work chosen to end the evening was the final scene from *Die Meistersinger*, with its ringing couplet from Hans Sachs, in which he denounces foreign insincerity and foreign frivolity (*Wälschen Dunst mit wälschen Tand*). This lack of courtesy—though the words were really nonsense when this very concert was given to show that foreign art could not be ignored—would not be worth while raking up if it did not further serve to show how regrettable is the indifference of French artists who take part in these festivals. And this mistake would never have occurred if they had taken care to acquaint themselves with the programme beforehand and put their veto upon it.

I have mentioned this little incident partly because my views were shared by many Alsatians in the audience, who expressed their annoyance to me afterwards. But, putting it aside, our French artists ought not to have consented to let our music be represented by a mutilated score of *Les Béatitudes* and by Charpentier's *Impressions d'Italie*, for the latter, though a brilliantly clever work, is not of the first rank, and was too easily crushed by one of Wagner's most stupendous compositions.

If people wish to institute a joust between French and German art, let it be a fair one, I repeat; let Wagner be matched with Berlioz, and Strauss with Debussy, and Mahler with Dukas or Magnard.

.        .        .        .        .        .

Such were the conditions of the combat; and they were, whether intentionally or not, unfavourable to France. And yet to the eyes of an impartial observer the result was full of hope and encouragement for us.

I have never bothered myself in art with questions of nationality. I have not even concealed my preference for German music; and I consider, even to-day, that Richard Strauss is the foremost musical composer in Europe. Having said this, I am freer to speak of the strange impression that I had at the Strasburg festival—an impression of the change that is coming over music, and the way that French art is silently setting about taking the place of German art.

"*Wälschen Dunst und wälschen Tand.*" . . . How that reproachful speech seems to be misplaced when one is listening to the honest thought expressed in César Franck's music. In *Les Béatitudes*, nothing, or next to nothing, was done for art's sake. It is the soul speaking to the soul. As Beethoven wrote, at the end of his mass in D, "*Vom Herzen . . . zu Herzen!*" ("It comes from the heart to go to the heart"). I know no one but Franck in the last century, unless it is Beethoven, who has possessed in so high a degree the virtue of being himself and speaking only the truth without thought of his public. Never before has religious faith been expressed with such sincerity. Franck is the only musician besides Bach who has really *seen* the Christ, and who can make other people see him too. I would even venture to say that his Christ is simpler than Bach's ; for Bach's thoughts are often led away by the interest of developing his subject, by certain habits of composition, and by repetitions and clever devices, which weaken his strength. In Franck's music we get Christ's speech itself, unadorned and in all its living force. And in the wonderful harmony between the music and the sacred words we hear the voice of the world's conscience. I once heard someone say to Mme. Cosima Wagner that certain passages in *Parsifal*, particularly the chorus " *Durch Mitleid wissend*," had a quality that was truly religious and the force of a revelation. But I find a greater force and a more truly Christian spirit in *Les Béatitudes*.

And here is an astonishing thing. At this German musical festival it was a Frenchman who represented not only serious music moulded in a classical form, but a religious spirit and the spirit of the Gospels. The characters of two nations have been reversed. The Germans have so changed that they are only able to appreciate this seriousness and religious faith with difficulty. I watched the audience on this occasion ; they listened politely, a little astonished and bored, as if to say, " What business has this Frenchman with depth and piety of soul ? "

"There is no doubt," said Henri Lichtenberger, who sat by me at the concert, "our music is beginning to bore the Germans."

It was only the other day that German music enjoyed the privilege of boring us in France.

And so, to make up for the austere grandeur of *Les Béatitudes* they had it immediately followed by Gustave Charpentier's *Impressions d'Italie.* You should have seen the relief of the audience. At last they were to have some French music—as Germans understand it. Charpentier is, of all living French musicians, the most liked in Germany; he is indeed the only one who is popular with artists and the general public alike. Shall I say that the sincere pleasure they take in his orchestration and the gay life of his subjects is enhanced a little by a slight disdain for French frivolity—*wälschen Tand?*

"Now listen to that," said Richard Strauss to me during the third movement of *Impressions d'Italie;* "that is the true music of Montmartre, the utterance of fine words . . . Liberty! . . . Love! . . . which no one believes."

And on the whole he found the music quite charming, and, without doubt, in the depths of his heart approved of this Frenchman according to conventional notions that are current in Germany alone. Strauss is really very fond of Charpentier, and was his patron in Berlin; and I remember how he showed childish delight in *Louise* when it was first performed in Paris.

But Strauss, and most other Germans, are quite on the wrong track when they try to persuade themselves that this amusing French frivolity is still the exclusive property of France.  They really love it because it has become German ;  and they are quite unconscious of the fact.  The German artists of other times did not find much pleasure in frivolity ; but I could have easily shown Strauss his liking for it by taking examples from his own works.   The Germans of to-day have but little in common with the Germans of yesterday.

I am not speaking of the general public only The German public of to-day are devotees of Brahms and Wagner, and everything of theirs seems good to them ; they have no discrimination, and, while they applaud Wagner and encore Brahms, they are, in their hearts, not only frivolous, but sentimental and gross.   The most striking thing about this public is their cult of power since Wagner's death. When listening to the end of *Die Meistersinger* I felt how the haughty music of the great march reflected the spirit of this military nation of shop-keepers, bursting with rude health and complacent pride.

The most remarkable thing of all is that German artists are gradually losing the power of understanding their own splendid classics and, in particular, Beethoven.  Strauss, who is very shrewd and knows exactly his own limitations, does not willingly enter Beethoven's domain, though he feels his spirit in a much more living way than any of the other German *Kapellmeister*.  At the Strasburg festival he contented himself with conducting, besides his own symphony, the *Oberon Overture* and a Mozart

concerto. These performances were interesting ;
a personality like his is so curious that it is quite
amusing to find it coming out in the works he conducts. But how Mozart's features took on an
offhand and impatient air ; and how the rhythms
were accentuated at the expense of the melodic
grace. In this case, however, Strauss was dealing
with a concerto, where a certain liberty of interpretation is allowed. But Mahler, who was less
discreet, ventured upon conducting the whole of
the Beethoven concert. And what can be said of
that evening ? I will not speak of the *Concerto for
pianoforte, in G major,* which Busoni played with
a brilliant and superficial execution that took away
all breadth from the work ; it is enough to note that
his interpretation was enthusiastically received by
the public. German artists were not responsible
for that performance ; but they were responsible
for that fine cycle of *Lieder, An die entfernte Geliebte,*
which was bellowed by a Berlin tenor at the top of
his voice, and for the *Choral Symphony,* which was,
for me, an unspeakable performance. I could never
have believed that a German orchestra conducted
by the chief *Kapellmeister* of Austria could have
committed such misdeeds. The time was incredible : the scherzo had no life in it ; the adagio
was taken in hot haste without leaving a moment
for dreams ; and there were pauses in the finale
which destroyed the development of the theme and
broke the thread of its thought. The different parts
of the orchestra fell over one another, and the whole
was uncertain and lacking in balance. I once

severely criticised the neo-classic stiffness of Weingartner ; but I should have appreciated his healthy
equilibrium and his effort to be exact after hearing
this neurasthenic rendering of Beethoven. No ; we
can no longer hear Beethoven and Mozart in Germany to-day, we can only hear Mahler and Strauss.

Well, let it be so. We will resign ourselves. The
past is past. Let us leave Beethoven and Mozart,
and speak of Mahler and Strauss.

. . . . . .

Gustav Mahler is forty-six years old.[1] He is a
kind of legendary type of German musician, rather
like Schubert, and half-way between a school-
master and a clergyman. He has a long, clean-
shaven face, a pointed skull covered with untidy
hair, a bald forehead, a prominent nose, eyes that
blink behind his glasses, a large mouth and thin
lips, hollow cheeks, a rather tired and sarcastic
expression, and a general air of asceticism. He is
excessively nervous, and silhouette caricatures of
him, representing him as a cat in convulsions in
the conductor's desk, are very popular in Germany.

He was born at Kalischt in Bohemia, and became
a pupil of Anton Bruckner at Vienna, and afterwards *Hofoperndirecktor* ("Director of the Opera")
there. I hope one day to study this artist's work
in greater detail, for he is second only to Strauss as
a composer in Germany, and the principal musician
of South Germany.

His most important work is a suite of sym-

[1] This essay was written in 1905.

phonies; and it was the fifth symphony of this suite that he conducted at the Strasburg festival. The first symphony, called *Titan*, was composed in 1894. The construction of the whole is on a massive and gigantic scale; and the melodies on which these works are built up are like rough-hewn blocks of not very good quality, but imposing by reason of their size, and by the obstinate repetition of their rhythmic design, which is maintained as if it were an obsession. This heaping-up of music both crude and learned in style, with harmonies that are sometimes clumsy and sometimes delicate, is worth considering on account of its bulk. The orchestration is heavy and noisy; and the brass dominates and roughly gilds the rather sombre colouring of the great edifice. The underlying idea of the composition is neo-classic, and rather spongy and diffuse. Its harmonic structure is composite: we get the style of Bach, Schubert, and Mendelssohn fighting that of Wagner and Bruckner; and, by a decided liking for canon form, it even recalls some of Franck's work. The whole is like a showy and expensive collection of bric-à-brac.

The chief characteristic of these symphonies is, generally speaking, the use of choral singing with the orchestra. "When I conceive a great musical painting (*ein grosses musikalisches Gemälde*)," says Mahler, "there always comes a moment when I feel forced to employ speech (*das Wort*) as an aid to the realisation of my musical conception."

Mahler has got some striking effects from this combination of voices and instruments, and he did well to seek inspiration in this direction from Beethoven and Liszt. It is incredible that the nineteenth century should have put this combination to so little use ; for I think the gain may be poetical as well as musical.

In the *Second Symphony in C minor*, the first three parts are purely instrumental ; but in the fourth part the voice of a contralto is heard singing these sad and simple words :

> *" Der Mensch liegt in grösster Noth !*
> *Der Mensch liegt in grösster Pein !*
> *Je lieber möcht' ich im Himmel sein !"* [1]

The soul strives to reach God with the passionate cry :   *" Ich bin von Gott und will wieder zu Gott."* [2]

Then there is a symphonic episode (*Der Rufer in der Wüste*), and we hear " the voice of one crying in the wilderness " in fierce and anguished tones. There is an apocalyptic finale where the choir sing Klopstock's beautiful ode on the promise of the Resurrection :

> *"Aufersteh'n, ja, aufersteh'n wirst du, mein Staub, nach*
> *kurzer Ruh !"* [3]

The law is proclaimed with :

> *"Was entstanden ist, dass mus vergehen,*
> *Was vergangen, auferstehen !"* [4]

[1] Man lies in greatest misery ;
Man lies in greatest pain ;
I would I were in Heaven !

[2] I come from God, and shall to God return.

[3] Thou wilt rise again, thou wilt rise again, O my dust, after a little rest.

[4] What is born must pass away ;
What has passed away must rise again.

And all the orchestra, the choirs, and the organ,
join in the hymn of Eternal Life.

In the *Third Symphony*, known as *Ein Sommer-
morgentraum* (" A Summer Morning's Dream "),
the first and the last parts are for the orchestra
alone ; the fourth part contains some of the best
of Mahler's music, and is an admirable setting of
Nietzsche's words :

> " *O Mensch ! O Mensch ! Gib Acht ! gib Acht !*
> *Was spricht die tiefe Mitternacht ?* "[1]

The fifth part is a gay and stirring chorus founded
on a popular legend.

In the *Fourth Symphony in G major*, the last part
alone is sung, and is of an almost humorous character, being a sort of childish description of the joys
of Paradise.

In spite of appearances, Mahler refuses to con-
nect these choral symphonies with programme-
music. Without doubt he is right, if he means that
his music has its own value outside any sort of
programme ; but there is no doubt that it is always
the expression of a definite *Stimmung*, of a conscious
mood ; and the fact is, whether he likes it or not,
that *Stimmung* gives an interest to his music
far beyond that of the music itself. His personality seems to me far more interesting than his
art.

This is often the case with artists in Germany ;
Hugo Wolf is another example of it. Mahler's

---

[1] O Man ! O Man ! Have care ! Have care !
What says dark midnight ?

case is really rather curious. When one studies his works one feels convinced that he is one of those rare types in modern Germany—an egoist who feels with sincerity. Perhaps his emotions and his ideas do not succeed in expressing themselves in a really sincere and personal way ; for they reach us through a cloud of reminiscences and an atmosphere of classicism. I cannot help thinking that Mahler's position as director of the Opera, and his consequent saturation in the music that his calling condemns him to study, is the cause of this. There is nothing more fatal to a creative spirit than too much reading, above all when it does not read of its own free will, but is forced to absorb an excessive amount of nourishment, the larger part of which is indigestible. In vain may Mahler try to defend the sanctuary of his mind ; it is violated by foreign ideas coming from all parts, and instead of being able to drive them away, his conscience, as conductor of the orchestra, obliges him to receive them and almost embrace them. With his feverish activity, and burdened as he is with heavy tasks, he works unceasingly and has no time to dream. Mahler will only be Mahler when he is able to leave his administrative work, shut up his scores, retire within himself, and wait patiently until he has become himself again—if it is not too late.

His *Fifth Symphony*, which he conducted at Strasburg, convinced me, more than all his other works, of the urgent necessity of adopting this course. In this composition he has not allowed

himself the use of the choruses, which were one of
the chief attractions of his preceding symphonies.
He wished to prove that he could write pure music,
and to make his claim surer he refused to have any
explanation of his composition published in the
concert programme, as the other composers in the
festival had done ; he wished it, therefore, to be
judged from a strictly musical point of view. It
was a dangerous ordeal for him.

Though I wished very much to admire the work
of a composer whom I held in such esteem, I felt
it did not come out very well from the test. To
begin with, this symphony is excessively long—
it lasts an hour and a half—though there is no apparent justification for its proportions. It aims at
being colossal, and mainly achieves emptiness. The
*motifs* are more than familiar. After a funeral
march of commonplace character and boisterous
movement, where Beethoven seems to be taking
lessons from Mendelssohn, there comes a scherzo, or
rather a Viennese waltz, where Chabrier gives old
Bach a helping hand. The adagietto has a rather
sweet sentimentality. The rondo at the end is presented rather like an idea of Franck's, and is the
best part of the composition ; it is carried out in
a spirit of mad intoxication and a chorale rises up
from it with crashing joy ; but the effect of the
whole is lost in repetitions that choke it and make
it heavy. Through all the work runs a mixture of
pedantic stiffness and incoherence ; it moves along
in a desultory way, and suffers from abrupt checks
in the course of its development and from super-

fluous ideas that break in for no reason at all, with the result that the whole hangs fire.

Above all, I fear Mahler has been sadly hypnotised by ideas about power—ideas that are getting to the head of all German artists to-day. He seems to have an undecided mind, and to combine sadness and irony with weakness and impatience, to be a Viennese musician striving after Wagnerian grandeur. No one expresses the grace of *Ländler* and dainty waltzes and mournful reveries better than he ; and perhaps no one is nearer the secret of Schubert's moving and voluptuous melancholy ; and it is Schubert he recalls at times, both in his good qualities and certain of his faults. But he wants to be Beethoven or Wagner. And he is wrong ; for he lacks their balance and gigantic force. One saw that only too well when he was conducting the *Choral Symphony*.

But whatever he may be, or whatever disappointment he may have brought me at Strasburg, I will never allow myself to speak lightly or scoffingly of him. I am confident that a musician with so lofty an aim will one day create a work worthy of himself.

. . . . . . .

Richard Strauss is a complete contrast to Mahler. He has always the air of a heedless and discontented child. Tall and slim, rather elegant and super-cilious, he seems to be of a more refined race than most other German artists of to-day. Scornful, *blasé* with success, and very exacting, his bearing towards other musicians has nothing of Mahler's

Q

winning modesty. He is not less nervous than
Mahler, and while he is conducting the orchestra
he seems to indulge in a frenzied dance which
follows the smallest details of his music—music
that is as agitated as limpid water into which a
stone has been flung. But he has a great advantage over Mahler ; he knows how to rest after
his labours. Both excitable and sleepy by nature,
his highly-strung nerves are counterbalanced by his
indolence, and there is in the depths of him a Ba-
varian love of luxury. I am quite sure that when
his hours of intense living are over, after he has
spent an excessive amount of energy, he has hours
when he is only partially alive. One then sees his
eyes with a vague and sleepy look in them ; and
he is like old Rameau, who used to walk about for
hours as if he were an automaton, seeing nothing
and thinking of nothing.

At Strasburg Strauss conducted his *Sinfonia
Domestica*, whose programme seems boldly to defy
reason, and even good taste. In the symphony he
pictures himself with his wife and his boy (" *Meiner
lieben Frau und unserm Jungen gewidmet* ").
" I do not see," said Strauss, " why I should not
compose a symphony about myself ; I find myself
quite as interesting as Napoleon or Alexander."
Some people have replied that everybody else might
not share his interest. But I shall not use that
argument ; it is quite possible for an artist of
Strauss's worth to keep us entertained. What
grates upon me more is the way in which he speaks
of himself. The disproportion between his subject

and the means he has of expressing it is too strong.
Above all, I do not like this display of the inner and
secret self. There is a want of reticence in this
*Sinfonia Domestica*. The fireside, the sitting-room,
and the bedchamber, are open to all-comers. Is
this the family feeling of Germany to-day ? I admit
that the first time I heard the work it jarred upon
me for purely moral reasons, in spite of the liking
I have for its composer. But afterwards I altered
my first opinion, and found the music admirable.
Do you know the programme ?

The first part shows you three people : a man, a
woman, and a child. The man is represented by
three themes : a *motif* full of spirit and humour, a
thoughtful *motif*, and a *motif* expressing eager and
enthusiastic action. The woman has only two
themes : one expressing caprice, and the other love
and tenderness. The child has a single *motif*, which
is quiet, innocent, and not very defined in character ;
its real value is not shown until it is developed. . . .
Which of the two parents is he like? The family
sit round him and discuss him. " He is just like his
father " (*Ganz der Papa*), say the aunts. " He is the
image of his mother " (*Ganz die Mama*), say the
uncles.

The second part of the symphony is a scherzo
which represents the child at play ; there are
terribly noisy games, games of Herculean gaiety,
and you can hear the parents talking all over the
house. How far we seem from Schumann's good
little children and their simple-hearted families !
At last the child is put to bed ; they rock him to

sleep, and the clock strikes seven. Night comes.
There are dreams and some uneasy sleep. Then a
love scene. . . . The clock strikes seven in the
morning. Everybody wakes up, and there is a
merry discussion. We hear a double fugue in which
the theme of the man and the theme of the woman
contradict each other with exasperating and ludi-
crous obstinacy ; and the man has the last word.
Finally there is the apotheosis of the child and
family life.

Such a programme serves rather to lead the listener astray than to guide him. It spoils the idea of
the work by emphasising its anecdotal and rather
comic side. For without doubt the comic side is
there, and Strauss has warned us in vain that he
did not wish to make an amusing picture of married
life, but to praise the sacredness of marriage and
parenthood ; but he possesses such a strong vein
of humour that it cannot help getting the better
of him. There is nothing really grave or religious
about the music, except when he is speaking of the
child ; and then the rough merriment of the man
grows gentle, and the irritating coquetry of the
woman becomes exquisitely tender. Otherwise
Strauss's satire and love of jesting get the upper
hand, and reach an almost epic gaiety and strength.

But one must forget this unwise programme, which
borders on bad taste and at times on something
even worse. When one has succeeded in forgetting
it one discovers a well-proportioned symphony in
four parts—Allegro, Scherzo, Adagio, and Finale in
fugue form—and one of the finest works in contem-

porary music.　It has the passionate exuberance
of Strauss's preceding symphony, *Heldenleben,* but
it is superior in artistic construction ; one may even
say that it is Strauss's most perfect work since *Tod
und Verklärung* (" Death and Transfiguration "),
with a richness of colouring and technical skill that
*Tod und Verklärung* did not possess.　One is dazzled
by the beauty of an orchestration which is light
and pliant, and capable of expressing delicate shades
of feeling ;　and this struck me the more after the
solid massiveness of Mahler's orchestration, which
is like heavy unleavened bread.　With Strauss
everything is full of life and sinew, and there is
nothing wasted.　Possibly the first setting-out of his
themes has rather too schematic a character ; and
perhaps the melodic utterance is rather restricted
and not very lofty ;　but it is very personal, and one
finds it impossible to disassociate his personality
from these vigorous themes that burn with youthful
ardour, and cut the air like arrows, and twist themselves in freakish arabesques.　In the adagio de-
picting night, there is, though in very bad taste,
much seriousness and reverie and stirring emotion.
The fugue at the end is of astonishing sprightliness ;
and is a mixture of colossal jesting and heroic pastoral poetry worthy of Beethoven, whose style it
recalls in the breadth of its development.　The
final apotheosis is filled with life ; its joy makes the
heart beat.　The most extravagant harmonic effects
and the most abominable discords are softened and
almost disappear in the wonderful combination of
*timbres.*　It is the work of a strong and sensual

artist, the true heir of the Wagner of the *Meister-singer.*

. . . . . .

Upon the whole, these works make one see that, in spite of their apparent audacity, Strauss and Mahler are beginning to make a surreptitious retreat from their early standpoint, and are abandoning the symphony with a programme. Strauss's last work will lose nothing by calling itself quite simply *Sinfonia Domestica*, without adding any further information. It is a true symphony; and the same may be said of Mahler's composition. But Strauss and Mahler are already reforming themselves, and are coming back to the model of the classic symphony.

But there are more important conclusions to be drawn from a hearing of this kind. The first is that Strauss's talent is becoming more and more exceptional in the music of his country. With all his faults, which are considerable, Strauss stands alone in his warmth of imagination, in his unquenchable spontaneity and perpetual youth. And his knowledge and his art are growing every day in the midst of other German art which is growing old. German music in general is showing some grave symptoms. I will not dwell on its neurasthenia, for it is passing through a crisis which will teach it wisdom ; but I fear, nevertheless, that this excessive nervous excitement will be followed by torpor. What is really disquieting is that, in spite of all the talent that still abounds, Germany is fast losing her

chief musical endowments.  Her melodic charm has
nearly disappeared.  One could search the music of
Strauss, Mahler, or Hugo Wolf, without finding a
melody of any real value, or of any true originality,
outside its application to a text, or a literary idea,
and its harmonic development.  And besides that,
German music is daily losing its intimate spirit ;
there are still traces of this spirit in Wolf, thanks
to his exceptionally unhappy life ; but there is
very little of it in Mahler, in spite of all his efforts
to concentrate his mind on himself ; and there is
hardly any at all in Strauss, although he is the most
interesting of the three composers.  German musicians have no longer any depth.

I have said that I attribute this fact to the
detestable influence of the theatre, to which nearly
all these artists are attached as *Kapellmeister*, or
directors of opera.  To this they owe the melo-
dramatic character of their music, even though it is
on the surface only—music written for show, and
aiming chiefly at effect.

More baneful even than the influence of the
theatre is the influence of success.  These musicians
have nowadays too many facilities for having their
music played.  A work is played almost before it is
finished, and the musician has no time to live with
his work in solitude and silence.  Besides this, the
works of the chief German musicians are supported
by tremendous booming of some kind or another :
by their *Musikfeste*, by their critics, their press, and
their " Musical Guides " (*Musikführer*), which are
apologetic explanations of their works, scattered

abroad in millions to set the fashion for the sheep-
like public.  And with all this a musician grows soon
contented with himself, and comes to believe any
favourable opinion about his work.  What a difference from Beethoven, who, all his life, was hammer-
ing out the same subjects, and putting his melodies
on the anvil twenty times before they reached their
final form.  That is where Mahler is so lacking.  His
subjects are a rather vulgarised edition of some of
Beethoven's ideas in their unfinished state.  But
Mahler gets no further than the rough sketch.

And, lastly, I want to speak of the greatest danger
of all that menaces music in Germany ; *there is too
much music in Germany.*  This is not a paradox.
There is no worse misfortune for art than a super-
abundance of it.  The music is drowning the musicians.  Festival succeeds festival : the day after the
Strasburg festival there was to be a Bach festival
at Eisenach ; and then, at the end of the week, a
Beethoven festival at Bonn.  Such a plethora of concerts, theatres, choral societies, and chamber-music
societies, absorbs the whole life of the musician.
When has he time to be alone to listen to the music
that sings within him ?  This senseless flood of
music invades the sanctuaries of his soul, weakens
its power, and destroys its sacred solitude and the
treasures of its thought.

You must not think that this excess of music
existed in the old days in Germany.  In the time
of the great classic masters, Germany had hardly
any institutions for the giving of regular concerts,
and choral performances were hardly known.  In

the Vienna of Mozart and Beethoven there was only a single association that gave concerts, and no *Chorvereine* at all, and it was the same with other towns in Germany. Does the wonderful spread of musical-culture in Germany during the last century correspond with its artistic creation ? I do not think so ; and one feels the inequality between the two more every day.

Do you remember Goethe's ballad of *Der Zauberlehrling* (*L'Apprenti Sorcier*) which Dukas so cleverly made into music ? There, in the absence of his master, an apprentice set working some magic spells, and so opened sluice-gates that no one could shut ; and the house was flooded.

This is what Germany has done. She has let loose a flood of music, and is about to be drowned in it.

# CLAUDE DEBUSSY

## PELLÉAS ET MÉLISANDE

THE first performance of *Pelléas et Mélisande* in Paris, on April 30th, 1902, was a very notable event in the history of French music ; its importance can only be compared with that of the first performance of Lully's *Cadmus et Hermione,* Rameau's *Hippolyte et Aricie,* and Gluck's *Iphigénie en Aulide ;* and it may be looked upon as one of the three or four red-letter days in the calendar of our lyric stage.[1]

The success of *Pelléas et Mélisande* is due to many things. Some of them are trivial, such as fashion, which has certainly played its part here as it has in all other successes, though it is a relatively weak part ; some of them are more important, and arise from something innate in the spirit of French genius ; and there are also moral and æsthetic reasons for its success, and. in the widest sense, purely musical reasons.

. . . . . .

In speaking of the moral reasons of the success

[1] May I be allowed to say that I am trying to write this study from a purely historical point of view, by eliminating all personal feeling—which would be of no value here. As a matter of fact, I am not a Debussyite ; my sympathies are with quite another kind of art. But I feel impelled to give homage to a great artist, whose work I am able to judge with some impartiality.

of *Pelléas et Mélisande*, I would like to draw your attention to a form of thought which is not confined to France, but which is common nowadays in a section of the more distinguished members of European society, and which has found expression in *Pelléas et Mélisande*. The atmosphere in which Maeterlinck's drama moves makes one feel the melancholy resignation of the will to Fate. We are shown that nothing can change the order of events ; that, despite our proud illusions, we are not master of ourselves, but the servant of unknown and irresistible forces, which direct the whole tragi-comedy of our lives. We are told that no man is responsible for what he likes and what he loves—that is if he knows what he likes and loves—and that he lives and dies without knowing why.

These fatalistic ideas, reflecting the lassitude of the intellectual aristocracy of Europe, have been wonderfully translated into music by Debussy ; and when you feel the poetic and sensual charm of the music, the ideas become fascinating and intoxicating, and their spirit is very infectious. For there is in all music an hypnotic power which is able to reduce the mind to a state of voluptuous submission.

The cause of the artistic success of *Pelléas et Mélisande* is of a more specially French character, and marks a reaction that is at once legitimate, natural, and inevitable ; I would even say it is vital—a reaction of French genius against foreign art, and especially against Wagnerian art and its awkward representatives in France.

Is the Wagnerian drama perfectly adapted to German genius ? I do not think so ; but that is a question which I will leave German musicians to decide. For ourselves, we have the right to assert that the form of Wagnerian drama is antipathetic to the spirit of French people—to their artistic taste, to their ideas about the theatre, and to their musical feeling. This form may have forced itself upon us, and, by the right of victorious genius, may have strongly influenced the French mind, and may do so again ; but nothing will ever make it anything but a stranger in our land.

It is not necessary to dwell upon the differences of taste. The Wagnerian ideal is, before everything else, an ideal of power. Wagner's passional and intellectual exaltation and his mystic sensualism are poured out like a fiery torrent, which sweeps away and burns all before it, taking no heed of barriers. Such an art cannot be bound by ordinary rules ; it has no need to fear bad taste—and I commend it. But it is easy to understand that other ideals exist, and that another art might be as expressive by its proprieties and niceties as by its richness and force. And this former art—our own—is not so much a reaction against Wagnerian art as a reaction against its caricatures in France and the consequent abuse of an ill-regulated power.

Genius has a right to be what it will—to trample underfoot, if it wishes, taste and morals and the whole of society. But when those who are not geniuses wish to do the same thing they only make themselves ridiculous and odious. There have been too many monkey Wagners in France. During the last ten or twenty years scarcely one French musician has escaped Wagner's influence. One understands only too well the revolt of the French mind, in the name of naturalness and good taste, against exaggerations and extremes of passion, whether sincere or not. *Pelléas et Mélisande* came as a manifestation of this revolt. It is an uncompromising reaction against over-emphasis and excess, and against anything that oversteps the limits of the imagination. This distaste of exaggerated words and sentiments results in what is like a fear of showing the feelings at all, even when they are most deeply stirred. With Debussy the passions almost whisper ; and it is by the imperceptible vibrations of the melodic line that the love in the hearts of the unhappy couple is shown, by the timid " Oh, why are you going ? " at the end of the first act, and the quiet " I love you, too," in the last scene but one. Think of the wild lamentations of the dying Ysolde, and then of the death of Mélisande, without cries and without words.

From a scenic point of view, *Pelléas et Mélisande* is also quite opposed to the Bayreuth ideal. The vast proportions—almost immoderate proportions—of the Wagnerian drama, its compact structure and the intense concentration of mind which from beginning to end holds these enormous works and their ideology together, and which is often displayed at the expense of the action and even the emotions, are as far removed as they can be from the French love of clear, logical, and temperate action. The little pictures of *Pelléas et Mélisande*, small and sharply cut, each marking without stress a new stage in the evolution of the drama, are built up in quite a different way from those of the Wagnerian theatre.

And, as if he wished to accentuate this antagonism, the author of *Pelléas et Mélisande* is now writing a *Tristan*, whose plot is taken from an old French poem, the text of which has been recently brought to light by M. Bédier. In its calm and lofty strain it is a wonderful contrast to Wagner's savage and pedantic, though sublime poem.

But it is especially by the manner in which they conceive the respective relationships of poetry and music to opera that the two composers differ. With Wagner, music is the kernel of the opera, the glowing focus, the centre of attraction ; it absorbs everything, and it stands absolutely first. But that is not the French conception. The musical stage, as we conceive it in France (if not what we actually possess), should present such a combination of the arts as go to make an harmonious whole. We demand that an equal balance shall be kept between poetry and music ; and if their equilibrium must be a little upset, we should prefer that poetry was not the loser, as its utterance is more conscious and rational. That was Gluck's aim ; and because he realised it so well he gained a reputation among the French public which nothing will destroy. Debussy's strength lies in the methods by which he has approached this ideal of musical temperateness and disinterestedness, and in the way he has placed his genius as a composer at the service of the drama. He has never sought to dominate Maeterlinck's poem, or to swallow it up in a torrent of music ; he has made it so much a part of himself that at the present time no Frenchman is able to think of a passage in the play without Debussy's music singing at the same time within him.

But apart from all these reasons that make the work important in the history of opéra, there are purely musical reasons for its success, which are of deeper significance still.[1] *Pelléas et Mélisande* has brought about a reform in the dramatic music of France. This reform is concerned with several things, and, first of all, with recitative.

In France we have never had—apart from a few attempts in *opéra-comique*—a recitative that exactly expressed our natural speech. Lully and Rameau took for their model the high-flown declamation of the tragedy stage of their time. And French opera for the past twenty years has chosen a more dangerous model still—the declamation of Wagner, with its vocal leaps and its resounding and heavy accentuation. Nothing could be more displeasing in French. All people of taste suffered from it, though they did not admit it. At this time, Antoine, Gémier, and Guitry were making theatrical declamation more natural, and this made the exaggerated declamation of the French opera appear more ridiculous and more archaic still. And so a

---

[1] That is for musicians. But I am convinced that with the mass of the public the other reasons have more weight—as is always the case.

reform in recitative was inevitable. Jean-Jacques
Rousseau had foreseen it in the very direction in
which Debussy[1] has accomplished it. He showed in
his *Lettre sur la musique française* that there was no
connection between the inflections of French speech,
" whose accents are so harmonious and simple," and
"the shrill and noisy intonations" of the recitative
of French opera. And he concluded by saying that
the kind of recitative that would best suit us should
" wander between little intervals, and neither raise
nor lower the voice very much ; and should have
little sustained sound, no noise, and no cries of any
description—nothing, indeed, that resembled singing, and little inequality in the duration or value of
the notes, or in their intervals." This is the very
definition of Debussy's recitative.

The symphonic fabric of *Pelléas et Mélisande*
differs just as widely from Wagner's dramas. With
Wagner it is a living thing that springs from one
great root, a system of interlaced phrases whose
powerful growth puts out branches in every direction, like an oak. Or, to take another simile, it is
like a painting, which though it has not been exe-
cuted at a single sitting, yet gives us that impression ;
and, in spite of the retouching and altering to which
it has been subjected, still has the effect of a compact whole, of an indestructible amalgam, from

---

[1] We must also note that during the first half of the seventeenth century people of taste objected to the very theatrical
declamation of French opera. " Our singers believe," wrote
Mersenne, in 1636, " that the exclamations and emphasis used
by the Italians in singing savour too much of tragedies and
comedies, and so they do not wish to employ them."

which nothing can be detached. Debussy's system, on the contrary, is, so to speak, a sort of classic impressionism—an impressionism that is refined, harmonious, and calm ; that moves along in musical pictures, each of which corresponds to a subtle and fleeting moment of the soul's life ; and the painting is done by clever little strokes put in with a soft and delicate touch. This art is more allied to that of Moussorgski (though without any of his roughness) than that of Wagner, in spite of one or two reminiscences of *Parsifal*, which are only extraneous traits in the work. In *Pelléas et Mélisande* one finds no persistent *leitmotifs* running through the work, or themes which pretend to translate into music the life of characters and types ; but, instead, we have phrases that express changing feelings, that change with the feelings. More than that, Debussy's harmony is not, as it was with Wagner and all the German school, a fettered harmony, tightly bound to the despotic laws of counterpoint ; it is, as Laloy[1] has said, a harmony that is first of all harmonious, and has its origin and end in itself.

As Debussy's art only attempts to give the impression of the moment, without troubling itself with what may come after, it is free from care, and takes its fill in the enjoyment of the moment. In the garden of harmonies it selects the most beautiful flowers ; for sincerity of expression takes a second

---

[1] No other critic has, I think, discerned so shrewdly Debussy's art and genius. Some of his analyses are models of clever intuition. The thought of the critic seems to be one with that of the musician.

R

place with it, and its first idea is to please. In this
again it interprets the æsthetic sensualism of the
French race, which seeks pleasure in art, and does
not willingly admit ugliness, even when it seems
to be justified by the needs of the drama and of
truth. Mozart shared the same thought : " Music,"
he said, " even in the most terrible situations,
ought never to offend the ear ; it should charm it
even there; and, in short, always remain music."

As for Debussy's harmonic language, his
originality does not consist, as some of his foolish
admirers have said, in the invention of new chords,
but in the new use he makes of them. A man is not
a great artist because he makes use of unresolved
sevenths and ninths, consecutive major thirds and
ninths, and harmonic progressions based on a scale
of whole tones ; one is only an artist when one
makes them say something. And it is not on
account of the peculiarities of Debussy's style—of
which one may find isolated examples in great composers before him, in Chopin, Liszt, Chabrier, and
Richard Strauss—but because with Debussy these
peculiarities are an expression of his personality,
and because *Pelléas et Mélisande*, " the land of
ninths," has a poetic atmosphere which is like no
other musical drama ever written.

Lastly, the orchestration is purposely restrained,
light, and divided, for Debussy has a fine disdain for
those orgies of sound to which Wagner's art has
accustomed us ; it is as sober and polished as a fine
classic phrase of the latter part of the seventeenth
century. *Ne quid nimis* (" Nothing superfluous "

is the artist's motto. Instead of amalgamating the
*timbres* to get a massive effect, he disengages their
separate personalities, as it were, and delicately
blends them without changing their individual
nature. Like the impressionist painters of to-day,
he paints with primary colours, but with a delicate
moderation that rejects anything harsh as if it were
something unseemly.

. . . . . .

I have given more than enough reasons to account for the success of *Pelléas et Mélisande* and the
place that its admirers give it in the history of opera.
There is every reason to believe that the composer
has not been as acutely conscious of his musico-
dramatic reform as his disciples have been. The
reform with him has a more instinctive character ;
and that is what gives it its strength. It responds
to an unconscious yet profound need of the French
spirit. I would even venture to say that the historical importance of Debussy's work is greater than its
artistic value. His personality is not without faults,
and the gravest are perhaps negative faults—the
absence of certain qualities, and even of the strong
and extravagant faults which made the heroes of the
art world, like Beethoven and Wagner. His voluptuous nature is at once changeable and precise ; and
his dreams are as clear and delicate as the art of a
poet of the Pleiades in the sixteenth century, or of
a Japanese painter. But among al' his gifts he has
a quality which I have not found so evident in any
other musician—except perhaps Mozart; and this

quality is a genius for good taste. Debussy has it in
excess, so that he almost sacrifices the other elements
of art to it, until the passionate force of his music,
even its very life, seems to be impoverished. But
one must not deceive oneself ; that impoverishment
is only apparent, and in all his work there are evi-
dences that his passion is only veiled. It is only the
trembling of the melodic line, or the orchestration
which, like a shadow passing before the eyes, tells
us of the drama that is being played in the hearts
of his characters. This lofty shame of emotion is
something as rare in opera as a Racine tragedy is
in poetry—they are works of the same order, and
both of them perfect flowers of the French spirit.
Anyone who lives in foreign parts and is curious
to know what France is like and understand her
genius should study *Pelléas et Mélisande* as they
would study Racine's *Bérénice*.

Not that Debussy's art entirely represents French
genius any more than Racine's does ; for there is
quite another side to it which is not represented
there ; and that side is heroic action, the intoxication of reason and laughter, the passion for light,
the France of Rabelais, Molière, Diderot, and in
music, we will say—for want of better names—the
France of Berlioz and Bizet. To tell the truth, that
is the France I prefer. But Heaven preserve me
from ignoring the other ! It is the balance between
these two Frances that makes French genius. In
our contemporary music, *Pelléas et Mélisande* is at
one end of the pole of our art and *Carmen* is at the
other. The one is all on the surface, all life, with no

shadows, and no underneath. The other is below
the surface, bathed in twilight, and enveloped in
silence. And this double ideal is the alternation
between the gentle sunlight and the faint mist that
veils the soft, luminous sky of the Isle of France.

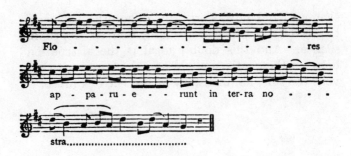

Flo  .  .  .  .  .  .  .  .  .  .  .  .  .  .  res

ap - pa - ru - e - - - runt in ter-ra no - - -

stra.........................................

# THE AWAKENING

## A SKETCH OF THE MUSICAL MOVEMENT IN PARIS
### SINCE 1870

IT is not possible in a few pages to give an account
of forty years of active and fruitful life without
many omissions, and also without a certain dryness
entailed by lists of names. But I have purposely
abstained from trying to arouse interest by any
artifices of writing and treatment, as I wish to let
deeds speak for themselves.

I want to show, by this simple account, the
splendid efforts made by musicians in France since
1870, and the growth of the faith and energy that
has recreated French music. Such an awakening
seems to me a fine thing to look upon, and very
comforting. But few people in France realise it,
outside a handful of musicians. It is to the public
at large I dedicate these pages, so that they may
know what a generation of artists with large hearts

246

and strong determination have done for the honour
of our race. The nation must not be allowed to
forget what she owes to some of her sons.

But you must not accuse me of contradicting
myself if in another work, which will appear at the
same time as this one,[1] I indulge in some sarcasm
over the failings and absurdities of French music
to-day. I think that for the last ten years French
musicians have rather imprudently and prematurely proclaimed their victory, and that, in a
general way, their works—apart from three or four
—are not worth as much as their endeavours. But
their endeavours are heroic ; and I know nothing
finer in the whole history of France. May they
continue ! But that is only possible by practising
a virtue—modesty. The completion of a part is
not the completion of the whole.

## PARIS AND MUSIC

The nature of Paris is so complex and unstable
that one feels it is presumptuous to try to define it.
It is a city so highly-strung, so ingrained with
fickleness, and so changeable in its tastes, that a
book that truly describes it at the moment it is
written is no longer accurate by the time it is
published. And then, there is not only one Paris ;
there are two or three Parises—fashionable Paris,
middle-class Paris, intellectual Paris, vulgar Paris—
all living side by side, but intermingling very little.
If you do not know the little towns within the great

---

[1] *Jean-Christophe à Paris*, 1904.

Town, you cannot know the strong and often inconsistent life of this great organism as a whole.

If one wishes to get an idea of the musical life
of Paris, one must take into account the variety of
its centres and the perpetual flow of its thought—
a thought which never stops, but is always over-
shooting the goal for which it seemed bound.   This
incessant change of opinion is scornfully called
" fashion " by the foreigner.   And there is, without
doubt, in the artistic aristocracy of Paris, as in all
great towns, a herd of idle people on the watch for
new fashions—in art, as well as in dress—who wish
to single out certain of them for no serious reason
at all.   But, in spite of their pretensions, they have
only an infinitesimal share in the changes of artistic
taste.   The origin of these changes is in the Parisian
brain itself—a brain that is quick and feverish,
always working, greedy of knowledge, easily tired,
grasping to-day the splendours of a work, seeing
to-morrow its defects, building up reputations as
rapidly as it pulls them down, and yet, in spite of
all its apparent caprices, always logical and sincere.
It has its momentary infatuations and dislikes, but
no lasting prejudices ;   and, by its curiosity, its
absolute liberty, and its very French habit of
criticising everything, it is a marvellous barometer,
sensitive to all the hidden currents of thought in the
soul of the West, and often indicating, months in
advance, the variations and disturbances of the
artistic and political world.

And this barometer is registering what is happening just now in the world of music, where a move-

ment has been making itself felt in France for several years, whose effect other nations—perhaps more musical nations—will not feel till later. For the nations that have the strongest artistic traditions are not necessarily those that are likely to develop a new art. To do that one must have a virgin soil and spirits untrammelled by a heritage from the past. In 1870 no one had a lighter heritage to bear than French musicians ; for the past had been forgotten, and such a thing as real musical education did not exist.

The musical weakness of that time was a very curious thing, and has given many people the impression that France has never been a musical nation. Historically speaking, nothing could be more wrong. Certainly there are races more gifted in music than others ; but often the seeming differences of race are really the differences of time ; and a nation appears great or little in its art according to what period of its history we consider. England was a musical nation until the Revolution of 1688 ; France was the greatest musical nation in the sixteenth century ; and the recent publications of M. Henry Expert have given us a glimpse of the originality and perfection of the Franco-Belgian art during the Renaissance. But without going back as far as that, we find that Paris was a very musical town at the time of the Restoration, at the time of the first performance of Beethoven's symphonies at the Conservatoire, and the first great works of Berlioz, and the Italian Opera. In Berlioz's *Mémoires* you can read about the enthusiasm, the tears, and the feeling, that the performances of Gluck's and Spontini's operas aroused ; and in the same book one sees clearly that this musical warmth lasted until 1840, after which it died down little by little, and was succeeded by complete musical apathy in the second Empire—an apathy from which Berlioz suffered cruelly, so that one may even say he died crushed by the indifference of the public. At this time Meyerbeer was reigning at the Opera. This incredible weakening of musical feeling in France, from 1840 to 1870, is nowhere better shown than in its romantic and realistic writers, for whom music was an hermetically sealed door. All these artists were " *visuels*," for whom music was only a noise. Hugo is supposed to have said that Germany's inferiority was measured by its superiority in music.[1] " The elder Dumas detested," Berlioz says, " even bad music."[2] The journal of the Goncourts calmly reflects the almost universal scorn of literary men for music. In a conversation which took place in 1862 between Goncourt and Théophile Gautier, Goncourt said :

" We confessed to him our complete infirmity, our musical deafness—we who, at the most, only liked military music."

---

[1] One must at least do Hugo the justice of saying that he always spoke of Beethoven with admiration, although he did not know him. But he rather exalts him in order to take away from the importance of a poet—the only one in the nineteenth century—whose fame was shading his own ; and when he wrote in his *William Shakespeare* that " the great man of Germany is Beethoven " it was understood by all to mean " the great man of Germany is not Goethe."

[2] Written in a letter to his sister, Nanci, on 3 April, 1850.

"Well," said Gautier, "what you tell me pleases me very much. I am like you; I prefer silence to music. I have only just succeeded, after having lived part of my life with a singer,. in being able to tell good music from bad; but it is all the same to me."[1]

And he added:

"But it is a very curious thing that all other writers of our time are like this. Balzac hated music. Hugo could not stand it. Even Lamartine, who himself is like a piano to be hired or sold, holds it in horror!"

It needed a complete upheaval of the nation—a political and moral upheaval—to change that frame of mind. Some indication of the change was making itself felt in the last years of the second Empire. Wagner, who suffered from the hostility or indifference of the public in 1860, at the time when *Tannhäuser* was performed at the Opera, had already found, however, a few understanding people in Paris who discerned his genius and sincerely admired him. The most interesting of the writers who first began to understand musical emotion is Charles Baudelaire. In 1861, Pasdeloup gave the first *Concerts populaires de musique classique* at the Cirque d'Hiver. The Berlioz Festival, organised by M. Reyer, on March 23rd, 1870, a year after Berlioz's death, revealed to France the grandeur of its greatest musical genius, and was the beginning of a campaign of public reparation to his memory.

The disasters of the war in 1870 regenerated the

---

[1] We remark, nevertheless, that that did not prevent Gautier from being a musical critic.

nation's artistic spirit. Music felt its effect immediately.[1] On February 24th, 1871, the *Société nationale de Musique* was instituted to propagate the works of French composers ; and in 1873 the *Concerts de l'Association artistique* were started under M. Colonne's direction ; and these concerts, besides making people acquainted with the classic composers of symphonies and the masters of the young French school, were especially devoted to the honouring of Berlioz, whose triumph reached its summit about 1880.[2] At this time Wagner's success, in its turn, began to make itself felt. For this M. Lamoureux, whose concerts began in 1882, was chiefly responsible. Wagner's influence considerably helped forward the progress of French art, and aroused a love for music in people other than musicians ; and, by his all-embracing personality and the vast domain of his work in art, not only engaged the interest of the musical world, but that of

---

[1] I wish to make known from the beginning that I am only noticing here the greater musical doings of the nation, and making no mention of works which have not had an important influence on this movement.

[2] In the meanwhile France saw the brilliant rise and extinction of a great artist—the most spontaneous of all her musicians— Georges Bizet, who died in 1875, aged thirty-seven. " Bizet was the last genius to discover a new beauty," said Nietzsche ; " Bizet discovered new lands—the Southern lands of music." *Carmen* (1875) and *L'Arlésienne* (1872) are masterpieces of the lyrical Latin drama. Their style is luminous, concise, and well-defined ; the figures are outlined with incisive precision. The music is full of light and movement, and is a great contrast to Wagner's philosophical symphonies, and its popular subject only serves to strengthen its aristocratic distinction. By its nature and its clear perception of the spirit of the race it was well in advance of its time. What a place Bizet might have taken in our art if he had only lived twenty years longer !

the theatrical world, and the world of poetry and the plastic arts. One may say that from 1885 Wagner's work acted directly or indirectly on the whole of artistic thought, even on the religious and intellectual thought of the most distinguished people in Paris. And a curious historical witness of its world-wide influence and momentary supremacy over all other arts was the founding of the *Révue Wagnérienne,* where, united by the same artistic devotion, were found writers and poets such as Verlaine, Mallarmé, Swinburne, Villiers de l'Isle Adam, Huysmans, Richepin, Catulle Mendès, Édouard Rod, Stuart Merrill, Ephraïm Mikhaël, etc., and painters like Fantin-Latour, Jacques Blanche, Odilon Redon ; and critics like Teodor de Wyzewa, H. S. Chamberlain, Hennequin, Camille Benoît, A. Ernst, de Fourcaud, Wilder, E. Schuré, Soubies, Malherbe, Gabriel Mourey, etc. These writers not only discussed musical subjects, but judged painting, literature, and philosophy, from a Wagnerian point of view. Hennequin compared the philosophic systems of Herbert Spencer and Wagner. Teodor de Wyzewa made a study of Wagnerian literature—not the literature that commentated and the paintings that illustrated Wagner's works, but the literature and the painting that were inspired by Wagner's principles—from Egyptian statuary to Degas's paintings, from Homer's writings to those of Villiers de l'Isle Adam ! In a word, the whole universe was seen and judged by the thought of Bayreuth. And though this folly scarcely lasted more than three or four years—the length of the life of that little magazine

—Wagner's genius dominated nearly the whole of French art for ten or twelve years.[1] An ardent musical propaganda by means of concerts was carried on among the public ; and the young intellectuals of the day were won over. But the finest service that Wagnerism rendered to French art was that it interested the general public in music ; although the tyranny its influence exercised became, in time, very stifling.

Then, in 1890, there were signs of a movement that was in revolt against its despotism. The great wind from the East began to drop, and veered to the North. Scandinavian and Russian influences were making themselves felt. An exaggerated infatuation for Grieg, though limited to a small number of people, was an indication of the change in public taste. In 1890, César Franck died in Paris. Belgian by birth and temperament, and French in feeling and by musical education, he had remained outside the Wagnerian movement in his own serene and fecund solitude. To his intellectual greatness and the charm his personal genius held for the little band of friends who knew and revered him he added the authority of his knowledge. Unconsciously he brought back to us the soul of Sebastian Bach, with its infinite richness and depth ; and through this he found himself the head of a school (without having wished it) and the greatest teacher of contemporary French music. After his death, his

---

[1] Its influence is shown, in varying degrees, in works such as M. Reyer's *Sigurd* (1884), Chabrier's *Gwendoline* (1886), and M. Vincent d'Indy's *Le Chant de la Cloche* (1886).

name was the means of rallying together the
younger school of musicians. In 1892, the *Chanteurs de Saint-Gervais*, under the direction of M.
Charles Bordes, reinstated to honour and popu-
larised Gregorian and Palestrinian music ; and,
following the initiative of their director, the *Schola
Cantorum* was founded in 1894 for the revival of
religious music. Ambition grew with success ; and
from the *Schola* sprang the *École Supérieure de
Musique*, under the direction of Franck's most
famous pupil, M. Vincent d'Indy. This school,
founded on a solid knowledge, not only of the
classics, but of the primitives in music, took from
its very beginning in 1900 a frankly national
character, and was in some ways opposed to German
art. At the same time, performances of Bach and
seventeenth- and eighteenth-century music became
more and more frequent ; and more intimate relationship with the artists of other countries, repeated
visits of the great *Kapellmeister*, foreign virtuosi and
composers (especially Richard Strauss), and, lastly,
of Russian composers, completed the education of
the Parisian musical public, who, after repeated
rebukes from the critics, became conscious of the
awakening of a national personality, and of an impatient desire to free itself from German tutelage.
By turns it gratefully and warmly received M.
Bruneau's *Le Rêve* (1891), M. d'Indy's *Fervaal*
(1898), M. Gustave Charpentier's *Louise* (1900)—
all of which seemed like works of liberation. But,
as a matter of fact, these lyric dramas were by no
means free from foreign influences, and especially

from Wagnerian influences. M. Debussy's *Pelléas et Mélisande*, in 1902, seemed to mark more truly the emancipation of French music. From this time on, French music felt that it had left school, and claimed to have founded a new art, which reflected the spirit of the race, and was freer and suppler than the Wagnerian art. These ideas, which were seized upon and enlarged by the press, brought about rather quickly a conviction in French artists of France's superiority in music. Is that conviction justified? The future alone can tell us. But one may see by this brief outline of events how real is the evolution of the musical spirit in France since 1870, in spite of the apparent contradictions of fashion which appear on the surface of art. It is the spirit of France that is, after long oppression and by a patient but eager initiation, realising its power and wishing to dominate in its turn.

I wanted at first to trace the broad line of the movement which for the last thirty years has been affecting French music; and now I shall consider the musical institutions that have had their share in this movement. You will not be surprised if I ignore some of the most celebrated, which have lost their interest in it, in order that I may consider those that are the true authors of our regeneration.

## MUSICAL INSTITUTIONS BEFORE 1870

It is not by any means the oldest and most celebrated musical institutions which have taken the largest share in this evolution of music in the last thirty years.

The *Académie des Beaux-Arts,* where six chairs are reserved for the musical section, could have played a very important part in the musical organisation of France by the authority of its name, and by the many prizes that it gives for composition and criticism, especially by the *Prix de Rome,* which it awards every year. But it does not play its part well, partly because of the antiquated statutes that govern it, by which a handful of musicians are associated with a great number of painters, sculptors, and architects, who are ignorant of music and mock at the musicians, as they did in the time of Berlioz ; and partly because it is the custom of the Academy that the little group of musicians shall be trained in a very conservative way. One of the names of these musicians is justly celebrated—that of M. Saint-Saëns ; but there are others whose fame is of poorer quality, and others still who have no fame at all. And the whole forms a little group, which though it does not put any actual obstacles in the way of the progress of art, yet does not look upon it favourably, but remains rather apart in an indifferent or even hostile spirit.

The *Conservatoire national de Musique et de Déclamation,* which dates from the last years of the *Ancien Régime* and the Revolution, was designed by its patriotic and democratic origin to serve the cause of national art and free progress.[1] It was

---

[1] One knows that the Conservatoire originated in *L'École gratuite de musique de la garde nationale parisienne,* founded in 1792 by Sarrette, and directed by Gossec. It was then a civic and military school, but, according to Chénier, was changed into the *Institut national de musique* on 8 November, 1793, and into

S

for a long time the corner-stone of the edifice of
music in Paris. But although it has always num-
bered in its ranks many illustrious and devoted professors—among whom it recognised, a little late, the
founder of the young French school, César Franck—
and though the majority of artists who have made
a name in French music have received its teaching,
and the list of laureates of Rome who have come
from its composition classes includes all the heads
of the artistic movement to-day in all its diversity,
and ranges from M. Massenet to M. Bruneau, and
from M. Charpentier to M. Debussy—in spite of all
this, it is no secret that, since 1870, the official
action with regard to the movement amounts to
almost nothing ; though we must at least do it
justice, and say that it has not hindered it.[1] But
if the spirit of this academy has often destroyed the
effect of the excellent teaching there, by making
success in academic competitions the chief aim of
the professors and their pupils, yet a certain freedom

the *Conservatoire* on 3 August, 1795. This Republican Conservatoire made it its business to keep in contact with the spirit of
the country, and was directly opposed to the Opera, which was
of monarchical origin. See M. Constant Pierre's work *Le
Conservatoire national de musique* (1900), and M. Julien Tiersot's
very interesting book *Les Fêtes et les Chants de la Révolution
française* (1908).

[1] You must remember that I am speaking here of *official*
action only ; for there have always been masters among the
Conservatoire teaching staff who have united a fine musical
culture with a broad-minded and liberal spirit. But the influence
of these independent minds is, generally speaking, small ; for
they have not the disposing of academic successes ; and when,
by exception, they have a wide influence, like that of César
Franck, it is the result of personal work outside the Conservatoire
—work that is, as often as not, opposed to Conservatoire principles.

has always reigned in the institution. And though this freedom is mainly the result of indifference, it has, however, permitted the more independent temperaments to develop in peace—from Berlioz to M. Ravel. One should be grateful for this. But such virtues are too negative to give the Conservatoire a high place in the musical history of the Third Republic ; and it is only lately, under the direction of M. Gabriel Fauré, that it has endeavoured, not without difficulty, to get back its place at the head of French art, which it had lost, and which others had taken.

The *Société des Concerts du Conservatoire*, founded in 1828 under the direction of Habeneck, has had its hour of glory in the musical history of Paris. It was through this society that Beethoven's greatness was revealed to France.[1] It was at the Conservatoire that the early important works of Berlioz were first given : *La Fantastique, Harold*, and *Roméo et Juliette*. It was there, nearer our own time, that Saint-Saëns's *Symphonie avec Orgue* and César Franck's *Symphonie* were played for the first time. But for a long time the Conservatoire seemed to take its name too literally, and to restrict its sphere to that of a museum for classical music. In later

---

[1] It is to be noted that since 1807 the Conservatoire pupils have made Beethoven's symphonies familiar to Parisians. The *Symphony in C minor* was performed by them in 1808 ; the *Heroic* in 1811. It was in connection with one of these performances that the *Tablettes de Polymnie* gave a curious appreciation of Beethoven, which is quoted by M. Constant Pierre : " This composer is often grotesque and uncouth, and sometimes flies majestically like an eagle and sometimes crawls along stony paths. It is as though one had shut up doves and crocodiles together."

years, however, the *Société des Concerts*, with M.
Marty, began to consider new works. Its orchestra,
composed of eminent instrumentalists, enjoys a
classical fame ; though it is now no longer alone in
the excellence of its performances, and has perhaps
lost a little the secret that it claimed to possess for
the interpretation of great classical works. It
excels in works of a neo-classic character, like those
of M. Saint-Saëns, which are stronger in style and
taste than in life and passion. The Conservatoire
concerts have also a relative superiority over other
concerts in Paris in the performance of choral works,
which up to the present have been very second-rate.
But these concerts are not easy of access for the
general public, as the number of seats for sale is
very limited. And so the society is representative
of a little public whose taste is, broadly speaking,
conservative and official ; and the noise of the
strife outside its doors only reaches its ears slowly,
and with a deadened sound.

The influence of the Conservatoire is, in music
especially, an influence of the past and of the
Government. One may say much the same of the
Opera. This ancient association, which bears the
imposing name of *Académie nationale de Musique*
and dates from 1669, is a sort of national institution
which is more concerned with the history of official
art than with living art. The satire with which
Jean-Jacques describes, in his *Nouvelle Héloïse*, the
stiff solemnity and mournful pomp of its performances has not lost much of its truth. What is
lacking in the Opera to-day is the enthusiasm that

accompanied its former musical struggles in the times of the " *Encyclopédistes* " and the " *guerre des coins.*" The great battles of art are now fought outside its doors ; and it has become by degrees a showy *salon*, a little faded perhaps, where the public is more interested in itself than in the performance. In spite of the enormous sums that it swallows up every year (nearly four million francs),[1] only one or two new pieces are produced in a year, and they are rarely works that are representative of the modern school. And though it has at last admitted Wagner's dramas into its repertory, one can no longer consider these works, half a century old, to be in the vanguard of music. The most esteemed masters of the French school, such as Massenet, Reyer, Chausson, and Vincent d'Indy, had to seek refuge in the Théâtre de la Monnaie at Brussels before they could get their works received at the Opera in Paris. And the classical composers fare no better. Neither *Fidelio* nor Gluck's tragedies—with the exception of *Armide*, which was put on under pressure of fashion—are represented ; and when by chance they give *Freischütz* or *Don Juan*, one wonders if it would not have been better to let them rest in oblivion, rather than treat them sacrilegiously by adding, cutting, introducing ballets and new recitatives, and deforming their style so as to bring them " up to date."[2] In spite of the changes of

---

[1] This is according to M. Rivet's report on the *Beaux-Arts* in 1906. The Opera employs 1370 people, and its expenses are about 3,988,000 francs. The annual grant of the State comes to about 800,000 francs.

[2] On the occasion of the revival of *Don Juan* in 1902, the

taste and the campaign of the press, the Opera has
remained to this day as it was in the time of Meyerbeer and Gounod and their disciples. But it would
be foolish to pretend that it has not its public. The
receipts show well enough that *Faust* is in greater
favour than *Siegfried* or *Tristan*, not to speak of the
more recent works of the new French school, which
cannot be acclimatised there.

Without doubt, the enormous stage at the Opera
does not lend itself well to modern musical dramas,
which are intimate and concentrated, and would be
lost in its immense space, which is more adapted for
formal processions like the marches in the *Prophète*
and *Aïda*. Besides this, there is the conventional
acting of the majority of the singers, the dull life-
lessness of the choruses, the defective acoustics,
and the exaggerated utterance and gestures of the
actors, demanded by the great dimensions of the
place—all of which is a serious obstacle to the conception of a living and simple art. But the chief
obstacle will always lie in the very nature of such a
theatre—a theatre of luxury and vanity, created
for a set of snobs, whose least interest is the music,
who have not enough intellect to create a fashion,
but who servilely follow every fashion after it is
thirty years old. Such a theatre no longer counts
in the history of French music ; and its next
directors will need a vast amount of ingenuity and
energy to get a semblance of life into such a dead
colossus.

*Revue Musicale* counted up the pages that had been added to
the original score. They came to two hundred and twenty-
eight.

But it is quite another affair with the Opéra-Comique. This theatre has taken a very active part in the development of modern music. Without renouncing its classic traditions, or its delightful repertory of the old *opéra-comiques*, it has had understanding enough, under the judicious management of M. Albert Carré, to hold itself open for any interesting productions in dramatic music. It takes no side among the different schools ; and the representatives of the old-fashioned light opera with their songs elbow the leaders of the advanced school. No association has done more important work, among musical dramas as well as musical comedies, during the last twenty years. In this theatre, which produced *Carmen* in 1875, *Manon* in 1884, and the *Roi d'Ys* in 1888, were played the principal dramas of M. Bruneau, as well as M. Charpentier's *Louise*, M. Debussy's *Pelléas et Mélisande*, and M. Dukas's *Ariane et Barbebleue*. It may seem astonishing that such works should have found a place at the Opéra-Comique and not at the Opera. But if two musical theatres of different kinds exist, one of which pretends to have the monopoly of great art, while the other with a simpler and more intimate character seeks only to please, it is always the latter that has a better chance of development and of making new discoveries ; for the first is oppressed by traditions that become ever stiffer and more pedantic, while the other with its simplicity and lack of pretension is able to accommodate itself to any manner of life. How many artists have revolutionised their times while they were merely looked upon as people who amused! Frescobaldi and Philipp Emanuel Bach brought fresh life to art, but were scorned by the so-called representatives of fine art ; Mozart's *opere buffe* have more of truth and life in them than his *opere serie ;* and there is as much dramatic power in an *opéra-comique* like *Carmen* as in all the repertory of grand Opera to-day. And so the Opéra-Comique theatre has become the home of the boldest experiments in musical drama. The most daring or the most violent ventures into musical realism, after the manner of Charpentier or Bruneau, and the subtle fantasies of a delicate art of dreams, like that of Debussy, have found a welcome there. It has also been open to various kinds of foreign art : Humperdinck's *Hänsel und Gretel*, Verdi's *Falstaff*, the works of Puccini, Mascagni, and the young Italian school, Richard Strauss's *Feuersnot*, Rimsky-Korsakow's *Snégourotchka*, have all been played. And they have even given the classic masterpieces of opera there : *Fidelio*, *Orfeo*, *Alceste*, the two *Iphigénies ;* and taken more pains with them and mounted them with more pious zeal than they do at the Opera. The operas themselves are more at home there, too, for the size of the theatre is more like that of the eighteenth-century theatres. It is true that the stage rather lacks depth ; but the ingenuity of the director and the admirable scenic artists he employs has succeeded in making one forget this defect, and accomplished marvels. No theatre in Paris has more artistic staging, and some of the scenery that has been designed lately is a masterpiece of its kind. The Opéra-Comique has also the advantage of excellent conductors, and one of them, M. Messager, who is now Director, has, by his clever interpretations, greatly contributed to the success of the works of the new school.

## NEW MUSICAL INSTITUTIONS

### 1. *The Société Nationale*

Before 1870, French music had already in the Opera and the Opéra-Comique (without counting the various endeavours of the Théâtre Lyrique) an outlet which was nearly enough for the needs of her dramatic productions. Even when musical taste was most decadent, the works of Gounod, Ambroise Thomas, and Massé, had always upheld the name of French *opéra-comique*. But what was almost entirely lacking was an outlet for symphonic music and chamber-music. " Before 1870," wrote M. Saint-Saëns in *Harmonie et Mélodie*, " a French composer who was foolish enough to venture on to the ground of instrumental music had no other means of getting his works performed than by himself arranging a concert for them." Such was Berlioz's case ; for he had to gather together an orchestra and hire a room each time he wished to get a hearing for his great symphonies. The financial result was often disastrous : the performance of the *Damnation de Faust* in 1846 was, for example, a complete failure, and he had to give it up. The Conservatoire, which was formerly more hospitable, rather reluctantly performed a portion of *L'Enfance du Christ;* but it gave young composers no encouragement.

The first man who attempted to make the symphony popular, M. Saint-Saëns tells us in his *Portraits et Souvenirs,* was Seghers, a dissentient member of the *Société des Concerts du Conservatoire,* who during several years (1848–1854) was conductor of the *Société de Sainte-Cécile,* which had its quarters in a room in the rue de la Chaussée d'Antin. There he had performed Mendelssohn's *Symphonie Italienne,* the overtures to *Tannhäuser* and *Manfred,* Berlioz's *Fuite en Égypte,* and Gounod's and Bizet's early works. But lack of money cut short his efforts.

Pasdeloup took up the work. After having been conductor for the *Société des jeunes artistes du Conservatoire* since 1851, in the Salle Herz, he founded, in 1861, at the Cirque d'Hiver, with the financial support of a rich moneylender, the first *Concerts populaires de musique classique.* Unhappily, says M. Saint-Saëns, Pasdeloup, even up to 1870, made an almost exclusive selection of German classical works. He raised an impenetrable barrier before the young French school, and the only French works he played were symphonies by Gounod and Gouvy, and the overtures of *Les Francs-Juges* and *La Muette.* It was impossible to set up a rival society against him ; and an exclusive monopoly in music was, therefore, held by him. According to M. Saint-Saëns he was a mediocre musician, and had, in spite of his passion for music, "immense incapacity." In *Harmonie et Mélodie* M. Saint-Saëns says : "The few chamber-music societies that existed were also closed to all new-comers ; their programmes only contained the names of undisputed celebrities, the writers of classic symphonies. In those times one had really to be devoid of all common sense to write music."

A new generation was growing up, however,—a generation that was serious and thoughtful, that was more attracted by pure music than by the theatre, that was filled with a burning desire to found a national art. To this generation M. Saint-Saëns and M. Vincent d'Indy belong. The war of 1870 strengthened these ideas about music, and, while the war was still raging, there sprang from them the *Société Nationale de Musique*.

One must speak of this society with respect, for it was the cradle and sanctuary of French art.[1] All that was great in French music from 1870 to 1900 found a home there. Without it, the greater part of the works that are the honour of our music would never have been played ; perhaps they would not ever have been written. The Society possessed the rare merit of being able to anticipate public opinion by ten or eleven years, and in some ways it has formed the public mind and obliged it to honour those whom the Society had already recognised as great musicians.

The two founders of the Society were Romaine

[1] The facts which follow are taken from the archives of the *Société Nationale de Musique*, and have been given me by M. Pierre de Bréville, the Society's secretary.

Bussine, professor of Singing at the Conservatoire, and M. Camille Saint-Saëns. And, following their initiative, César Franck, Ernest Guiraud, Massenet, Garcin, Gabriel Fauré, Henri Duparc, Théodore Dubois, and Taffanel, joined forces with them, and at a meeeting on 25 February, 1871, agreed to found a musical society that should give hearings to the works of living French composers exclusively. The first meetings were interrupted by the doings of the Commune ; but they began again in October, 1871. The Society's early statutes were drawn up by Alexis de Castillon, a military officer and a talented composer, who, after having served in the war of 1870 at the head of the *mobiles* of Eure-et-Loire, was one of the founders of French chamber-music, and died prematurely in 1873, aged thirty-five. It was these statutes, signed by Saint-Saëns, Castillon, and Garcin, that gave the Society its title of *Société Nationale de Musique,* and its device, *"Ars gallica."* This is what the statutes say about the aims of the Society :

" The aim of the Society is to aid the production and the popularisation of all serious musical works, whether published or unpublished, of French composers ; to encourage and bring to light, so far as is in its power, all musical endeavour, whatever form it may take, on condition that there is evidence of high, artistic aspiration on the part of the author. . . . It is in brotherly love, with complete forgetfulness of self, and with the firm intention of aiding one

another as far as they can, that the members of
the Society will co-operate, each in his own
sphere of ʾction, for the study and performance
of the works which they· shall be called upon to
select and to interpret."

The first Committee was made up as follows :
President, Bussine ; Vice-President, Saint-Saëns ;
Secretary, Alexis de Castillon ; Under-Secretary,
Jules Garcin ; Treasurer, Lenepveu. The members
of the Committee were : César Franck, Théodore
Dubois, E. Guiraud, Fissot, Bourgault-Ducoudray,
Fauré, and Lalo.

The first concert was given on 25 November,
1871, in the Salle Pleyel; and it is worthy of note
that the first work played was a trio of César Franck's.
Since then the Society has given three hundred and
fifty performances of chamber-music or orchestral
works. The best known French composers and
virtuosi have taken part as executants, among
others : César Franck, Saint-Saëns, Massenet, Bizet,
Vincent d'Indy, Fauré, Chabrier, Guiraud, Debussy,
Lekeu, Lamoureux, Chevillard, Taffanel, Widor,
Messager, Diémer, Sarasate, Risler, Cortot, Ysaye,
etc. And among the compositions that have been
played for the first time it is enough to mention the
following :

César Franck : Nearly the whole of his works,
including his Sonata, Trio, Quartette, Quintette,
Symphonic Variations, Preludes and Fugues, Mass,
*Rédemption, Psyché,* and a part of *Les Béatitudes.*

Saint-Saëns : *Phaéton, Second Symphony,* Sonatas,

Persian Melodies, the *Rapsodie d'Auvergne*, and a quartette.

Vincent d'Indy : The trilogy of *Wallenstein*, the *Poême des Montagnes*, the *Symphonie sur un thème montagnard*, and quartettes.

Chabrier : Part of *Gwendoline*.

Lalo : Fragments of the *Roi d'Ys*, Rhapsodies and Symphonies.

Bruneau : *Penthésilée, La Belle au Bois Dormant.*

Chausson : *Viviane, Hélène, La Tempête.* a quartette and a symphony.

Debussy : *La Damoiselle élue*, the *Prélude à l'après-midi d'un faune*, a quartette, pieces for the pianoforte, and melodies.

Dukas : *L'Apprenti Sorcier*, and a sonata for the pianoforte.

Lekeu : *Andromède.*

Alberic Magnard : Symphonies and a quartette.

Ravel : *Schéhérazade, Histoires Naturelles*, etc.

Saint-Saëns was director with Bussine until 1886. But from 1881 the influence of Franck and his disciples became more and more felt ; and Saint-Saëns began to lose interest in the efforts of the new school. In 1886 there was a division of opinion about a proposition of Vincent d'Indy's to introduce the works of classical masters and foreign composers into the programmes. This proposition was adopted ; but Saint-Saëns and Bussine sent in their resignations. Franck then became the true president, although he refused the title ; and after his death, in 1890, Vincent d'Indy took his place. Under these two directors a quite important place was given to old and classical music by composers such as Palestrina, Vittoria, Josquin, Bach, Händel, Rameau, Gluck, Beethoven, Schumann, Liszt, and Brahms. Foreign contemporary music only occupied a very limited place. Wagner's name only appears once, in a transcription of the *Venusberg* for the pianoforte ; and Richard Strauss's name figures only against his Quartette. Grieg had his hour of popularity there about 1887, as well as the Russians—Moussorgski, Borodine, Rimsky-Korsakow, Liadow, and Glazounow—whom M. Debussy has perhaps helped to make known to us. At the present moment the Society seems more exclusively French than ever ; and the influence of M. Vincent d'Indy and the school of Franck is predominant. That is only natural ; the *Société Nationale* most truly earned its title to glory by discerning César Franck's genius ; for the Society was a little sanctuary where the great artist was honoured at a time when he was ignored or laughed at by the rest of the world. This character of a sanctuary was kept even after victory. In its general programme of 1903–1904, the Society reminded us with pride that it had remained faithful to the promises made in 1871 ; and it added that if, in order to permit its members to keep abreast of the general progress of art, it had little by little allowed classical masterpieces and modern foreign works of interest on its programmes, it had, however, always kept its guest-chamber open, and shaped many a future reputation there.

Nothing is truer. The *Société Nationale* is indeed

a guest-chamber, where for the past thirty years a guest-chamber art and guest-chamber opinions have been formed ; and from it some of the profoundest and most poetic French music has been derived, such as Franck's and Debussy's chamber-music. But its atmosphere is becoming daily more rarefied. That is a danger. It is to be feared that this art and thought may be absorbed by the decadent subtleties or pedantic scholasticism which is apt to accompany all coteries—in short, that its music will be salon-music rather than chamber-music. Even the Society itself seems to have felt this at times ; and at different periods has sought contact with the general public, and put itself into direct communication with it. " It becomes more and more necessary," wrote M. Saint-Saëns, " that French composers should find something intermediate between an intimate hearing of their music and a performance of it before the general public—something which would not be a speculative thing like a big concert, but which would be analogous to the artistic attraction of an exhibition of painting, and which would dare everything. It is a new aim for the *Société Nationale*." But it does not seem that it has yet attained this goal, nor that it is near attaining it, despite some not quite happy attempts.

But at least the *Société Nationale* has gloriously achieved the task it set itself. In thirty years it has created in Paris a little centre of earnest composers of symphonies and chamber-music, and a cultured public that seems able to understand them.

## 2. *The Grand Symphony Concerts*

Although it was an urgent matter that young French composers should unite to withstand the general indifference of the public, it was more urgent still that that indifference should be attacked, and that music should be brought within reach of ordinary people. It was a matter of taking up and completing Pasdeloup's work in a more artistic and more modern spirit.

A publisher of music, Georges Hartmann, feeling the forces that were drawing together in French art, gathered about him the greater part of the talented men of the young school—Franck, Bizet, Saint-Saëns, Massenet, Delibes, Lalo, A. de Castillon, Th. Dubois, Guiraud, Godard, Paladilhe, and Joncières—and undertook to produce their works in public. He rented the Odéon theatre, and got together an orchestra, the conductorship of which he entrusted to M. Édouard Colonne. And on 2 March, 1873, the *Concert National* was inaugurated in a musical matinée, where M. Saint-Saëns played his *Concerto in G minor* and Mme. Viardot sang Schubert's *Roi des Aulnes*. In the first year six ordinary concerts were given, and, besides that, two sacred concerts with choirs, at which César Franck's *Rédemption* and Massenet's *Marie-Magdeleine* were performed. In 1874 the Odéon was abandoned for the Châtelet. This venture attracted some attention, and the concerts were patronised by the public ; but the financial results were not

T

great.[1]  Hartmann was discouraged and wished to give the whole thing up.  But M. Édouard Colonne conceived the idea of turning his orchestra into a society, and of continuing the work under the name of *Association Artistique*.  Among the artist-founders were MM. Bruneau, Benjamin Godard, and Paul Hillemacher.  Its early days were full of struggle ; but owing to the perseverance of the Association all obstacles were finally overcome. In 1903 a festival was held to celebrate its thirtieth anniversary.  During these thirty years it had given more than eight hundred concerts, and had performed the works of about three hundred composers, of which half were French. ˙ The four composers most frequently heard at the Châtelet were Saint-Saëns, Wagner, Beethoven, and Berlioz.[2]

Berlioz is almost the exclusive property of the Châtelet.  Not only have they performed his works there more frequently than anywhere else,[3] but they are better understood there than in other places. The Colonne orchestra and its conductor, gifted with great warmth of spirit,—though it is sometimes a little intemperate—are rather bothered by works of a classic nature and by those that show contemplative feeling ; but they give wonderful ex-

---

[1] It must be remembered that the prices of the seats were much cheaper than they are to-day ; the best were only three francs.

[2] There were about 340 performances of Saint-Saëns' works, 380 of Wagner's, 390 of Beethoven's, and 470 of Berlioz's.  I owe these details to the kind information of M. Charles Malherbe and M. Léon Petitjean, the secretary of the Colonne concerts.

[3] The *Damnation de Faust* alone was given in its entirety a hundred and fifty times in thirty years.

pression to Berlioz's tumultuous romanticism, his poetic enthusiasm, and the bright and delicate colouring of his paintings and his musical landscapes. Although Berlioz has his place at the Chevillard and Conservatoire concerts, it is to the Châtelet that his followers flock ; and their enthusiasm has not been affected by the campaign that for several years has been directed against Berlioz by some French critics under the influence of the younger musical party—the followers of d'Indy and Debussy.

It is also at the Châtelet that the keenest musical passion has been preserved in the public, even to this day. Thanks to the size of the theatre, which is one of the largest in Paris, and to the great number of cheap seats, you may always find there a number of young students who make the most interested kind of public possible. And the music is something more than a pleasure to them—it is a necessity. There are some that make great sacrifices in order to have a seat at the Sunday concerts. And many of these young men and women live all the week on the thought of forgetting the world for a few hours in musical enjoyment. Such a public did not exist in France before 1870. It is to the honour of the Châtelet and the Pasdeloup concerts to have created it.

Édouard Colonne has done more than educate ꭲusical taste in France ; for no one has worked ꭓarder than he to break down the barriers that ꭓeparated the French public from the art of other ꭓands ; and, at the same time, he has himself helped

to make French art known to foreigners. When he
himself was conducting concerts all over Europe
he entrusted the conductorship at the Châtelet to
the great German *Kapellmeister* and to foreign
composers—to Richard Strauss, Grieg, Tschaikow-
sky, Hans Richter, Hermann Levi, Mottl, Nikisch,
Mengelberg, Siegfried Wagner, and many others.
No other conductor has done so much for Parisian
music during the last thirty years ; and we must
not forget it.[1]

The Lamoureux concerts have had from the beginning a very different character from the Colonne
concerts. That difference lies partly in the personality of the two conductors, and partly in the
fact that the Lamoureux concerts, although of later
date than the Colonne concerts by less than ten
years, represent a new generation in music. The
progress of the musical public was singularly rapid :
hardly had they explored the rich treasure-house
of Berlioz's music than they were making discoveries
in the world of Wagner. And in that world they
needed a new guide, who had intimate knowledge of
Wagner's art and of German art in general. Charles
Lamoureux was that guide. In 1873 he conducted
special performances of Bach and Händel, given by
the *Société de l'Harmonie sacrée*. After leaving the
conductorship of the Opera, he inaugurated, on
21 October, 1881, at the Château-d'Eau theatre,
the *Société des Nouveaux Concerts*. These concerts
had at first very comprehensive programmes of

---

[1] It is known that M. Colonne has now a helper in M. Gabriel
Pierné, who will succeed him when he retires.

every kind of music and every kind of school. At the first concert there were works of Beethoven, Händel, Gluck, Sacchini, Cimarosa, and Berlioz. In the first year Lamoureux had Beethoven's *Ninth Symphony* performed, as well as a large part of *Lohengrin*, and numerous works of young French musicians. Various compositions of Lalo, Vincent d'Indy, and Chabrier, were performed there for the first time. But it was especially to the study of Wagner's works that Lamoureux most gladly devoted himself. It was he who gave the first hearings of Wagner in their entirety in France, such as the first and second act of *Tristan*, in 1884-1885. The Wagnerian battle was still going on at that time, as the notice printed at the head of the programme of *Tristan* shows.

" The management of the *Société des Nouveaux Concerts* is desirous of avoiding any disturbance during the performance of the second act of *Tristan*, and urgently and respectfully begs that the audience will abstain from giving any mark of their approval or disapproval before the end of the act."

The same year, in the Eden theatre, to which the concerts had been transferred, Lamoureux conducted, for the first time in Paris, the first act of the *Walküre*. In these concerts the tenor, Van Dyck, made his *début;* later, he was one of the leading performers at Bayreuth. In 1886-1887 Lamoureux rehearsed and conducted the only performance of *Lohengrin* at the Eden theatre. Disturbances in the streets prevented further performances. Lamoureux then established himself in the concert-room of the Cirque des Champs Élysées, where for eleven years he has given what are called the *Concerts-Lamoureux*. He continued to spread the knowledge of Wagner's works, and has sometimes had the help of some of the most celebrated of the Bayreuth artists, among others, that of Mme. Materna and Lilli Lehmann. At the end of the season of 1897 Lamoureux wished to disband his orchestra in order to conduct concerts abroad. But the members of the orchestra decided to remain together under the name of the *Association des Concerts-Lamoureux*, with Lamoureux's son-in-law, M. Camille Chevillard, as conductor. But Lamoureux was not long before he returned to the conductorship of the concerts, which had now returned to the Château-d'Eau theatre ; and a few months before his death, in 1899, he conducted the first performance of *Tristan* at the Nouveau theatre. And so he had the happiness of being present at the complete triumph of the cause for which he had fought so stubbornly for nearly twenty years.[1]

Lamoureux's performances of Wagner's works have been among the best that have ever been given. He had a regard for the work as a whole and a care for its details, to which the Colonne orchestra did not quite attain. On the other hand, Lamoureux's

[1] My statements may be verified by the account published in the *Revue Éolienne* of January, 1902, by M. Léon Bourgeois, secretary of the Committee of the *Association des Concerts-Lamoureux*.

defect was the exuberant liveliness with which he interpreted compositions of a romantic nature. He did not fully understand these works ; and although he knew much more about classic art than his rival, he rendered its letter rather than its spirit, and paid such sedulous attention to detail that music like Beethoven's lost its intensity and its life. But both his talents and his defects fitted him to be an excellent interpreter of the young neo-Wagnerian school, the principal representatives of which in France were then M. Vincent d'Indy and M. Emmanuel Chabrier. Lamoureux had need, to a certain extent, to be himself directed either by the living traditions of Bayreuth, or by the thought of modern and living composers ; and the greatest service he rendered to French music was his creation, thanks to his extreme care for material perfection, of an orchestra that was marvellously equipped for symphonic music.

This seeking for perfection has been carried on by his successor, M. Camille Chevillard, whose orchestra is even more refined still. One may say, I think, that it is to-day the best in Paris. M. Chevillard is more attracted by pure music than Lamoureux was ; and he rightly finds that dramatic music has been occupying too large a place in Parisian concerts. In a letter published by the *Mercure de France*, in January, 1903, he reproaches the educators of public taste with having fostered a liking for opera, and with not having awakened a respect for pure music : " Any four bars from one of Mozart's quartettes have," he says, " a greater

educational value than a showy scene from an opera."
No one in Paris conducts classic works better than
he, especially the works that possess clean, plastic
beauty; and in Germany itself it would be
difficult to find anyone who would give a more
delicate interpretation of some of Händel's and
Mozart's symphonic works. His orchestra has kept,
moreover, the superiority that it had already acquired in its repertory of Wagner's works. But
M. Chevillard has communicated a warmth and
energy of rhythm to it that it did not possess before.
His interpretations of Beethoven, even if they are
somewhat superficial, are very full of life. Like
Lamoureux, he has hardly caught the spirit of
French romantic works—of Berlioz, and still less
of Franck and his school; and he seems to have
but lukewarm sympathy for the more recent
developments of French music. But he understands
well the German romantic composers, especially
Schumann, for whom he has a marked liking;
and he tried, though without great success, to
introduce Liszt and Brahms into France, and was
the first among us to attract real attention to
Russian music, whose brilliant and delicate colouring he excels in rendering. And, like M. Colonne,
he has brought the great German *Kapellmeister*
among us—Weingartner, Nikisch, and Richard
Strauss, the last mentioned having directed the
first performance in Paris of his symphonic poems,
*Zarathustra, Don Quixote,* and *Heldenleben,* at the
Lamoureux concerts.

Nothing could have better completed the musical

education of the public than this continuous defile, for the past ten years, of *Kapellmeister* and foreign virtuosi, and the comparisons that their different styles and interpretations afforded. Nothing has better helped forward the improvement of Parisian orchestras than the emulation brought about by the meetings between Parisian conductors and those of other countries. At present our own conductors are worthy rivals of the best in Germany. The string instruments are good ; the wood has kept its old French superiority ; and though the brass is still the weakest part of our orchestras, it has made great progress. One may still criticise the grouping of orchestras at concerts, for it is often defective ; there is a disproportion between the different families of instruments and, in consequence, between their different sonorities, some of which are too thin and others too dull. But these defects are fairly common all over Europe to-day. Unhappily, more peculiar to France is the insufficiency or poor quality of the choirs, whose progress has been far from keeping pace with that of the orchestras. It is to this side of music that the directors of concerts must now bring their efforts to bear.

The Lamoureux Concerts have not had as stable a dwelling-place as the Châtelet Concerts. They have wandered about Paris from one room to another —from the Cirque d'Hiver to the Cirque d'Été, and from the Château-d'Eau to the Nouveau Théâtre. At the present moment they are in the Salle Gaveau, which is much too small for them. In spite of the progress of music and musical taste, Paris has not yet a concert-hall, as the smallest provincial towns in Germany have; and this shameful indifference, unworthy of the artistic renown of Paris, obliges the symphonic societies to take refuge in circuses or theatres, which they share with other kinds of performers, though the acoustics of these places are not intended for concerts. And so it happens that for six years the Chevillard Concerts have been given at the back of a music-hall, which has the same entrance, and which is only separated from the concert-room by a small passage, so that the roaring choruses of a *danse du ventre* may mingle with an adagio of Beethoven's or a scene from the Tetralogy. Worse than this, the smallness of the place into which these concerts have been crammed has been a serious obstacle in the way of making them popular. Nevertheless, in the promenade and galleries of the Nouveau Théâtre, in later years, arose what may be called a little war over concertos. It was rather a curious episode in the history of the musical taste of Paris, and merits a few words here. In every country, but especially in those countries that are least musical, a virtuoso profits by public favour, often to the detriment of the work he is performing; for what is most liked in music is the musician. The virtuoso—whose importance must not be underrated, and who is worthy of honour when he is a reverential and sympathetic interpreter of genius—has too often taken a lamentable part, especially in Latin countries, in the degrading of musical taste; for empty virtuosity makes a desert of art. The

fashion of inept fantasias and acrobatic variations
has, it is true, gone by ; but of late years virtuosity
has returned in an offensive way, and, sheltering
itself under the solemn classical name of " concertos," it usurped a place of rather exaggerated
importance in symphony concerts, and especially
in M. Chevillard's concerts—a place which Lamoureux would never have given it. Then the
younger and more enthusiastic part of the public
began to revolt ; and very soon, with perfect impartiality and quite indiscriminately, began to hiss
famous and obscure virtuosi alike in their performance of any concerto, whether it was splendid
or detestable. Nothing found favour with them—
neither the playing of Paderewski, nor the music of
Saint-Saëns and the great masters. The management of the concerts went its own way and tried
in vain to put out the disturbers, and to forbid
them entry to the concert-room ; and the battle
went on for a long time, and critics were drawn into
it. But in spite of its ridiculous excesses, and the
barbarism of the methods by which the parterre
expressed its opinions, that quarrel is not without
interest. It proved how a passion and enthusiasm
for music had been roused in France ; and the
passion, though unjust in its expression, was more
fruitful and of far greater worth than indifference.

.    .    .    .    .    .

### 3. The Schola Cantorum

The Lamoureux Concerts had served their purpose, and, in their turn, their heroic mission came

to an end. They had forced Wagner on Paris; and Paris, as always, had overshot the mark, and could swear by no one but Wagner. French musicians were translating Gounod's or Massenet's ideas into Wagner's style; Parisian critics repeated Wagner's theories at random, whether they understood them or not—generally when they did not understand them. A reaction was inevitable directly Paris was well saturated with Wagner; and it came about in 1890, among a chosen few, some of whom had been, and were even still, under Wagner's influence. It was at first only a mild reaction, and showed itself in a return to the classics of the past and to the great primitives in music.

There had been several attempts in this direction before, but none of them had succeeded in making any impression on the mass of the public. In 1843, Joseph Napoléon Ney, Prince of Moszkowa, founded in Paris a society for the performance of religious and classical vocal music. This society, which the Prince himself conducted in his own house, set itself to perform the vocal works of the sixteenth and seventeenth centuries.[1] In 1853, Louis Niedermeyer founded in Paris an *École de musique religieuse et classique*, which strove "to form singers, organists, choirmasters, and composers of music, by the study of the classic works of the great masters of the fifteenth, sixteenth, and seventeenth

---

[1] It published, in eleven volumes, the ancient works that it performed. Before this experiment there had been the *Concerts historiques de Fétis*, preceded by lectures, which were inaugurated in 1832, and failed; and these were followed by Amédée Méreaux's *Concerts historiques* in 1842–1844.

centuries." This school, subsidised by the State, was a nursery for some real musicians. It reckoned among its pupils some noted composers, conductors, organists, and historians; among others, M. Gabriel Fauré, M. André Messager, M. Eugène Gigout, and M. Henry Expert. M. Saint-Saëns was a professor there, and became its president. Nearly five hundred organists, choir-masters, and professors of music of the Conservatoire and other French colleges were trained there. But this school, serious in intention, and a refuge for the classic spirit in the midst of the prevailing bad taste, did not trouble itself about influencing the public, and, in fact, almost ignored it.

Lamoureux attempted in 1873 to perform the great choral works of Bach and Händel; and in 1878 the celebrated French organist, M. Alexandre Guilmant, ventured to give concerts at the Trocadéro for the organ and orchestra, which were devoted to religious music of the seventeenth and eighteenth centuries. But the deplorable acoustics of the concert-room had a prejudicial effect on the works that were performed there; and the public did not respond very warmly to M. Guilmant's efforts, and seemed from the first only to find an historical interest in the masterpieces, and to miss their depth and life altogether.

Then a pupil of Franck's, M. Henry Expert, who began his admirable works on Musical History in 1882, laid the foundation of the *Société J.-S. Bach*, in order to spread the knowledge of ancient music written between the twelfth and eighteenth cen-

turies. And he succeeded in interesting in his under-
taking, not only the principal French musicians,
such as César Franck, Saint-Saëns, and Gounod,
but also foreigners, such as Hans von Bülow,
Tschaikowski, Grieg, Sgambati, and Gevaert. Unhappily this society never got farther than arranging what it wanted to do, and only sketched
out the plans that were realised later by Charles
Bordes.

The general public were not really interested in
the art of the old musicians until the *Association
des Chanteurs de Saint-Gervais* was founded in 1892
by Charles Bordes, the choirmaster of the church of
Saint-Gervais. The immediate success and the
noisy renown of the Society were due to other things
besides the talent of its conductor, who combined
with a lively artistic intelligence both common-
sense and energy and a remarkable gift for organisation—it was due partly to the help of favourable
circumstances, partly to the surfeit of Wagnerism,
of which I have just spoken, and partly to the birth
of a new religious art, which had sprung up since
the death of César Franck round the memory of
that great musician.

It is not my intention here to write an appreciation of César Franck's genius, but it is not possible
to understand the musical movement in Paris of
the last fifteen years if one does not take into account
the importance of his teaching. The organ class
at the Conservatoire, where in 1872 Franck succeeded his old master Benoist, was for a long time,
as M. Vincent d'Indy says, " the true centre for the

study of Composition at the Conservatoire. Many of his fellow-workers could never bring themselves to look upon him as one of themselves, because he had the boldness to see in art something other than the means of earning a living. Indeed, César Franck was not of them ; and they made him feel this." But the young students made no mistake about the matter. " At this time," M. d'Indy also tells us,[1] " that is to say from 1872 to 1876, the three courses of Advanced Musical Composition were given by three professors who were not at all fitted for their work. One was Victor Massé, a composer of simple light operas and a man with no understanding of a symphony, who was very frequently ill and had to entrust his teaching to one of his pupils ; another was Henri Reber, an oldish musician with narrow and dogmatic ideas ; and the third was François Bazin, who was not capable of distinguishing in his pupil's fugues a false answer from a true one, and whose highest title to glory is derived from a composition called *Le Voyage en Chine*. So it is not surprising that César Franck's teaching, founded on that of Bach and Beethoven, but admitting, as well, imagination and all new and liberal ideas, did, at that time, draw to him all young minds that had lofty ambitions and that were really in love with their art. And so, quite unconsciously, the master attracted to himself all the sincere and artistic talent that was scattered

[1] The following information was given by M. Vincent d'Indy at a lecture held on 20 February, 1903, at the *École des Hautes Études sociales*—a lecture which later became a chapter in M. d'Indy's book, *César Franck* (1906).

about the different classes of the Conservatoire, as well as that of his outside pupils."

Among those who received his direct teaching[1] were Henri Duparc, Alexis de Castillon, Vincent d'Indy, Ernest Chausson, Pierre de Bréville, Augusta Holmes, Louis de Serres, Charles Bordes, Guy Ropartz, and Guillaume Lekeu. And if to these we add the pupils in the organ classes, who also came under his influence, we have, among others, Samuel Rousseau, Gabriel Pierné, Auguste Chapuis, Paul Vidal, and Georges Marty ; and also the virtuosi who were for some time intimate with him, such as Armand Parent and Eugène Ysaye, to whom Franck dedicated his violin sonata. And if one thinks, too, of the artists who, though not his pupils, felt his power—artists such as Gabriel Fauré, Alexandre Guilmant, Emmanuel Chabrier, and Paul Dukas—one may see that nearly the whole musical generation of Paris of that time took its inspiration from César Franck. And it was largely with the intention of perpetuating his teaching that his pupils, Charles Bordes and Vincent d'Indy, and his friend, Alexandre Guilmant, founded in 1894, four years after his death, the *Schola Cantorum*, which has kept his memory alive ever since.

" Our revered father, Franck," said Vincent d'Indy, in a speech, " is in some ways the grandfather of the *Schola Cantorum ;* for it is his system of teaching that we apply and try to carry on here."[2]

---

[1] A complete list may be found in M. d'Indy's book.
[2] *Tribune de Saint-Gervais*, November, 1900.

The influence of Franck was twofold : it was artistic and moral. On the one hand he was, if I may so put it, an admirable professor of musical architecture ; he founded a school of symphony and chamber-music such as France had never had before, which in certain directions was newer and more daring than that of the German symphony writers. And, on the other hand, he exercised by his own character a memorable influence over all those who came into contact with him. His profound faith, that fine, indulgent, and calm faith, shone round him like a glory. The Catholic party, who were awakening to new life in France just then, tried, after his death, to identify his ideals with their own. But this was, as we have said elsewhere,[1] to narrow Franck's mind ; for its great charm lay in its harmonious union of religion and liberty, which never limited its artistic sympathies to an exclusive ideal. The composer's son, M. Georges César-Franck, has in vain protested against this monopoly of his father, and says :

" According to certain writers, who wish to reduce everything to a dead level and deduce all things from a single cause, César Franck was a mystic whose true domain was religious music. Nothing could be wider of the mark. The public is given to generalisations, and is too easily gulled. They will judge a composer on a single work, or a group of works, and class him once and for all. . . . In reality, my father was a man of all-round

[1] See the Essay on *Vincent d'Indy*.

U

accomplishments. As a finished musician, he was master of every form of composition. He wrote both religious and secular music—melodies, dances, pastorales, oratorios, symphonic poems, symphonies, sonatas, trios, and operas. He did not confine his attention to any particular kind of work to the exclusion of other kinds ; he was able to express himself in any way he chose." [1]

But as what was really religious in him found itself in agreement with a current of thought that was rather powerful at that time, it was inevitable that this one side of his genius should be first brought to light, and that religious music should be the first to benefit by his work. And also one of the early manifestos [2] of the *Schola Cantorum* dealt with the reform of sacred music by carrying it back to great ancient models ; and its first decision was as follows : " Gregorian chant shall rest for all time the fountain-head and the base of the Church's music, and shall constitute the only model by which it may be truly judged." [3]    They

[1] *Revue d'histoire et de critique musicale*, August–September, 1901.

[2] " The *Schola Cantorum* aims at creating a modern music truly worthy of the Church " (First number of the *Tribune de Saint-Gervais*, the monthly bulletin of the *Schola Cantorum*, January, 1895).

[3] The Schola had in mind here the vigorous work of the French Benedictines, which had been done in silence for the past fifty years ; it was thinking, too, of the restoration of the Gregorian chant during 1850 and 1860 by Dom Guéranger, the first abbot of Solesmes, a work continued by Dom Jausions and Dom Pothier, the abbot of Saint-Wandrille, who published in 1883 the *Mélodies Grégoriennes*, the *Liber Gradualis*, and the *Liber Antiphonarius*. This work was finally brought to a happy

added to this, however, music *à la Palestrina*, and any music that conformed to its principles or was inspired by its example. Such archaic ideas would certainly never create a new kind of religious music, but at least they have helped to restore the old art ; and they received their official consecration in the famous letter written by Pope Pius X on the Reform of Sacred Music.

The achievement of an artistic ideal so restricted as this would not have sufficed, however, to assure the success of the *Schola Cantorum*, nor establish its authority with a public that was, whatever people may say, only lukewarm in its religion, and that would only interest itself in the religious art of other days as it would in a passing fashion. But the spirit of curiosity and the meaning of modern life began to weigh little by little with the Schola's principles. After singing Palestrinian and Gregorian chants at the Church of Saint-Gervais during Holy Week, they played Carissimi, Schütz, and the Italian and German masters of the seventeenth century. Then came Bach's cantatas ; and their performance, given by M. Bordes in the Salle d'Harcourt, attracted large audiences and started the cult of this master in Paris. Then they sang Rameau and Gluck ; and, finally, all ancient music, sacred or secular, was approved. And so this little school,

conclusion by Dom Schmitt, and Dom Mocquereau, the prior of Solesmes, who in 1889 began his monumental work, the *Paléographie Musicale*, of which nine volumes had appeared in 1906. This great Benedictine school is an honour to France by the scientific work it has lately done in music. The school is at present exiled from France.

which had been consecrated to the cult of ancient
religious music, and had made so modest a beginning,[1] developed into a School of Art capable of
satisfying modern wants ; and in 1900, when
M. Vincent d'Indy became president of the. *Schola*,
it was decided to move the school into larger
premises in the Rue Saint-Jacques.

The programme of this new school was explained
by M. Vincent d'Indy in his Inauguration speech
on 2 November, 1900, and showed how he based
the foundations of musical teaching upon history.

" Art, in its journey across the ages, is a micro-
cosm which has, like the world itself, successive
stages of youth, maturity, and old age ; but it
never dies—it renews itself perpetually.   It is
not like a perfect circle ; it is like a spiral, and
in its growth is always mounting higher.   I
believe in making students follow the same path
that art itself has followed, so that they shall
undergo during their term of study the same
transformations that music itself has undergone
during the centuries.   In this way they will come
out much better armed for the difficulties of
modern art, since they will have lived, so to
speak, the life of art, and followed the natural
and inevitable order of the forms that made up
the different epochs of artistic development."

[1] When Charles Bordes opened the first *Schola Cantorum* in
the Rue Stanislas he was without help or resources, and had
exactly thirty-seven francs and fifty centimes in hand.   I
mention this detail to give an idea of the splendidly courageous
and confident spirit that Charles Bordes possessed.

M. d'Indy claims that this system may be applied as successfully to instrumentalists and singers as to future composers. " For it is as profitable for them to know," he says, " how to sing a liturgic monody properly, or to be able to play a Corelli sonata in a suitable style, as it is for composers to study the structure of a motet or a suite." M. d'Indy, moreover, obliged all students, without distinction, to attend the lectures on vocal music ; and, besides that, he instituted a special class to teach the conducting of orchestras—which was something quite new to France. His object, as he clearly said, was to give a new form to modern music by means of a knowledge of the music of the past.

On this subject he says :

" Where shall we find the quickening life that will give us fresh forms and formulas ? The source is not really difficult to discover. Do not let us seek it anywhere but in the decorative art of the plainsong singers, in the architectural art of the age of Palestrina, and in the expressive art of the great Italians of the seventeenth century. It is there, and *there alone*, that we shall find melodic craft, rhythmic cadences, and a harmonic magnificence that is really new—if our modern spirit can only learn how to absorb their nutritious essence. And so I prescribe for all pupils in the School the careful study of classic forms, because *they alone* are able to give the elements of a new life to our music, which will be founded on principles that are sane, solid, and trustworthy."[1]

This fine and intelligent eclecticism was likely to develop a critical spirit, but was rather less adapted to form original personalities. In any case, however, it was excellent discipline in the formation of musical taste; and, in truth, the *École Supérieure de musique* of the Rue Saint-Jacques became a new Conservatoire, both more modern and more learned than the old Conservatoire, and freer, and yet less free, because more self-satisfied. The school developed very quickly. From having twenty-one pupils in 1896, it had three hundred and twenty in 1908. Eminent musicians and professors learned in the history and science of music taught there, and M. d'Indy himself took the Composition classes.[2] And in its short career the *Schola* may already be credited with the training of young composers, such as MM. Roussel, Déodat de Séverac, Gustave Bret, Labey, Samazeuilh, R. de Castéra, Sérieyx, Alquier, Coindreau, Estienne, Le Flem, and Groz; and to these may be added M. d'Indy's private pupils, Witkowski, and one of the foremost of modern composers, Alberic Magnard.

Outside the influence that the School exercises by its teaching, its propaganda by means of concerts and publications is very active. From its founda-

---

[1] *Tribune de Saint-Gervais*, November, 1900.
[2] There are actually nine courses of Composition at the *Schola*—five for men and four for women. M. d'Indy takes eight of them, as well as a mixed class for orchestra.

tion up to 1904 it had given two hundred performances in one hundred and thirty provincial towns ;
more than one hundred and fifty concerts in Paris,
of which fifty were of orchestral and choral music,
sixty of organ music, and forty of chamber-music.
These concerts have been well attended by enthusiastic and appreciative audiences, and have been a
school for public taste. One does not look for perfect execution there,[1] but for intelligent interpretations and a thirst for a fuller knowledge of the great
works of the past. They have revived Monteverde's
*Orfeo* and his *Incoronazione di Poppea,* which had
been forgotten these three centuries ; and it was
following an interest created by repeated performances of Rameau at the *Schola*[2] that *Dardanus* was
performed at Dijon under M. d'Indy's direction,
*Castor et Pollux* at Montpellier under M. Charles
Bordes' direction, and that in 1908 the Opera at
Paris gave *Hippolyte et Aricie.* Branches of the
*Schola* have been started at Lyons, Marseilles,
Bordeaux, Avignon, Montpellier, Nancy, Épinal,
Montluçon, Saint-Chamond, and Saint-Jean-de-

---

[1] The orchestra is mainly composed of pupils ; and, by a
generous arrangement, the financial profits from rehearsals and
performances are divided among the pupils who take part in
them, and credited to their account. And so besides the exhibi-
tioners the *Schola* has a great number of pupils who are not well
off, but who manage by these concerts to defray almost the
entire expenses of their education there. " The concerts serve
more especially as æsthetic exercises for the pupils, and as a
means of according them teaching at small expense to themselves." I owe this information and all that precedes it to the
kindness of M. J. de la Laurencie, the general secretary of the
*Schola,* whom I should like to thank.

[2] The *Schola* has even performed, in an open-air theatre,
Rameau's *La Guirlande.*

Luz.[1]  A publishing house has been associated with
the School at Paris ; and from this we get Reviews,
such as the *Tribune de Saint-Gervais ;* publications
of old music, such as the *Anthologie des maîtres
religieux primitifs des XVe, XVIe, et XVIIe siècles,*
edited by Charles Bordes ;  the *Archives des maîtres
de l'orgue des XVIe, XVIIe, et XVIIIe siècles,*
edited by Alexandre Guilmant and André Pirro ;
the *Concerts spirituels de la Schola,* the new editions
of *Orfeo,* and the *Incoronazione di Poppea,* edited by
M. Vincent d'Indy ;  and publications of modern
music, such as the *Collection du chant populaire,*
the *Répertoire moderne de musique vocale et d'orgue,*
and, notably, the *Édition mutuelle,* published by the
composers themselves, whose property it is.

And all this shows such a marvellous activity and
gives evidence of such whole-hearted enthusiasm
that I cannot bring myself to join issue with the
critics who have lately attacked the *Schola,* though
their attacks have been in some degree merited.
Pettiness is to be found even in great artists, and
imperfection in every human work ;  and defects
reveal themselves most clearly after a victory has
been won.  The *Schola* has not escaped the critical
periods that accompany growth, through which

[1] One may add to this list the choral societies of Nantes and
Besançon, which are bodies of the same order as the *Chanteurs
de Saint-Gervais.*  And we may also attribute to the influence
of the *Schola* an independent society, the *Société J. S. Bach,*
started in Paris by an old *Schola* pupil, M. Gustave Bret, which,
since 1905, has devoted itself to the performance of the great
works of Bach.  It is not one of the least merits of the *Schola*
that it has helped to form good amateur choirs of the same type
as the choral societies of Germany.

every work must pass if it is to triumph and endure. Without doubt, the sudden illness and premature retirement of the founder of the work, M. Charles Bordes, deprived the *Schola* of one of its most active forces—a force that was perhaps necessary for the school's successful development. For this man had been the school's life and soul, and retired, worn out by the heavy labours which he had borne alone during ten years.[1]

But M. d'Indy, like a courageous apostle, has continued the direction of the *Schola* with a firm hand and unwearying care, despite his varied activities as composer, professor, and *Kapellmeister;* and he is one of the surest and most reliable guides for a young school of French music. And if his mind is rather given to abstractions, and his moods are sometimes rather combative, and certain prejudices (which are not always musical ones) make him lean towards ideals of reason and immovable faith—and if at times his followers unconsciously distort his ideas, and try to dam the stream which flows from life itself, I am convinced it is only the

[1] M. Charles Bordes did not even then give up his labours altogether. Though obliged to retire to the south of France for his health's sake, he founded, in November, 1905, the *Schola* of Montpellier. This *Schola* has given about fifteen concerts a year, and has performed some of Bach's cantatas, scenes from Rameau's and Gluck's operas, Franck's oratorios, and Monteverde's *Orfeo.* In 1906 M. Bordes organised an open-air performance of Rameau's *Guirlande.* In January, 1908, he produced *Castor et Pollux* at the Montpellier theatre. The man's activity was incredible, and nothing seemed to tire him. He was planning to start a dramatic training-school at Montpellier for the production of seventeenth and eighteenth century operas, when he died, in November, 1909, at the age of forty-four, and so deprived French art of one of its best and most unselfish servants.

passing evidence of a reaction, perhaps a natural
one, against the exaggerations they have encountered, and that the *Schola* will always know how to
avoid the rocks where revolutionaries of the past
have run aground and become the conservatives
of the morrow. I hope the *Schola* will never grow
into the kind of aristocratic school that builds walls
about itself, but will always open wide its doors
and welcome every new force in music, even to
such as have ideals opposed to its own. Its future
renown and the well-being of French art can only
thus be maintained.

.   .   .   .   .   .

### 4. *The Chamber-Music Societies*

On parallel lines with the big symphony concerts
and the new *conservatoires*, societies were formed to
spread the knowledge of, and form a taste for,
chamber-music. This music, so common in Germany, was almost unknown in Paris before 1870.
There was nothing but the Maurin Quartette, which
gave five or six concerts every winter in the Salle
Pleyel, and played Beethoven's last quartettes
there. But these performances only attracted a
small number of artists[1] ; and so far as the general
public was concerned the *Société des derniers quar-*

---

[1] The quality of the audience atoned, it is true, for its small
numbers. Berlioz used to come to these concerts with his
friends, Damcke and Stephen Heller ; and it was after one of
these performances, when he had been very stirred by an *adagio*
in the E flat quartette, that he burst out with, " What a man !
He could do everything, and the others nothing ! "

*tuors de Beethoven* had the reputation for devoting itself to a singular and incomprehensible kind of music that had been written by a deaf man.

The true founder of chamber-music concerts in Paris was M. Émile Lemoine, who started the society called *La Trompette*. He has given us a history of his work in the *Revue Musicale* (15 October, 1903). He was an engineer at the École Polytechnique ; and after he had left school he formed, about 1860, a quartette society of earnest amateurs, though they were not very skilled performers. This little society continued to meet regularly, and after perfecting itself little by little, finally opened its doors to the general public, which attended the concerts in gradually increasing numbers. Then *La Trompette* came into being. It prospered from the day that M. Saint-Saëns—who was at that time a young man—made its acquaintance. He was pleased with these gatherings, and became an intimate friend of Lemoine ; and he interested himself in the society, and induced other celebrated artists to take an interest in it, too. Among its early friends were MM. Alphonse Duvernoy, Diémer, Pugno, Delsart, Breitner, Delaborde, Ch. de Bériot, Fissot, Marsick, Loëb, Rémy, and Holmann. With such patronage, *La Trompette* soon acquired fame in the musical world, and " it represented in classical chamber-music the semi-official part played by the *Société des Concerts du Conservatoire* in classical orchestral music. Rubinstein, Paderewski, Eugène d'Albert, Hans von Bülow, Arthur de Greef, Mme. Essipoff, and Mme. Menter, never missed getting a

hearing there when their tours led them to Paris ;
and to figure on the programme of *La Trompette*
was like the consecration of an artist.'' Such a
society naturally contributed a great deal to the
spread of classical chamber-music in Paris. M.
Lemoine writes :

" Classical music was so little known to the
musical public that even the audiences of *La
Trompette*, cultured as they were, did not at all
understand Beethoven's last quartettes ; and my
friends jeered at my taste for enigmas. This
only made me the more determined that they
should hear one of these great works at each
concert. And sometimes I would give the same
work at two or three concerts running if I thought
it had not been properly appreciated. In that
case I used to say before the performance : ' It
seems to me that such-and-such a work has not
been quite understood at the last hearing ; and
as it is a really marvellous work, I am sure that
your feeling is that you do not know it sufficiently.
So I have included it in to-day's programme.' "[1]

These performances of sonatas, trios, and quartettes, were attentively listened to by an audience
of five or six hundred persons, the greater part of

---

[1] The name, *La Trompette*, was also the pretext for embellish-
ing chamber-music, by introducing the trumpet among the other
instruments. To this end M. Saint-Saëns wrote his fine septette
for piano, trumpet, two violins, viola, violoncello, and double
bass ; and M. Vincent d'Indy his romantic suite in D for trumpet,
two flutes, and string instruments.

them cultured people, students from the poly-
technics and universities, who formed the kernel
of a very discerning and enthusiastic public for
chamber-music.

By degrees, following the example of Émile
Lemoine, other quartette societies were formed ;
and at present they are so numerous that it would
be difficult to name them all. And then there sprang
up the same spirit of intelligent curiosity that
had induced the French *Kapellmeister* of the symphony concert societies sometimes to introduce
their German and Russian colleagues as conductors ;
and for this purpose the *Nouvelle Société Phil-
harmonique de Paris* was founded, in 1901, on the
initiative of Dr. Fränkel and under the direction of
M. Emmanuel Rey, to give a hearing in Paris to
the principal foreign quartette players. And the
profit was as great in one case as in the other ; and
the friendly rivalry between French quartette
players and those of other countries bore good fruit,
and gave us a fuller understanding of the inner
character of German music.

## 5. *Musical Learning and the University*

While this movement was going on in the artistic
world, scholars were taking their share in it, and
music was beginning to invade the University.

But the thing was brought about with some
difficulty ; for among these serious people music
did not count as a serious study. Music was thought

of as an agreeable art, a social accomplishment,·
and the idea of making it the subject of scientific
teaching must have been received with some amusement. Even up to the present time, general histories of Art have refused to accord music a place,
so little was thought of it ; and other arts were
indignant at being mentioned in the same breath
with it. This is illustrated in the eternal dispute
among M. Jourdain's masters, when the fencing-
master says :

> "And from this we know what great con-
> sideration is due to us in a State ; and how the
> science of Fencing is far above all useless sciences,
> such as dancing and music."

The first lectures on Æsthetics and Musical
History were not given in France until after the
war of 1870.[1] They were then given at the Conservatoire, and, until quite lately, were the only lectures
on Music of any importance in Paris. Since 1878
they have been given in a very excellent way by
M. Bourgault-Ducoudray ; but, as is only natural
in a school of music, their character is artistic rather
than scientific, and takes the form of a sort of
illustration of the practical work that is done at
the Conservatoire. And as for Parisian musical
criticism as a whole, it had, thirty years ago, an

[1] On 12 September, 1871, at the suggestion of Ambroise
Thomas. The first lecturer was Barbereau, who, however, only
lectured for a year. He was succeeded by Gautier, Professor of
Harmony and Accompaniment, who in turn was replaced, in
1878, by M. Bourgault-Ducoudray.

almost exclusively literary character, and was
without technical precision or historical knowledge.

There again, on the territory of science, as on
that of art, a new generation of musicians had
sprung up since the war, a group of men versed in
the history and æsthetics of music such as France
had never known before. About 1890 the result of
their labours began to appear. Henry Expert
published his fine work, *Maîtres Musiciens de la
Renaissance*, in which he revived a whole century
of French music. Alexander Guilmant and André
Pirro brought to daylight the works of our seventeenth and eighteenth century organists. Pierre
Aubry studied mediæval music. The admirable
publications of the Benedictines of Solesmes awoke
at the *Schola* and in the world outside it a taste
for the study of religious music. Michel Brenet
attacked all epochs of musical history, and produced, by his solid learning, some fine work. Julien
Tiersot began the history of French folk-song, and
rescued the music of the Revolution from oblivion.
The publisher Durand set to work on his great
editions of Rameau and Couperin. Towards 1893 the
study of Music was introduced at the Sorbonne by
some young professors, who made the subject the
theses for their doctor's degree.[1]

[1] The first three theses on Music accepted at the Sorbonne
were those of M. Jules Combarieu on *The Relationship of Poetry
and Music*, of M. Romain Rolland on *The Beginnings of Opera
before Lully and Scarlatti*, and of M. Maurice Emmanuel on
*Greek Orchestics*. There followed, several years afterwards, M.
Louis Laloy's *Aristoxenus of Tarento and Greek Music* and M.

This movement with regard to musical study grew rapidly ; and the first International Congress of Music, held in Paris at the time of the Universal Exhibition of 1900, gave historians of music an opportunity of realising their influence. In a few years, teaching about music was to be had everywhere. At first there were the free lectures of M. Lionel Dauriac and M. Georges Houdard at the Sorbonne, those of MM. Aubry, Gastoué, Pirro, and Vincent d'Indy at the *Schola* and the *Institut Catholique ;* and then, at the beginning of 1902, there was the little Faculty of Music of the *École des Hautes Études sociales*, making a centre for the efforts of French scholars of music ; and, in 1900, two official courses of lectures on Musical History and Æsthetics were given at the Collège de France and the Sorbonne.

The progress of musical criticism was just as rapid. Professors of faculties, old pupils of the École Normale Supérieure, or the École des Chartes, such as Henri Lichtenberger, Louis Laloy, and Pierre Aubrey, examined works of the past, and even of the present, by the exact methods of historical criticism. Choir-masters and organists of great erudition, such as André Pirro and Gastoué, and composers like Vincent d'Indy, Dukas, Debussy, and some others, analysed their art with the confi-dence that the intimate knowledge of its practice

Jules Écorcheville's *Musical Æsthetics, from Lully to Rameau* and *French Instrumental Music of the Seventeenth Century*, M. André Pirro's *Æsthetics of Johann Sebastian Bach*, and M. Charles Lalo's *Sketch of Scientific Musical Æsthetics*.

brings. A perfect efflorescence of works on music appeared. A galaxy of distinguished writers and a public were found to support two separate collections of Biographies of Musicians (which were issued at the same time by different publishers), as well as five or six good musical journals of a scientific character, some of which rivalled the best in Germany. And, finally, the French section of the *Société Internationale de Musique,* which was founded in 1899 in Berlin to establish communication between the scholars of all countries, found so favourable a ground with us that the number of its adherents in Paris alone is now over one hundred.

.　　.　　.　　.　　.　　.

## 5. *Music and the People*

Thus music had almost come back to its own, as far as the higher kind of teaching and the intellectual world were concerned. It remained for a place to be found for it in other kinds of teaching ; for there, and especially in secondary education, its advance was less sure. It remained for us to make it enter into the life of the nation and into the people's education. This was a difficult task, for in France art has always had an aristocratic character ; and it was a task in which neither the State nor musicians were very interested. The Republic still continued to regard music as something outside the people. There had even been opposition shown during the last thirty years towards any

X

attempt at popular musical education. In the old days of the Pasdeloup concerts one could pay seventy-five centimes for the cheapest places, and have a seat for that ; but at some of the symphony concerts to-day the cheapest seats are two and four francs. And so the people that sometimes came to the Pasdeloup concerts never come at all to the big concerts to-day.

And that is why one should applaud the enterprise of Victor Charpentier, who, in March, 1905, founded a Symphonic Society of amateurs called *L'Orchestre*, to give free hearings for the benefit of the people. And in that Paris, where forty years ago one would have had a good deal of trouble to get together two or three amateur quartettes, Victor Charpentier has been able to count on one hundred and fifty good performers,[1] who under his direction, or that of Saint-Saëns or Gabriel Fauré, have already given seventeen free concerts, of which ten were given at the Trocadéro.[2] It is to be hoped that the State will help forward such a generous work for the people in a rather more practical way than it has done up till now.[3]

[1] There are ninety violins, fifteen violas, and fifteen violoncellos. Unfortunately it is much more difficult to get recruits for the wood wind and brass.

[2] They have performed classical music of composers like Bach, Händel, Gluck, Rameau, and Beethoven ; and modern music of composers like Berlioz, Saint-Saëns, Dukas, etc. This Society has just installed itself in the ancient chapel of the Dominicans of the Faubourg-Saint-Honoré, who have given them the use of it.

[3] Of late years there has been a veritable outburst of concerts at popular prices—some of them in imitation of the German *Restaurationskonzerte*, such as the Concerts-Rouge, the Concerts-

Attempts have been made at different times to found a *Théâtre Lyrique Populaire*. But up to the present time none has succeeded. The first attempts were made in 1847. M. Carvalho's old Théâtre-Lyrique was never a financial success, though quite distinguished performances of operas were given there, such as Gounod's *Faust* and Gluck's *Orfeo*, with Mme. Viardot as an interpreter and Berlioz as conductor ; and the directors who followed Carvalho—Rety, Pasdeloup, etc.—did not succeed any better. In 1875 Vizentini took over the Gaîté, with a grant of two hundred thousand francs and excellent artists ; but he had to give it up. Since then all sorts of other schemes have been tried by Viollet-le-Duc, Guimet, Lamoureux, Melchior de Vogüé and Julien Goujon, Gabriel Parisot, Colonne and Milliet, Deville, Lagoanère, Corneille,

Touche, etc., where classical and modern symphony music may be heard. These concerts are increasing fast, and have great success among a public that is almost exclusively *bourgeois*, but they are yet a long way behind the popular performances of Händel in London, where places may be had for sixpence and threepence.

I do not attach very much importance to the courageous, though not always very intelligent movement of the Universités Populaires, where since 1886 a collection of amateurs, of fashionable people and artists, meet to make themselves heard, and pretend to initiate the people into what are sometimes the most complicated and aristocratic works of a classic or decadent art. While honouring this propaganda—whose ardour has now abated somewhat—one must say that it has shown more goodwill than common-sense. The people do not need amusing, still less should they be bored ; what they need is to learn something about music. This is not always easy ; for it is not noisy deeds we want, but patience and self-sacrifice. Good intentions are not enough. One knows the final failure of the *Conservatoire populaire de Mimi Pinson*, started by Gustave Charpentier, for giving musical education to the work-girls of Paris.

Gailhard, and Carré ; but none of them achieved any success. At the moment, a new attempt is being made ; and this time the thing seems to show every sign of being a success.

But whatever may be the educational value of the theatre and concerts, they are not complete enough in themselves for the people. To make their influence deep and enduring it must be combined with teaching. Music, no less than every other expression of thought, has no use for the illiterate.

So in this case there was everything to be done. There was no other popular teaching but that of the numerous Galin-Paris-Chevé schools. These schools have rendered great service, and are continuing to render it ; but their simplified methods are not without drawbacks and gaps. Their purpose is to teach the people a musical language different from that of cultured people ; and although it may not be as difficult as is supposed to go from a knowledge of the one to a knowledge of the other, it is always wrong to raise up a fresh barrier—however small it is—between the cultured people and the other people, who in our own country are already too widely separated.

And besides, it is not enough to know one's letters ; one must also have books to read. What books have the people had ?—so far songs sung at the café concerts and the stupid répertoires of choral societies. The folk-song had practically disappeared, and was not yet ready for re-birth ; for the populace, even more readily than the cultured people, are inclined to blush at anything which suggests " popularity."[1]

It is nearly twenty-five years since M. Bourgault-Ducoudray, who was one of the people who fostered the growth of choral singing in France, pointed out, in an account of the teaching of singing, the usefulness of making children sing the old popular airs of the French provinces, and of getting the teachers to make collections of them. In 1895, as the result of a meeting organised by the *Correspondance générale de l'Instruction primaire*, delightful collections of folk-songs were distributed in the schools. The melodies were taken from old airs collected by M. Julien Tiersot, and M. Maurice Buchor had put some fresh and sparkling verses to them. " M. Buchor," I wrote at the time, " will enjoy a pleasure not common to poets of our day : his songs will soar up into the open air, like the lark in his *Chanson de labour*. The populace may even recognise its own spirit in them, and one day take possession of them, as if they were of their own contriving."[2] This prediction has been almost com-

---

[1] M. Maurice Buchor relates an anecdote which typifies what I mean. " I begged the conductor of a good men's choral society," he says, " to have one of Händel's choruses sung. But he seemed to hesitate. I had made the suggestion tentatively, and then tried to enlarge on the sincerity and breadth of its musical idea. ' Ah, very good,' he said, ' if you really want to hear it, it is easily done ; but I was afraid that perhaps it was rather too popular.' " (*Poème de la Vie Humaine :* Introduction to the Second Series, 1905.) One may add to this the words of a professor of singing in a primary school for Higher Education in Paris : " Folk-music—well, it is very good for the provinces." (Quoted by Buchor in the Introduction to the Second Series of the *Poème*, 1902.)

[2] Taken from the *Supplément à la Correspondance générale de l'Instruction primaire*, 15 December, 1894.

pletely realised, and M. Buchor's songs are now the property of all the people of France.

But M. Buchor did not remain content to be a poet of popular song. During the last twelve years he has made, with untiring energy, a tour of all the Écoles Normales in France, returning several times to places where he found signs of good vocal ability. In each school he made the pupils sing his songs—in unison, or in two or three parts, sometimes massing the boys' and girls' schools of one town together. His ambition grew with his success; and to the folk-song melodies[1] he began gradually to add pieces of classical music. And to impress the music better on the singers he changed the existing words, and tried to find others, which by their moral and poetic beauty more exactly translated the musical feeling.[2] And at last he

[1] Three series of these *Chants populaires pour les Écoles* have already been published.

[2] I reserve my opinion, from an artist's point of view, on this plagiarising of the words of songs. On principle I condemn it absolutely. But, in this case, it is Hobson's choice. *Primum vivere, deinde philosophari.* If our contemporary musicians really wished the people to sing, they would have written songs for them; but they seem to have no desire to achieve honour that way. So there is nothing else to be done but to have recourse to the musicians of other days; and even there the choice is very limited. For France formerly, like the France of to-day, had very few musicians who had any understanding of a great popular art. Berlioz came nearest to understanding the meaning of it; and he is not yet public property, so his airs cannot be used. It is curious, and rather sad, that out of eighty pieces chosen by M. Buchor only nine of them are French; and this is reckoning the Italians, Lully and Cherubini, as Frenchmen. M. Buchor has had to go to German classical musicians almost entirely, and, generally speaking, his choice has been a happy one. With a sure instinct he has given the preference to popular geniuses like Händel and Beethoven. We may ask why he did

composed and grouped together twenty-four poems
in his *Poème de la Vie humaine*[1]—fine odes and songs,
written for classic airs and choruses, a vast repertory of the people's joys and sorrows, fitting the
momentous hours of family or public life. With a
people that has ancient musical traditions, as Germany has, music is the vehicle for the words and
impresses them in the heart ; but in France's case
it is truer to say that the words have brought the
music of Händel and Beethoven into the hearts of
French school-children. The great thing is that the
music has really got hold of them, and that now one
may hear the provincial Écoles Normales performing
choruses from *Fidelio*, *The Messiah*, Schumann's

not keep their words ; but we must remember that at any rate
they had to be translated ; and though it may seem rash to
change the subject of a musical masterpiece, it is certain that
M. Buchor's clever adaptations have resulted in driving the fine
thoughts of Händel and Schubert and Mozart and Beethoven
into the memories of the French people, and making them part
of their lives. Had they heard the same music at a concert they
would probably not have been very much moved. And that
makes M. Buchor in the right. Let the French people enrich
themselves with the musical treasures of Germany until the
time comes when they are able to create a music of their own !
This is a kind of peaceful conquest to which our art is accustomed.
" Now then, Frenchmen," as Du Bellay used to say, " walk
boldly up to that fine old Roman city, and decorate (as you have
done more than once) your temples and altars with its spoils."
Besides, let us remember that the German masters of the eighteenth century, whose words M. Buchor has plagiarised, did not
hesitate to plagiarise themselves ; and in turning the Berceuse
of the *Oratorio de Noël* into a *Sainte famille humaine*, M. Buchor
has respected the musical ideas of Bach much more than Bach
himself did when he turned it into a *Dialogue between Hercules
and Pleasure.*

[1] The *Poème* has been published in four parts :—I. *De la
naissance au mariage* ("From Birth to Marriage ") ; II. *La Cité*
("The City ") ; III. *De l'âge viril jusqu'à la mort* ("From Man-
hood to Death ") ; IV. *L'Idéal* ("Ideals "). 1900–1906.

*Faust*, or Bach cantatas.[1] The honour of this remarkable achievement, which no one could have believed possible twenty years ago, belongs almost entirely to M. Maurice Buchor.[2]

M. Buchor's endeavours have been the most extensive and the most fruitful, but he is not alone in individual effort. There was, twenty years ago, in the suburbs of Paris and in the provinces, a large number of well-meaning people who devoted themselves to the work of musical education with sincerity and splendid enthusiasm. But their good works were too isolated, and were swamped by the

[1] The last chorus of *Fidelio* has been recently sung by one hundred and seventy school-children at Douai; a grand chorus from *The Messiah* by the Écoles Normales of Angoulême and Valence; and the great choral scene and the last part of Schumann's *Faust* by the two Écoles Normales of Limoges. At Valence, performances are given every year in the theatre there before an audience of between eight hundred and a thousand teachers.

Outside the schools, especially in the North, a certain number of teachers of both sexes have formed choral societies among work-girls and co-operative societies, such as *La Fraternelle* at Saint Quentin.

In a general way one may say that M. Maurice Buchor's campaign has especially succeeded in departments like that of Aisne and Drôme, where the ground has been prepared by the Academy Inspector. Unhappily in many districts the movement receives a lively opposition from music-teachers, who do not approve of this mnemotechnical way of learning poetry with music, without any instruction in solfeggio or musical science. And it is quite evident that this method would have its defects if it were a question of training musicians. But it is really a matter of training people who have some music in them; and so the musicians must not be too fastidious. I hope that great musicians will one day spring from this good ground—musicians more human than those of our own time, musicians whose music will be rooted in their hearts and in their country.

[2] We must not forget M. Bourgault-Ducoudray, who was his forerunner with his *Chants de Fontenoy*, collections of songs for the Écoles Normales.

apathy of the people about them ; though sometimes they kindled little fires of love and understanding in art, which only needed coaxing in order to burn brightly ; and even their less happy efforts generally succeeded in lighting a few sparks, which were left smouldering in people's hearts.[1]

At length, as a result of these individual efforts, the State began to show an interest in this educational movement, although it had for so long stood apart from it.[2] It discovered, in its turn, the educational value of singing. A musical test was instituted at the examination for the *Brevet supérieur*[3] which made the study of solfeggio a more serious matter in the Écoles Normales. In 1903 an endeavour was made to organise the teaching of music in the schools and colleges in a more rational way.[4] In 1904, following the suggestions of M. Saint-

[1] Mention must especially be made of little groups of young students, pupils of the Universities or the larger schools, who are devoting themselves at present to the moral and musical instruction of the people. Such an effort, made more than a year ago at Vaugirard, resulted in the *Manécanterie des petits chanteurs de la Croix de bois*, a small choir of the children of the people, who in the poor parishes go from one church to another singing Gregorian and Palestrinian music.

[2] It is hardly necessary to recall the unfortunate statute of 15 March, 1850, which says : " Primary instruction *may* comprise singing."

[3] By the decree of 4 August, 1905. At the same time, a programme and pedagogic instructions were issued. The importance of musical dictation and the usefulness of the Galin methods for beginners were urged. Let us hope that the State will decide officially to support M. Buchor's endeavours, and that it will gradually introduce into schools M. Jacques-Delacroze's methods of rhythmic gymnastics, which have produced such astonishing results in Switzerland.

[4] M. Chaumié's suggestion. See the *Revue Musicale*, 15 July, 1903.

Saëns and M. Bourgault-Ducoudray, class singing
was incorporated with other subjects in the programme of teaching,[1] and a free school of choral
singing was started in Paris under the honorary
chairmanship of M. Henry Marcel, director of the
Beaux-Arts, and under the direction of M. Radi-
guer. Quite lately a choral society for young
school-girls has been formed, with the Vice-Provost
as president and a membership of from six to seven
hundred young girls, who since 1906 have given
an annual concert under the direction of M. Gabriel
Pierné. And lastly, at the end of 1907, an association of professors was started to undertake the
teaching of music in the institutions of public instruction ; its chairman was the Inspector-General,
M. Gilles, and its honorary presidents were M.
Liard and M. Saint-Saëns. Its object is to aid the
progress of musical instruction by establishing a
centre to promote friendly relations among professors of music ; by centralising their interests
and studies ; by organising a circulating library of
music and a periodical magazine in which questions
relating to music may be discussed ; by establishing
communication between French professors and
foreign professors ; and by seeking to bring together professors of music and professors in other
branches of public teaching.

All this is not much, and we are yet terribly
behindhand, especially as regards secondary teaching, which is considered less important than primary

[1] *Revue Musicale*, December 15, 1903, and 1 and 15 January,
1904.

teaching.[1] But we are scrambling out of an abyss of ignorance, and it is something to have the desire to get out of it. We must remember that Germany has not always been in its present plethoric state of musical prosperity. The great choral societies only date from the end of the eighteenth century. Germany in the time of Bach was poor—if not poorer—in means for performing choral works than France to-day. Bach's only executants were his pupils at the Thomasschule at Leipsic, of which barely a score knew how to sing.[2] And now these people gather together for the great *Männergesangsfeste* (choral festivals) and the *Musikfeste* (music festivals) of Imperial Germany.

Let us hope on and persevere. The main thing is that a start has been made ; the thing that remains is to have patience and—persistence.

### THE PRESENT CONDITION OF FRENCH MUSIC

We have seen how the musical education of France is going on in theatres, in concerts, in schools, by lectures and by books ; and the Parisian's rather restless desire for knowledge seems to be satisfied for the moment. The mind of Paris has made a journey—a hasty journey, it is true—

---

[1] " In this," says M. Buchor, " as in many other things, the children of the people set an example to the children of the middle classes." That is true ; but one must not blame the middle-class children so much as those in authority, who, " in this, as in many other things," have not fulfilled their duties.

[2] *The Passion according to St. Matthew* was given first of all by two little choirs, consisting of from twelve to sixteen students, including the soloists.

through the music of other countries and other times,[1] and is now becoming introspective. After a mad enthusiasm over discoveries in strange lands, music and musical criticism have regained their self-possession and their jealous love of independence. A very decided reaction against foreign music has been shown since the time of the Universal Exhibition of 1900. This movement is not unconnected, consciously or unconsciously, with the nationalist train of thought, which was stirred up in France, and especially in Paris, somewhere about the same time. But it is also a natural development in the evolution of music. French music felt new vigour springing up within her, and was astonished at it ; her days of preparation were over, and she aspired to fly alone ; and, in accordance with the eternal rule of history, the first use she made of her newly-acquired strength was to defy her teachers. And this revolt against foreign influences was directed—one had expected it—against the strongest of the influences—the influence of German music as personified by Wagner. Two discussions in magazines, in 1903 and 1904, brought this state of mind curiously to light : one was an enquiry held by M. Jacques Morland in the *Mercure de France* (January, 1903) as to *The Influence of German Music in France ;* and the other was that of M. Paul Landormy in the *Revue Bleue* (March and April,

---

[1] It is hardly necessary to mention the curious attraction that some of our musicians are beginning to feel for the art of civilisations that are quite opposed to those of the West. Slowly and quietly the spirit of the Far East is insinuating itself into European music.

1904) as to *The Present Condition of French Music*. The first was like a shout of deliverance, and was not without exaggeration and a good deal of ingratitude; for it represented French musicians and critics throwing off Wagner's influence because it had had its day; the second set forth the theories of the new French school, and declared the independence of that school.

For several years the leader of the young school, M. Claude Debussy, has, in his writings in the *Revue Blanche* and *Gil Blas*, attacked Wagnerian art. His personality is very French—capricious, poetic, and *spirituelle*, full of lively intelligence, heedless, independent, scattering new ideas, giving vent to paradoxical caprice, criticising the opinions of centuries with the teasing impertinence of a little street boy, attacking great heroes of music like Gluck, Wagner, and Beethoven, upholding only Bach, Mozart, and Weber, and loudly professing his preference for the old French masters of the eighteenth century. But in spite of this he is bringing back to French music its true nature and its forgotten ideals—its clearness, its elegant simplicity, its naturalness, and especially its grace and plastic beauty. He wishes music to free itself from all literary and philosophic pretensions, which have burdened German music in the nineteenth century (and perhaps have always done so); he wishes music to get away from the rhetoric which has been handed down to us through the centuries, from its heavy construction and precise orderliness, from its harmonic and rhythmic formulas, and the

exercises of oratorical embroidery.  He wishes that
all about it shall be painting and poetry ; that it
shall explain its true feeling in a clear and direct
way ; and that melody, harmony, and rhythm
shall develop broadly along the lines of inner laws,
and not after the pretended laws of some intellectual arrangement.  And he himself preaches by
example in his *Pelléas et Mélisande*, and breaks with
all the principles of the Bayreuth drama, and gives
us the model of the new art of his dreams.  And on
all sides discerning and well-informed critics, such
as M. Pierre Lalo of *Le Temps*, M. Louis Laloy of
the *Revue Musicale* and the *Mercure Musicale*, and
M. Marnold of *Le Mercure de France*, have cham-
pioned his doctrines and his art.  Even the *Schola
Cantorum*, whose eclectic and archaic spirit is very
different from that of Debussy, seemed at first to
be drawn into the same current of thought ; and
this school which had so helped to propagate the
foreign influences of the past, did not seem to be
quite insensible to the nationalistic preoccupation
of the last few years.  So the *Schola* devoted itself
more and more—as was moreover its right and duty
—to the French music of the past, and filled its
concert programmes with French works of the
seventeenth and eighteenth centuries—with Marc
Antoine Charpentier, Du Mont, Leclair, Cléram-
bault, Couperin, and the French primitive composers for the organ, the harpsichord, and the
violin ; and with the works of dramatic composers,
especially of the great Rameau, who, after a period
of complete oblivion, suddenly benefited by this

excessive reaction, to the detriment of Gluck, whom
the young critics, following M. Debussy's example,
severely abused.[1]  There was even a moment when
the *Schola* took a decided share in the battle, and,
through M. Charles Bordes, issued a manifesto—
a *Credo*, as they called it—about a new art founded
on the ancient traditions of French music :

"We wish to have free speech in music—a
sustained recitative, infinite variety, and, in
short, complete liberty in musical utterance. We
wish for the triumph of natural music, so that it
shall be as free and full of movement as speech,
and as plastic and rhythmic as a classical dance."

It was open war against the metrical art of the
last three centuries, in the name of national tradition (more or less freely interpreted), of folk-song,
and of Gregorian chant. And "the constant
and avowed purpose of all this campaign was the
triumph of French music, and its cult."[2]
This manifesto reflects in its own way the spirit
of Debussy and his untrammelled musical impressionism ; and though it shows a good deal of
naïveté and some intolerance, there was in it a
strength of youthful enthusiasm that accorded

[1] There is no need to say that Rameau's genius justified all
this enthusiasm ; but one cannot help believing that it was
aroused, not so much on account of his musical genius as on
account of his supposed championship of the French music of
the past against foreign art ; though that art was well adapted
to the laws of French opera, as we may see for ourselves in
Gluck's case.
[2] *La Tribune de Saint-Gervais*, September, 1903.

with the great hopes of the time, and foretold glorious days to come and a splendid harvest of music.

Not many years have passed since then ; yet the sky is already a little clouded, the light not quite so bright. Hope has not failed ; but it has not been fulfilled. France is waiting, and is getting a little impatient. But the impatience is unnecessary ; for to found an art we must bring time to our aid ; art must ripen tranquilly. Yet tranquillity is what is most lacking in Parisian art. The artists, instead of working steadily at their own tasks and uniting in a common aim, are given up to sterile disputes. The young French school hardly exists any longer, as it has now split up into two or three parties. To a fight against foreign art has succeeded a fight among themselves : it is the deep-rooted evil of the country, this vain expenditure of force. And most curious of all is the fact that the quarrel is not between the conservatives and the progressives in music, but between the two most advanced sections : the *Schola* on the one hand, who, should it gain the victory, would through its dogmas and traditions inevitably develop the airs of a little academy ; and, on the other hand, the independent party, whose most important representative is M. Debussy. It is not for us to enter into the quarrel ; we would only suggest to the parties in question that if any profit is to result from their misunderstanding, it will be derived by a third party—the party in favour of routine, the party that has never lost favour with the great theatre-going public,—

a party that will soon make good the place it has
lost if those who aim at defending art set about
fighting one another.  Victory has been proclaimed
too soon ; for whatever the optimistic representatives of the young school may say, victory has not
yet been gained ; and it will not be gained for some
time yet—not until public taste is changed, not
while the nation lacks musical education, nor until
the cultured few are united to the people, through
whom their thoughts shall be preserved.  For not
only—with a few rare and generous exceptions—
do the more aristocratic sections of society ignore
the education of the people, but they ignore the very
existence of the people's soul.  Here and there, a
composer—such as Bizet and M. Saint-Saëns, or
M. d'Indy and his disciples—will build up symphonies and rhapsodies and very difficult pieces
for the piano on the popular airs of Auvergne,
Provence, or the Cevennes ; but that is only a whim
of theirs, a little ingenious pastime for clever artists,
such as the Flemish masters of the fifteenth century
indulged in when they decorated popular airs with
polyphonic elaborations.  In spite of the advance
of the democratic spirit, musical art—or at least
all that counts in musical art—has never been more
aristocratic than it is to-day.  Probably the phenomenon is not peculiar to music, and shows itself
more or less in other arts ; but in no other art is it
so dangerous, for no other has roots less firmly
fixed in the soil of France.  And it is no consolation
to tell oneself that this is according to the great
French traditions, which have nearly always been

Y

aristocratic. Traditions, great and small, are menaced to-day ; the axe is ready for them. Whoever wishes to live must adapt himself to the new conditions of life. The future of art is at stake. To continue as we are doing is not only to weaken music by condemning it to live in unhealthy conditions, but also to risk its disappearing sooner or later under the rising flood of popular misconceptions of music. Let us take warning by the fact that we have already had to defend music [1] when it was attacked at some of the parliamentary assemblies ; and let us remember the pitifulness of the defence. We must not let the day come when a famous speech will be repeated with a slight alteration— "The Republic has no need of musicians."

It is the historian's duty to point out the dangers of the present hour, and to remind the French musicians who have been satisfied with their first victory that the future is anything but sure, and that we must never disarm while we have a common enemy before us, an enemy especially dangerous in a democracy—mediocrity.

The road that stretches before us is long and difficult. But if we turn our heads and look back over the way we have come we may take heart. Which of us does not feel a little glow of pride at the thought of what has been done in the last thirty

---

[1] At any rate, certain forms of music—the highest. See the discussions at the Chambre des Députés on the budget of the Beaux-Arts in February, 1906 ; and the speeches of MM. Théodore Denis, Beauquier, and Dujardin-Beaumetz, on Religious Music, the Niedermeyer School, and the civic value of the organ.

years ? Here is a town where, before 1870, music
had fallen to the most miserable depths, which to-
day teems with concerts and schools of music—a
town where one of the first symphonic schools in
Europe has sprung from nothing, a town where an
enthusiastic concert-going public has been formed,
possessing among its members some great critics
with broad interests and a fine, free spirit—all this
is the pride of France. And we have, too, a little
band of musicians ; among them, in the first rank,
that great painter of dreams, Claude Debussy ;
that master of constructive art, Dukas ; that impassioned thinker, Alberic Magnard ; that ironic
poet, Ravel ; and those delicate and finished
writers, Albert Roussel and Déodat de Séverac ;
without mention of the younger musicians who
are in the vanguard of their art. And all this
poetic force, though not the most vigorous, is the
most original in Europe to-day. Whatever gaps
one may find in our musical organisation, still so
new, whatever results this movement may lead to,
it is impossible not to admire a people whom defeat
has aroused, and a generation that has accomplished
the magnificent work of reviving the nation's music
with such untiring perseverance and such steadfast
faith. The names of Camille Saint-Saëns, César
Franck, Charles Bordes, and Vincent d'Indy, will
remain associated before all others with this work
of national regeneration, where so much talent and
so much devotion, from the leaders of orchestras
and celebrated composers down to that obscure
body of artists and music-lovers, have joined

forces in the fight against indifference and routine. They have the right to be proud of their work. But for ourselves, let us waste no time in thinking about it. Our hopes are great. Let us justify them.